The Semi-Sovereign Presidency

TRANSFORMING AMERICAN POLITICS
Lawrence C. Dodd, Series Editor

Dramatic changes in political institutions and behavior over the past three decades have underscored the dynamic nature of American politics, confronting political scientists with a new and pressing intellectual agenda. The pioneering work of early postwar scholars, while laying a firm empirical foundation for contemporary scholarship, failed to consider how American politics might change or to recognize the forces that would make fundamental change inevitable. In reassessing the static interpretations fostered by these classic studies, political scientists are now examining the underlying dynamics that generate transformational change.

Transforming American Politics brings together texts and monographs that address four closely related aspects of change. A first concern is documenting and explaining recent changes in American politics—in institutions, processes, behavior, and policymaking. A second is reinterpreting classic studies and theories to provide a more accurate perspective on postwar politics. The series looks at historical change to identify recurring patterns of political transformation within and across the distinctive eras of American politics. Last and perhaps most importantly, the series presents new theories and interpretations that explain the dynamic processes at work and thus clarify the direction of contemporary politics. All of the books focus on the central theme of transformation—transformation in both the conduct of American politics and in the way we study and understand its many aspects.

FORTHCOMING TITLES

Broken Contract? Changing Relationships Between Citizens and Their Government in the United States, edited by Stephen C. Craig

Congress and the Administrative State, Second Edition, Lawrence C. Dodd and Richard L. Schott

The New American Politics, edited by Bryan D. Jones

Young Versus Old: Generational Gaps in Political Participation and Policy Preferences, Susan MacManus and Suzanne L. Parker

The Parties Respond: Changes in American Parties and Campaigns, Second Edition, edited by L. Sandy Maisel

Campaigns and Elections, edited by James A. Thurber and Candice J. Nelson

Cold War Politics, John Kenneth White

Bureaucratic Dynamics: The Role of the Bureaucracy in a Democracy, B. Dan Wood and Richard W. Waterman

The Semi-Sovereign Presidency

THE BUSH ADMINISTRATION'S STRATEGY
FOR GOVERNING WITHOUT CONGRESS

Charles Tiefer

Westview Press

BOULDER • SAN FRANCISCO • OXFORD

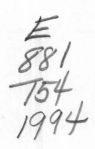

Transforming American Politics

Copyright © 1994 by Westview Press, Inc.

Published in 1994 in the United States of America by Westview Press, Inc., 5500 Central Avenue, Boulder, Colorado 80301-2877, and in the United Kingdom by Westview Press, 36 Lonsdale Road, Summertown, Oxford OX2 7EW

Library of Congress Cataloging-in-publication data
Tiefer, Charles.
    The semi-sovereign presidency : the Bush administration's strategy
for governing without Congress / Charles Tiefer.
        p.   cm. — (Transforming American politics)
    Includes bibliographical references and index.
    ISBN 0-8133-1930-7. — ISBN 0-8133-1931-5 (pbk.)
    1. United States—Politics and government—1989–1993.   2. Bush,
George, 1924–   . 3. Separation of powers—United States.
I. Title.   II. Series.
E881.T54   1994
320.973—dc20

93-6431
CIP

Printed and bound in the United States of America

The paper used in this publication meets the requirements
of the American National Standard for Permanence of Paper
for Printed Library Materials Z39.48-1984.

10   9   8   7   6   5   4   3   2   1

Contents

Preface

This book is the first analysis of the Bush Presidency's strategy regarding separation of powers—the constitutional relationship of president and Congress. The absence of prior studies on this subject owes partly to the natural lag time between the Bush Administration's start in 1989 and a sufficient record from which to draw conclusions. A record of presidential-congressional relations takes years to develop, and then more years are needed for analyzing its meaning. The delay also stems from the preoccupation of observers through 1990 with the significance of the Iran-contra scandal. Entirely appropriately, such works published in 1990 and 1991 as Harold Hongju Koh's *The National Security Constitution*, Michael J. Glennon's *Constitutional Diplomacy*, and Theodore Draper's *A Very Thin Line: The Iran-Contra Scandals* focused upon placing in historical and constitutional perspective the revelations of Iran-contra, which were still coming out at Oliver North's trial in 1989 and even as late as the indictment of Caspar Weinberger in 1992. Finally, the delay is owing to the illumination available only after the Clinton Administration allowed comparison with its sharply differing approach.

ACTIVE OR INACTIVE?

Moreover, the Bush Presidency's particular approach has required years to discern. Much critical reporting or analysis of the Bush Administration simply took it to task for asserted inactivity, weakness, or ineffectuality. One of the first books about the Bush Presidency, *Marching in Place: The Status Quo Presidency of George Bush*, published in spring 1992, gave good expression to this initially plausible view. Even the title told half the story: "The Status Quo Presidency." The text of the book told the other half, describing a president who wasn't *"doing* anything," was "in a holding pattern," and had a "minimalist strategy [that] dovetailed with his core beliefs. . . . that the best course was to do as little as possible; to 'do no harm,' rather than attempt reform at the risk of making things worse."[1]

Describing the Bush Presidency as minimalist does accord with part of the reality. By the late 1980s, political scientists began specific studies of the dynamics of "divided government," the phenomenon of a president from one party and a Congress with a majority from the other. Such divided government, unusual in the first half of the twentieth century, became the norm in the second half. As the studies reflected, divided government left presidents with the choice between activist styles of proposing and pushing major legislative programs, like those of President Truman in 1947–1948 and President Reagan in 1981–1982, and minimalist styles.

President Reagan had won the 1980 election by a decisive 10 percent margin in popular votes over the defeated incumbent president and with coattails that brought a big boost for the Republican Party in Congress. His mandate included his having helped elect the first Republican Senate majority since 1955. Using that mandate, President Reagan had moved a major legislative program of cutting taxes, raising military spending, and reducing social services spending. He had appointed controversial Cabinet nominees like Interior Secretary James Watt to implement a philosophy opposed to government protection of the environment.

In contrast, President Bush's election in 1988, with a smaller popular vote margin, weaker campaign themes, and the simultaneous election of a strong Democratic Congress, had put him in office without any such mandate. He could not engage in an activist quest for legislative action without risking defeat or at best compromise. A minimalist style allowed the president to avoid losses and to employ some powerful tools of full constitutional legitimacy that were principally anti-action in nature, such as vetoing and "veto bargaining." During his term, President Bush largely avoided the kinds of public appeals used by President Reagan and generally disdained moving a legislative program.

Yet taking minimalist as the whole description of the Bush Administration would overlook its most deliberate and strategic aspects. Worse, it would also mean actually being misled by the elements of the administration's strategy aimed at low visibility or surreptitious action. Although the Bush Administration lacked a mandate and avoided public appeals, it did not merely hold itself down to inactivity. It still wanted to exercise power in many policy contexts—the environment, civil rights, foreign affairs, and in late 1990 the initiation of war with Iraq.

Accordingly, President Bush had to exercise power in ways other than the struggles for public opinion and congressional enactments anticipated by the constitutional system. Unlike a president with a positive mandate or a desire for legislative activism, President Bush needed a strategy to exercise power without enacting new law and with shielding from Congress's oversight.

In the language of the Framers of the Constitution, President Bush needed an approach that would sustain a sovereign's claims to "personal rule." These are not the full claims of a leader who makes the grand changes and grand policies that can occur only with a supportive population and legislature behind them, like Henry VIII and the English Reformation, Franklin D. Roosevelt and the New Deal, or even Ronald Reagan in 1981–1982. Rather, these are the power claims of a sovereign who would accept a lesser scale of policymaking so long as he could work his will through internal and unaccountable channels. Such a strategy for a *semi-sovereign presidency* depends on personal staffs and special mechanisms outside the system of democratic checks and balances.

EXEMPLARS OF ADMINISTRATION STRATEGY

Chapter 1 starts the book with a statement of the Bush Presidency's strategy. President Bush's single clearest overall exposition and justification of his approach came in his Princeton Address of May 1991, which provides a convenient point of introduction. The chapter then continues with the origins of this strategy in President Bush's political situation and personal style. An overall chronology of the Bush Administration proceeds from the choice of a White House team in 1989, to the avoidance of issues of the midterm 1990 election, through the triumphal period of early 1991, and to the national reaction in 1992.

Chapter 2 then drops back in history to describe the barriers originally established in the Constitution against the claims of a sovereign leader and the conditions since World War II that undermined those barriers. It starts from the "personal rule" doctrines in England of Charles I and James II rejected by Anglo-American democracy. The Constitution and American practice through the midtwentieth century had reinforced that rejection by insistence upon the authority of laws and the accountability of officers. In the postwar era, two new postwar conditions—the Cold War and divided government—laid the foundation for the Bush Administration's approach.

Each of the following four chapters addresses in detail the Bush White House's pursuit of this approach in particular major issues. Chapter 3 discusses "signing statements," which are statements issued by the president at the time he signs newly enacted law. The Bush White House turned these into a major means of exercising power. They became the sovereign powers for shaping or escaping laws and for governing without Congress by voiding or revising key provisions in congressional enactments. Chapter 4 deals with the Council on Competitiveness, chaired by the vice president—the "Quayle Council"—which became the White House's internal and unaccountable tool of control, shielded from congressional oversight and public scrutiny, over environmental, health, and other regulatory matters.

The next two chapters concern the single most controversial national security issue of the Bush Administration: Iraq. Chapter 5 discusses how the White House managed the courtship of Saddam Hussein in 1989 and 1990 through the vehicle of National Security Council directives and committees and how the administration covered up that courtship in 1991 and 1992. Chapter 6 focuses on President Bush's initial effort in late 1990 to go to war with Iraq without congressional authorization, which expressed his ultimate claims to sovereign power. The chapter then addresses the significance of his surrendering in January 1991 to the requirements of the Constitution when he requested and obtained congressional authorization for the war.

Chapter 7 closes with assessments of the significance for the semi-sovereign approach of President Bush's crushing defeat in the 1992 election and of the prospects for similar presidential approaches in the future. The 1992 election defeat did constitute a national verdict against the Bush Administration and its strategy of governing without Congress. It seems likely that the Clinton Administration, with its mandate and desire for action through legislation and accountable policy change, will provide a respite for the separation of powers. However, in the long run that respite may well prove temporary, and White House abuses will likely recur. Because the courts cannot provide the full protection of the system of checks and balances, in the end Congress must do so.

AUTHOR'S PURPOSE

To explain briefly why I wrote this book, I should start by stating that it is most definitely not prepared in my official capacity as acting general counsel of the House of Representatives. This work reflects solely my personal views and does not represent the views of my office, the House of Representatives, or any House person or entity. Still, readers may find it helpful to know the nature of my work. The House of Representatives has an office of General Counsel to conduct litigation between Congress and the executive, among other matters. The office also advises on congressional investigations of the executive involving the separation of powers. I serve as solicitor of the House of Representatives, the position with primary responsibility to appear in court. I previously served as deputy in that office since 1984, following work in the corresponding Senate office beginning in 1979. I have therefore been immersed for the past fourteen years in the legal disputes between the branches of government, from legislative vetoes and the Gramm-Rudman Act to congressional investigations and executive privilege assertions.

During the Reagan Administration, as deputy House counsel I litigated successfully the cases challenging Attorney General Edwin Meese's doc-

trine that he and the president could declare laws unconstitutional and refuse to obey them. In 1987 I served as special deputy chief counsel on the
House Iran-contra committee, and in the six years afterward I represented
House committees in evidentiary proceedings for the Iran-contra criminal
cases. During President Bush's term, I assisted House committees with legal aspects of their inquiries regarding policy on Iraq and the Quayle
Council, among other matters. I was also involved in the general flow of
legal issues between President Bush and Congress on everything from the
administration's proposed constitutional amendment for the flag to its
keeping major legal opinions secret. It is precisely because my work allows no room for anything other than official views that I desired to write
a book in which I could express my views that are in no way official.

Memories of the last administration are still fairly clear in the minds of
readers. If they draw on their fresh memories as well as what is written
here and respond with their own views, whether similar to mine or different, then my purpose—to stimulate debate about the most recent presidency from a historical and constitutional perspective—will be more than
fulfilled.

Charles Tiefer

Acknowledgments

The whole of the manuscript was read carefully and thoughtfully by Louis Fisher, senior specialist in American government with the Congressional Research Service, and Thomas O. Sargentich, professor of law, Washington College of Law at American University. Most of the manuscript was read carefully and thoughtfully by James S. Liebman and Richard Briffault, assistant professors of law, Columbia University School of Law; and Irv Gornstein, appellate attorney, U.S. Department of Justice. In particular, Dr. Fisher and Professor Briffault gave me early conceptual guidance from their expert knowledge of presidential history in distinguishing what was special about the Bush Administration. Professors Sargentich and Liebman each painstakingly identified and corrected countless awkward passages and greatly refined the rough ideas, adding many insights of their own. These five individuals, who are distinguished authors in their own right, deserted their own projects to help me generously with mine. Individual chapters benefited from a reading, or other help provided, by specialists in particular areas: George Van Cleve, John Scheibel, Randy Bellows, and Prof. Michael J. Glennon. Of course, the responsibility for all inadequacies, and for the theories put forth, is mine alone, not that of these reviewers.

From the acquisitions editor at Westview Press, Jennifer Knerr, I received an extraordinarily high level of professional advice and encouragement. She also contributed her own close reading of the manuscript to show where to substitute research and thought for lawyer's jargon. The series editor, Lawrence C. Dodd, contributed dynamic suggestions from the political science world that served as a tonic to legalism. My copyeditor, Sarah Tomasek, labored prodigiously and proficiently to increase the text's readability and consistency. My project editors, Martha Robbins and Connie Oehring, provided conscientious and efficient oversight of the editorial production process. Research and secretarial assistance came cheerfully from Tambrey Zang, and in the final stages, other help came from Hillary Burchuk.

This book is a personal product in which my office took no part. However, I did draw on the work that I previously conducted as matters arose during the Bush Administration. Contributions to that work included House General Counsel Steven R. Ross's own subtle constitutional analysis of issues as they came up and ingenious research by Lenore Dick and Dina Green.

My sister, Leonore Tiefer, read the manuscript from a different perspective. As a professional lecturer, author, and clinician in psychology, she did her best to treat the manuscript for disorders of confused thinking and stylistic tedium. She applied her treatment to the text (and its writer) skillfully and supportively.

This book is dedicated to my mother, Rosalind Crost Tiefer. As a life-long teacher of history, she brought me up with as much as she could transmit of her own gift for seeing the eternal life of the past in the present. Characteristically, during the writing and after she read the manuscript, she offered much-needed encouragement on the theme that this was a lot more interesting than those legal briefs she usually received. This book is the fruit of her love and her intellect.

C. T.

1

An Overview of the Bush Presidency's Strategy

THE STRATEGY DESCRIBED IN
THE PRINCETON ADDRESS

In May 1991, at the very peak of his presidency, President Bush gave an address at Princeton University regarding the separation of powers. The warm, if not exultant, afterglow of the Persian Gulf War bathed the president in an aura of success and popular support. His public approval ratings hovered around a record level of 90 percent. Potential Democratic nominees for 1992 deserted the field rather than face him. His reelection seemed a foregone conclusion. Congress avoided confrontation. This was the moment—as it turned out, a unique one—when the president felt secure enough to provide to the nation an exposition and justification of his approach to the separation of powers.

In a sentence, President Bush's strategy consisted of having White House staffs, free from the accountability traditionally imposed on federal officers, employ novel mechanisms of power to trump the laws enacted by Congress. These mechanisms included signing statements, Quayle Council reviews, and National Security Directives and Committees. This approach satisfied the Bush Administration's aversion, for reasons both of political situation and personal style, to working with Congress or otherwise engaging in a struggle for public opinion. Where his predecessor, President Reagan, had delighted in public fighting with Congress to move his large-scale domestic programs or to let his Cabinet officers pursue missions that were comparatively open (until Iran-contra) in their ideological nature, President Bush's approach would avoid that democratic struggle. The scale of his actions might be smaller than a president with a strong mandate and a willingness to govern with Congress (at least domestically), but he would perform the action as a matter of personal rule, without the checks and balances involved in governing with Congress. He would achieve a semi-sovereign presidency.

This approach did not make a complete break with what prior postwar presidents had done. Two hallmarks of the postwar era, the Cold War and the divided government, had both contributed previously to an increased size and role for White House staff. Sherman Adams, McGeorge Bundy, Henry Kissinger, Hamilton Jordan, and Donald Regan all had potent roles. Strong and active presidents often used strong and active White House staffs in managing their efforts. To this postwar foundation, what President Bush brought was not greater activism than his predecessors, but the necessities born of his particular political situation and personal style. Other presidents, from Truman to Reagan, delighted in public arena combat to express activism. Their public appeals and legislative struggles balanced the internal workings of White House staffs with a large measure of domestic issue resolution in accountable channels. President Bush, because of his choice to avoid public arena combat, pushed further the tendency in the exercise of powers toward internal and unaccountable mechanisms.

President Bush's Princeton Address of May 1991 expounds this approach. As his jumping-off point in the Princeton Address for viewing the constitutional system, President Bush started with expression of blunt antagonism toward the flawed legislative branch. "Although our founders never envisioned a Congress that would churn out hundreds of thousands of pages worth of reports and hearings and documents and laws every year, they did understand that legislators would try to accumulate power," President Bush said. "[A] president . . . has an obligation to 'preserve, protect and defend' a 200-year-old system of constitutional government. The most common challenge to presidential powers comes from a predictable source, represented here by several able members of the United States Congress." Congress was the villain of the piece. His administration's approach would depict Congress as having taken on an excessive role and thereby having created a corresponding need to "protect" the presidency.

The president further described his frustration as follows: "Congress has also taken aggressive action against specific presidential powers . . . . It sometimes tries to manage Executive Branch—micromanage the Executive Branch—by writing too-specific directions for carrying out a particular law." Laws thus had the flaws of "micromanagement" and required presidential corrections. Previously, presidents had specific constitutional means for dealing within the system of checks and balances with laws they disliked. Before enactment, presidents could make public appeals over Congress, they could lobby about or bargain over proposed bills, and ultimately they could use the veto. After enactment, they could appoint officers willing, like President Reagan's Cabinet choices, to interpret the laws the president's way and to fight the ensuing oversight. President Reagan did have lapses from use of efforts within the system—notably,

Iran-contra—but these ultimately proved to be criminal and self-destructive.

President Bush had a different response in mind. In the Princeton Address, President Bush explained his chief tool for response to Congress: *"[On] many occasions during my presidency, I have stated that statutory provisions violating the Constitution have no binding legal force"* (emphasis added). He referred to his tool against bills that, unlike his record level of veto threats, operated outside the traditional system: Rather than to exercise his constitutional power of objection, these statements declared about the newly enacted law that particular provisions had "no binding legal force." Presidents prior to 1988 had used signing statements, but President Bush proclaimed and exercised the power of using them to a far greater extent and with far more potent tactics than anyone before. No tool more conveniently served the desire of this president to avoid a public arena fight for a legislative program while acting with freedom from constraint by laws.

His White House counsel would declare provisions violative of the Constitution in any of a vast array of laws on issues from trade to affirmative action. The White House counsel would also find a host of laws sufficiently open to constitutional question to justify presidential revision if not presidential voiding. At first President Bush issued scores and ultimately hundreds of statements declaring provisions in acts of Congress invalid or altering them. Taken overall, the 1989–1992 outpouring of signing statements that purported to strike down or revise new laws staked a major presidential claim to personal power and one that augmented and magnified other claims as part of the overall strategy.

As to congressional oversight, President Bush explained in the Princeton Address that "[o]versight, when properly exercised, helps keep the executive accountable. But when it proliferates wildly, it can confuse the public and make it more difficult for Congress and the president to do their jobs properly." What is the point at which the president must block congressional oversight so as not to "confuse the public" and make doing his job "more difficult"?

President Bush offered his view as follows: "It is the president who is responsible for guiding and directing the nation's foreign policy . . . . [and] performing this duty with 'secrecy and dispatch,' when necessary." Here he used a famous quote from one of the Federalist Papers to claim more than its author, John Jay, actually said,[1] but what mattered was the announced plan of action resulting from this claim. President Bush gave as caveats that he would not "keep Congress unnecessarily in the dark" and only when he found it "necessary" would he act with "secrecy." These caveats, superficially expressed as disclaimers of his exercise of power, unmistakably asserted a capability to decide when to make secret law and to shrug off unwanted oversight.

Such a philosophy took concrete form in his use of National Security Directives and the related system of unaccountable National Security Council (NSC) staff power. No matter illustrates this better than the administration's embrace of Saddam Hussein in 1989 and 1990, before the invasion of Kuwait. The Cold War's special requirements had laid the foundation for his administration's use of this mechanism, but now that mechanism had outlasted its original purposes. As will be seen, the courtship of Saddam Hussein followed the National Security Directive on Iraq policy, NSD-26, issued in late 1989, and the NSC Committee meetings of spring 1990 to implement it. The NSD established the policy without the need for engaging in debate with the public and Congress, as it was a mechanism shielded from oversight. When this courtship turned out to be the most embarrassing and questionable secret policy of Bush's entire term, the use of these NSC channels still served to block and delay the ensuing congressional investigations in 1991 and 1992.

Even the most purely domestic affairs involved novel power claims for the Bush White House outside the system of checks and balances. As President Bush added in his Princeton Address, "[t]he president's view of the whole ground includes a second responsibility—shaping the nation's domestic agenda." President Bush alluded only indirectly in this address to the vice president's role: "The president and vice president are the only officials elected to serve the entire nation." In practice, the president's methods on domestic policy involved Vice President Quayle and his own personal White House staff under the rubric of the Council on Competitiveness, known (because the vice president chaired it) as the Quayle Council.

Vice President Quayle provided the detailed justification for his role, about which the president's Princeton Address only hinted. In his own public statement in 1991, the vice president criticized the Cabinet departments and agencies, even though the president's own appointees headed them, as an excessive "federal bureaucracy." Vice President Quayle noted his "grandfather ['s] . . . [1971] editorial . . . titled, 'Will the Federal Bureaucracy Destroy Individual Freedom in America?'" He said, "So far, the answer to my grandfather's question is 'no.'" Echoing President Bush's philosophy about their special status, Vice President Quayle explained that "[t]his somewhat esoteric battle goes to the heart of democracy itself. The President and I . . . are elected by the people," whereas "[t]he iron triangle—special-interest groups, bureaucrats, and Congressional staff—are elected by nobody."

Accordingly, the vice president listed a number of areas, chiefly environment, health, and safety regulation, where his council's staff had effectively taken control of the law in this "somewhat esoteric battle" with those "bureaucrats." This council's staff emerged in the end as the supreme tool for White House control of the execution of regulatory laws by Cabinet departments. As the 1992 election approached and President Bush's capability for winning in public arena struggles dwindled, he formally imposed on all his Cabinet departments and agencies a moratorium supervised by the Quayle Council and the White House counsel.

Where did this strategy come from? How new was it? How much of it was the culmination of postwar presidential tendencies? How far did it deviate from the Constitution's plan for the presidency and from the historic practice from the time of the Framers to the present? How far did it transgress the rules and doctrines that distinguish claims of sovereign power from those within the system of checks and balances? The next chapter addresses these questions in a fuller perspective of American constitutional history. At this point it is appropriate to look at the Bush approach's roots in the president's political situation and personal style and then its development chronologically during President Bush's term.

ORIGINS OF THE STRATEGY

The particular origins of the strategy fall into two general categories: political forces surrounding the 1988 election and personal style, including previous experience. Each deserves separate attention.

Political Forces

George Bush came to the White House as perhaps the most extreme example in the postwar era of a president elected without a mandate. The post–World War II era has consisted largely of divided government, typically of a Republican president and a Democratic Congress. In 1988, though, the condition had reached a particularly intense point. Vice President Bush had watched the Democratic Party take a majority of the Senate in the 1986 election and retain a working Democratic majority in the House. After that election (i.e., in 1987 and 1988), the two chambers did not have a Democratic majority that was merely nominal in nature, but a solid majority that was at odds in legislative philosophy with the administration. Thus Vice President Bush had watched in 1987 and 1988 as the Democratic Congress enacted a whole legislative agenda largely against the desire of his predecessor: legislation on welfare, trade, arms control, aid to education, civil rights in housing, and renewal of the independent counsel statute.[2]

Then, President Bush had watched the Democratic Congress receive clear support in the 1988 election. Democrats won nineteen of the thirty-three Senate races, the fourth successive gain or draw by Senate Democrats since 1980. This created a 55-45 Democratic margin in the chamber, which neared their high pre-Reagan numbers. A small addition to the Democratic seats in the House created a large 260-175 Democratic margin.

In contrast, President Bush's own election victory failed, because of how he campaigned, to arm him to claim a mandate. He did receive 53 percent of the popular vote, 6 percentage points more than his opponent. Although this gave him a respectable showing, he had run behind the winners of the House races in 379 of the 435 congressional districts. Even in those few areas where he ran ahead of the winners, he had no particular coattails. President Bush had not staked his rise or governance on popular agreement with any clear policy program. As *Congressional Quarterly* put it, "[h]is inability to carry others into office may be partly due to his message, which was essentially a call to 'stay the course.'"[3]

Candidate Bush had chosen to back away from the firm ideology of the Reagan Administration by promising to be the "environmental president" and to run a "kinder, gentler" administration yet he embodied contradictions even on these issues by being a pro-business candidate. His choice of symbolic issues, notably expressed in the "Willie Horton" advertisement, the criticism of the American Civil Liberties Union (ACLU), and the flag enthusiasm, aroused racial divisions or nationalistic sentiments without signaling any kind of concrete legislative program.

One political scientist, to express the universal perception at the time of lack of a mandate or program, collected these contemporary headlines from a wide spectrum of publications:[4]

> Rough Road: Election Results Show Lack of a Consensus About President's Role (Wall Street Journal, 9 November 1988)
> Challenges for Bush: An Uncertain Agenda and a Wary Congress (New York Times, 10 November 1988)
> President-elect Starts Move Toward a "Bush Revolution" but Failure to Bolster GOP Position in Congress Will Make It Harder to Lead (Christian Science Monitor, 10 November 1988)
> What to Expect: The Outlook for the Bush Years: Reaganism Without Ideology, Persistence Without Brilliance—and Serious Trouble with Congress (Time, 21 November 1988)
> The Tough Tasks Ahead: George Bush Wins a Decisive Victory and a Personal Vindication, but No Clear Mandate (Newsweek, 21 November 1988)

A famous Doonesbury cartoon just before Bush's inaugural had him saying on his first day in office: "So far today, I've said the Pledge and I haven't furloughed any murderers. I've delivered on my entire mandate, and it isn't even lunch yet." President Bush proposed to Congress in the early months of his term what a political scientist described as a "modest" legislative agenda: "He proposed some modest new education programs, an increase in funding for the war on drugs, child-care legislation and a re-write of the Clean Air Act, which were on Congress's agenda in any case, plus legislation to bail out the savings-and-loan insurance fund and clean up nuclear weapons plants."[5] *Congressional Quarterly Almanac*'s computa-tions of the level of support in Congress for the president produced a re-sult for President Bush's first year fitting this starting point: "George Bush fared worse in Congress than any other first-year president elected in the postwar era," with support 11 percent less than the previous low point.[6] Thus the president started his term with a strongly opposed Congress, no mandate, and not much of a legislative program or legislative support.

Personal Style

Admirers, detractors, and objective observers alike contrast President Bush's personal style with his predecessor. President Reagan approached divided government by "appeal[ing] directly to the American people to show their support for his policies by lobbying their representatives on his behalf."[7] President Bush admitted his own problem with the "vision thing," and others noted that his "rhetorical skills . . . . pale, by contrast, however, with those of his immediate predecessor, whose dramatic tal-ents were honed over a lifetime."[8]

Although he lacked the tools for a style of popular appeals, what Presi-dent Bush did have, in the view of diverse observers, was a personal style best suited for "elite deal-making."[9] George Bush grew up in an elite set-ting of wealth and connection as the son of a senator from Connecticut. His family staked him initially with $300,000 for his start in business in the 1950s and soon tripled that. His connections helped him obtain a choice assignment to the House Ways and Means Committee during his brief House tenure (1966–1970). When he left this office after defeat in a 1970 senatorial race, he left the first and last post that he won by election on his own before the presidency.

At that point, his connections to President Nixon launched him on his appointed career.[10] In contrast to his limited career in elected office, he had an impressive list of appointed offices. He had served as United Na-tions ambassador, envoy to China, chairman of the Republican National Committee, and head of the Central Intelligence Agency, although he had held each post relatively briefly. Most important, of course, after Gover-nor Reagan picked him as a running mate, he served as vice president for eight years before becoming the first sitting vice president to win election to the presidency since 1836.

Thus he was no outsider, like Presidents Carter or Reagan, who had won the ultimate office by mobilizing public desires to change Washington. Rather, he rose as a very successful insider, an appointed and reappointed official, promoted to successive offices by the favors of Nixon, Ford, and Reagan. His proportion of "inside" executive experience to "outside" experience in the public arena or Congress was higher than any recent holder of the office.

Moreover, his personal style included changing and wavering in his public positions on major issues in a way that foreshadowed the usefulness of avoiding action in accountable channels. He had gone from anti–civil rights to pro– and back; from pro-choice views to an antiabortion position; and from scoring Reagan's tax and budget policies as "voodoo economics" to supporting them. There are diverse opinions of this style, particularly of his prepresidential career. Some view Bush as controlling his course by tactical flexibility: "As Bush was hit hard from left and right . . . . [h]e learned to use class and race, both to inoculate himself against charges of elitism and to take the initiative against more liberal opponents."[11] Others see his shifts as largely those of "hostage" to a Republican Party that was persistently, first in Texas in the 1960s and then nationally in the 1980s, well to his right. He was not deeply committed to the ideology of the dominant conservatives, like Barry Goldwater or Ronald Reagan, this analysis goes, but neither the Texas Republican Party of the 1960s nor the national party of the 1980s would support him if he advocated moderate views. Hence he adopted right-wing positions, but without the zeal of a true convert.

Analyzing Bush as a "hostage" helps in understanding his administration's style. It explains the relief from avoiding public and congressional battles that would inflame his internal contradictions as originally a moderate in a party with a dominant right wing. Acting outside the public-arena struggle would avoid or assuage criticism by his own party's right wing as well as keep at bay the Democratic Congress without his internal conflicts becoming a public focus.

Viewed thusly, his separation of powers strategy arose not only from dealing with divided government absent a mandate but also from having to soothe the estranged elements in his party. He could publicly support the Clean Air Act and then privately have the Quayle Council water down the implementing regulations. He could publicly accept the Civil Rights Act and then use the lower-visibility signing statement to revise it. Publicly he could take a general position opposing terrorist nations and then use an internal national security system to supervise the courtship of Iraq. A conservative admirer of his administration summed up how, when the president had accepted a bill containing a civil rights provision, the signing statement approach nevertheless let him "meet his duty," from the right-wing perspective: "President Bush has often used signing statements to meet his duty to enforce the Constitution . . . . [O]n a number of occasions Bush has objected to statutory language authorizing racial or gender preferences in violation of the Fourteenth Amendment's Equal Protection Clause."[12]

Furthermore, one particular scandal hung over the president from the first reform legislation of Congress that he undermined by a signing statement in 1989 to his final mass pardon in December 1992: the shadow of Iran-contra. He and his senior advisers had been very close to the Iran-contra scandal immediately preceding their start in office. Vice President Bush had been present at the key NSC meetings in August 1985 and January 1986 where he supported the arms-for-hostages deals with Iran. He had traveled to Honduras in 1985 to clinch a prohibited exchange of American aid to that country in return for its support of the contras. His national security aide as vice president, Donald I. Gregg, had a former CIA operative and frequent communicant, Felix Rodriguez, within Oliver North's illegal contra resupply operation.

Yet after exposure of the scandal in late 1986, Vice President Bush and his aides committed themselves to denials of activity and even of knowledge. Although running for president in 1988 may have necessitated that denial, his position left him with a severe legal vulnerability. Throughout his presidency, he and his aides lived with the constant threat inherent in their fellow officials falling prey to investigation and prosecution for parallel denials of Iran-contra knowledge. Rather than slackening over time, in 1991 and 1992 the independent counsel on the Iran-contra matter intensified his inquiry, using new sources of information and a deeper understanding of the 1986 postexposure cover-up for a new wave of indictments, notably of former secretary of defense Caspar Weinberger.

The Iran-contra debacle, and the subsequent investigations, served as the Bush Administration's formative national security experience on the eve of its taking office. C. Boyden Gray, who had gone on that 1985 trip to Honduras, served as the Bush counsel in the inquiries, making him "the guardian of what may be Mr. Bush's most precious official secret: his behavior in the Iran-contra scandal."[13] Brent Scowcroft served as one of the three members of the Tower Commission, the body established by President Reagan at the end of 1986 that prepared the administration's own account of the Iran-contra affair on terms very sympathetic to George Bush.[14]

From the Tower Commission report to the final 1992 pardon message, Gray as a lawyer and Scowcroft as a national security official defended the position that the scandal reflected nothing worse than some blunders of overzealous NSC staff. They declined to reform seriously any of the structural problems, including those of the NSC.[15] Thus the Bush Administration would expand the NSC staff role and the secrecy surrounding it as a means for exercising power without Congress. The Bush White House would spend four years avoiding any Iran-contra housecleaning and warding off the omnipresent shadow.

THE STRATEGY UNFOLDS

1989: Assembly of the Team and Early Experiences

At the start of President Bush's term in 1989, his choices for top White House staff of C. Boyden Gray, John Sununu, and Brent Scowcroft signaled a new course. President Bush consigned a large role to White House Counsel Gray, an attorney with no electoral or congressional experience but a taste for policymaking. Of all President Bush's White House staff, Gray had started with him the earliest in Bush's vice presidential term and stayed with him the longest. Gray became literally the éminence grise of the administration. The president armed him with a broad authorization to develop the most extreme aspects of the strategy, by creating channels for the White House counsel's staff to set policy and to build up executive prerogatives.

With Gray worked the president's two top White House lieutenants. Over time, John Sununu developed into a chief of staff in the mold of H. R. Haldeman (Nixon) and Donald Regan (Reagan): interested in centralized and closed internal management rather than like Richard Cheney (Ford) or Howard Baker (Reagan), who sought effective dealings with Congress.

Sununu became famous for contending relatively early in the president's term that it would be best for Congress to go home. As journalists note, "It was Sununu who had told conservatives that Congress could go home in 1990 and not come back to Washington until after 1992. By the middle of 1991 Sununu was simply shutting down any proposal or initiative well before it reached the Oval Office."[16] Wanting to govern with Congress having gone home—to forgo political interaction, new enactments, and expressions of opposition—constituted the very essence of the monarchical doctrine memorialized by Charles I when he too desired a period of personal rule without a legislature. Because the Constitution denied the president the power of the king to prorogue (adjourn) the legislature, Sununu could not have his wish directly. However, by building on the foundation of other postwar White Houses, he could seek to accomplish a similar result indirectly.

Scowcroft as national security adviser became "the man on whom Bush most relied in foreign and defense policy,"[17] with intense opposition to the task of engaging in an effort to shape public and congressional opinion. A reporter described Scowcroft's aversion to the press: "To say Scowcroft shuns personal publicity is to understate most seriously. 'Brent views journalists basically as he views the KGB,' says one longtime associate. 'Except that he probably thinks the KGB does what it does for more honorable motives.'"[18] Scowcroft marked his position early by his secret trips to China in 1989 to reassure leaders in Beijing, after the massacre in Tiananmen Square, of the Bush Administration's support. Scowcroft and the president incurred serious criticism at that time for deception of the press about those trips, which went beyond mere denials.[19] Nonetheless, the style of dealing directly and secretly with foreign leaders and fending off public and congressional scrutiny became the administrator's hallmark. With Gray as legal orchestrator of the pertinent doctrines and instruments, Sununu and Scowcroft each cooperated in the strategy of governing through internal means other than building support with the public or Congress.

Early experiences with Congress only confirmed the White House in its course. In March 1989, the Senate rejected the nomination of John Tower for secretary of defense. This was the first time the Senate had ever denied a first-term president his starting choice for a Cabinet post. In May and June 1989, the Senate held hearings on the nomination as ambassador to South Korea of Donald I. Gregg; these delved into his strained explanations of President Bush's asserted ignorance of Iran-contra. The Tower and Gregg disputes suggested that even in the field of national security President Bush would have to be wary of congressional hearings. Also, the House started hearings on the influence-peddling scandals in the Department of Housing and Urban Development, another reminder to the Bush Administration of the waiting perils of oversight.[20]

1990: National Security Focus

As noted previously, the Bush Administration entered office with a modest legislative agenda. Congress, however, had moved a major agenda in the previous two years. In particular, it had asserted itself on arms control through provisions in appropriations and authorizations. When the brief honeymoon period had passed, the Bush Administration soon had to address congressional intent to continue passing reform laws. Specifically, Congress now prepared to use the same tools as in the arms control issue on the new issue of reform of abuses exposed during the Iran-contra investigation and criminal trials.

To deal with these reform laws, the administration started making its claims of power outside the system of checks and balances to defeat such reforms.[21] In particular, President Bush used the tools honed by the White House counsel: statements declaring congressional enactments unconstitutional or revising the enactments into meaninglessness. President Bush's signing statement for the 1990 defense authorization bill showed how he would trump restrictions in law by wielding the equivalent of a line item veto.

Foreign affairs vis-à-vis the Soviet Union did not provide the Bush Administration with any great room for action. In 1989 and 1990, the Soviet role in Eastern Europe, the Soviet economy, and the centralism and Communist Party monopoly of power within the Soviet Union all collapsed from internal forces without President Bush having to take any pronounced action. Even German reunification, the great European issue of the postwar era, solved itself through West German spending and diplomacy with some American support. The more serious focuses in foreign affairs shifted elsewhere, as President Bush resorted to his style of secretive deal making even with unpopular regimes. Scowcroft's secret China missions foreshadowed the administration's style: They alienated the public when revealed afterward, they spurned a joint position with Congress, and they resorted to the NSC. This style applied to the most sensitive cockpit of foreign affairs: the Persian Gulf, particularly Iraq. There the Bush Administration's operating system received its fullest demonstration.

Employing the system of special White House staff mechanisms left over from the Cold War, President Bush secretly issued National Security Directive 26 in October 1989, the basis for marshaling the whole administration's support of Saddam Hussein. In the first half of 1990, Iraq grew more belligerent toward its neighbors, yet the White House clung to the NSD-26 policy of warding off congressional sanctions against Iraq. In spring 1990, the White House used its system of NSC committees to head off anti-Iraq action despite the growing congressional clamor.

After the invasion of Kuwait in August 1990, President Bush turned toward confrontation with Iraq. The president decided to deploy the forces for an offensive option. However, to avoid a public reaction in the November 1990 midterm congressional elections, he concealed this decision from the public until a few days after that election. Also, prior to the election President Bush made his deal with Congress to accept a tax increase in return for a spending ceiling, which eliminated the budget as a partisan issue in the election. By these two steps he removed what would have been the two main issues involving the administration in the 1990 election.

The 1990 election thereby came to embody the central paradox of President Bush's term. He enjoyed high personal popularity in the period leading up to the election (although this did drop temporarily with the breach of his "read my lips" pledge against new taxes). After a rocky few months in the initial polls, President Bush's approval ratings began in 1989 their long takeoff to levels of which his supposedly popular predecessor had only dreamed. By June 1989 the polls put President Bush's approval rating at 70 percent, which President Reagan had never seen; in 1990 it hit 80 percent; in 1991, after the wartime triumph of Desert Storm, it soared to the fabulous level of 90 percent.[22] As noted in 1991 by an analyst of the figures on public opinion, "Perhaps the biggest political surprise of the Bush administration has been the president's high standing in the polls."[23]

However, the president did not attempt to risk or to employ this popularity to move the public or Congress on policy. Even though his popularity had risen, as measured by the polls, in Congress his level of support, already a record low in 1989 for a first-term elected president, dropped in 1990 "16 percentage points below his 1989 score." This gave him "the worst two-year record in the 38-year history of the CQ presidential support vote study."[24] In the 1990 midterm election, he lost further ground in Congress. From the 1990 election, *Congressional Quarterly Almanac* noted, "Bush's hand was weakened. Republicans lost one Senate seat and eight House seats. . . . The GOP's greatest damage, however, sprang from its failure to meet its own expectations, announced . . . when [Bush's] soaring popularity held out the hope of defying history and gaining seats or breaking even."[25]

Rather than attempt to translate that popularity into support for action in the public arena, President Bush had avoided that arena. Instead of letting his plan for war with Iraq become an issue in 1990, he concealed the decision. Then, on November 8, less than a week after the 1990 election, President Bush announced an offensive buildup against Iraq. Concealing this major national decision until after the polls closed, in an unsubtle avoidance of electoral verdicts, provoked a "'mini-firestorm' of criticism" threatening to prove "as bitter as the conflicts between hawks and doves during the Vietnam War."[26] Up to the end of 1990, his administration followed by threatening to go to war without Congress. Only when faced with public pressure did the president finally give in, during January 1991, and ask Congress for authorization of the Persian Gulf War, which Congress provided.

After the war, in 1991 and 1992, the national security apparatus continued to employ its expanded powers by a rear-guard cover-up of the prewar courtship. President Bush's last two years also brought continued controversy over his protective attitude toward those implicated like him in denials of knowledge of Iran-contra. The hearings in September 1991 on President Bush's nomination of Robert M. Gates for Central Intelligence Agency director and the president's across-the-board Iran-contra pardons in December 1992 inevitably focused attention on his own Iran-contra role.

1991: Domestic Focus

From early 1991 on, national attention returned to domestic issues. President Bush spurned the golden opportunity of his record public approval levels by asking Congress only for a transportation bill and a crime bill. As observers noted later in a critical view on the eve of the 1992 election, "if these proposals were to be the crowning accomplishments of a second Bush term, they were awfully meager."[27] At that point, President Bush and his advisers had a rosy view of his reelection prospects. The Sununu strategy for reelection rested on three issues, alliteratively called "Kuwait, crime, and quotas."[28] Two out of these three—Iraq and civil rights opposition—were managed as much as possible through White House staff.

On the critical matter of the economy, the administration disdained serious legislative proposals. President Bush, without a fiscal and economic reform policy, found his administration with nothing to do as the unemployment rate began to climb. His reappointment in August 1991 of Federal Reserve Chairman Alan Greenspan, who responded slowly to the recession, was admitted later by insiders to result from botching the consideration of alternative appointees while the White House economics staff feuded with the Treasury secretary.[29]

Meanwhile, the multiyear struggle over civil rights legislation came to the forefront. President Bush had vetoed in 1990 a prior civil rights bill that rejected the Supreme Court's recent burdens of proof impeding job discrimination suits. The Senate fell one vote short of overriding his veto. President Bush left the long negotiations over a revised version of the bill to Sununu and Gray. By October 1991, the highly controversial confirmation hearings over the Supreme Court nomination of Clarence Thomas had made it all but impossible to stop the bill or avoid override of a second veto.[30]

Faced with a bill that he could no longer confidently veto, President Bush initially let the White House counsel circulate an astonishing draft executive order rolling back the government's chief mechanism for civil rights in employment. Even President Reagan had rejected that step as too far out. With the administration reeling from the impending fall of Sununu over travel improprieties, hostile public reaction to the draft order caused President Bush to back away from it.[31] Instead, the president declared that the Civil Rights Act of 1991 "codified" as law the burdens of proof impeding job discrimination suits that the act had been passed to supplant. President Bush pronounced this "codification" in a signing statement he labeled as "authoritative interpretive guidance" about the new act. By doing so, he attempted to seize the power to revise the meaning of new laws into something diametrically opposite to Congress's intent. He broke the deal made with Congress by his negotiators, and he set the stage for black voters to express much more antipathy to him at the polls in 1992 than they had in 1988.[32]

On another key domestic issue, environmental regulation, President Bush had initially started his term with the somewhat positive approach of shaping rather than blocking the Clean Air Act of 1990. However, even as early as June 1990 he gave the go-ahead for an active White House staff at the Quayle Council. In 1991, the council hit full stride in the blocking of regulations to carry out the environmental, safety, and health laws. It also stymied fulfillment of the president's 1988 campaign pledge of "no net loss" of wetlands. The Quayle Council waged a continuing campaign to weaken proposed regulations implementing the new clean air law into a version preferred by potential contributors to the Bush-Quayle reelection campaign who lobbied the White House.

By year's end, with the economy sluggish, President Bush's approval levels had declined sharply, from 89 percent in March, to 51 percent in November, to 40 percent in February 1992.[33] Yet the president still refused to offer serious legislative proposals: "Bush was frozen not only by conflicting advice, but by his fear of Congress. He worried aloud during White House strategy sessions that any legislation he initiated would only get mucked up by Congress. It would spend too much money and create new bureaucracies. Then his only options would be to accept a bill that would make things worse or to veto it and take political heat."[34]

1992: The Decline

The hard-hit economy of New Hampshire offered an open opportunity for a challenge, and Patrick Buchanan emerged to take advantage of it. In the midst of a primary challenge, President Bush's January 28, 1992, State of the Union Address constituted one of the last occasions for him to change his administration's approach. Instead, besides promising vetoes and shunning specific legislative proposals, he announced a three-month "experiment" with a moratorium in regulation. This initiative, perhaps the only firm aspect of his economic "competitiveness" policy, turned out to vest governmentwide control powers in the Quayle Council.

As the economy remained slow in spring and summer 1992, President Bush used the Quayle Council in an attempt to promote an anti-environmental policy as a pro-jobs policy. In March, published reports placed Gray at the heart of a White House staff effort at "using the regulatory powers of incumbency to score points with constituencies in key primary states."[35] The White House rebuffed Environmental Protection Agency administrator William Reilly's attempt at the Earth Summit in Rio de Janeiro for the United States to join the biodiversity treaty that had won worldwide acceptance. The Quayle Council staff and the White House counsel defeated Reilly's request.[36]

When Congress served up a largely noncontroversial set of appropriation bills in the fall, the president had nothing upon which to veto or to affect significantly with a signing statement. The White House counsel floated a legally amazing proposal that had the president claim to possess line-item veto power. A press report said, "White House counsel C.

Boyden Gray had led 'an aggressive and intense effort' in recent weeks to develop a legal foundation and tactical plan for provoking a court test."[37] This plan failed to materialize, perhaps because of the opposition of the new attorney general, William Barr. Even though Barr expressed in many contexts a passion for expansive views of presidential prerogatives, he conceded that the president could not exercise line-item veto power.

By the end of the congressional term in 1992, President Bush set a historic low in support from Congress. Congressional Quarterly's annual study of presidential strength on congressional votes concluded that President Bush's "dismal 43.0 percent" was "11 percentage points below his 1991 level—[and thus] was the worst performance of any president at any point in his term since CQ began keeping score 39 years ago." Even his own party's support dropped, which "was reflected most sharply by the decline in GOP support for Bush in the Senate, from 83 percent in 1991 to 75 percent in 1992."[38]

The election became a referendum on the question of which candidate would most likely produce change. By refusing to engage with Congress and public opinion, the Bush Administration, in its strategy for personal rule, contributed to a verdict against President Bush on that question. During the election came the notorious tampering with the passport office files of Bill Clinton, for which the White House gave such halting and changing explanations as to necessitate appointment—deferred until after the election—of an independent counsel to investigate. Also following the election came the December 1992 mass Iran-contra pardon by which President Bush protected himself from public examination about his contradictory Iran-contra stories.[39] The pardons came with a final presidential statement in the White House counsel's inimitable style that defiantly dismissed the investigation and prosecution of the illegal Iran-contra coverup—guilty pleas, jury convictions, and pending indictments all washed away together—as a wrongful interference with the White House's tools in foreign affairs for semi-sovereign rule.

The Clinton Administration's first year of 1993 presented a direct contrast with preceding years. On its major issues of health care and deficit reduction, the new administration engaged vigorously with Congress and the public. Its approach was clearly to govern by working with Congress rather than by unilateral fiat, even when events like the August 1993 razor-thin final passage of the deficit reduction bill, by single-vote margins in both the House and the Senate, suggested the new president's mandate had practical limits. The new administration also seemed to formulate and to conduct policy regarding the issues concerning overseas conflicts of late 1993—whether to use American forces in Bosnia, how long to keep such forces in Somalia—with attention to public and congressional concerns unlike the Iraq policy of 1989–1990. The White House systems for circumventing laws—signing statements and the Quayle Council—were, respectively, unused and dismantled. That first year of the new administration marked by contrast the different approach of the Bush Administration.

In turn, the Bush Administration's closing notes, during its campaign and then in the postelection Iran-contra pardons, recalled aptly the origins and course of its distinctive approach to governing without Congress. That course left open the question of how the American government had evolved to such a point.

2

From 1789 to 1988: President and Law Until the Bush Administration

Although the Bush Administration's semi-sovereign pretensions resulted from its own special situation, evaluating its strategy requires a historical perspective. After Vietnam and Watergate, the leading historian in this area, Arthur M. Schlesinger, Jr., conducted in *The Imperial Presidency* a broad survey of trends from the Framers to the 1970s, which showed that "Nixon displayed more monarchical yearnings than any of his predecessors." By 1990, in *The National Security Constitution: Sharing Power After the Iran-Contra Affair,* Harold Hongju Koh conducted a similar updated survey of presidential tendencies in national security (not domestic affairs).[1] These recent book-length surveys clear away the underbrush of detail to allow focusing on the particular subject pertinent from 1989 to 1992: the relation of the president to enacted law.

FROM THE FRAMERS TO 1945

The Danger of Personal Rule

At the Constitutional Convention in 1787, the Framers set out to replace the weak Articles of Confederation with a strong central government headed by a single ruler with potentially great power. Thus they faced the overriding problem of how to create centralized power yet at the same time check and restrain that power. For Congress's powers, structural checks and restraints more than sufficed. The Framers did not let Congress execute the laws, only make them. By dividing Congress between House and Senate, the Framers preserved the mutual checks of large and small states and guaranteed the divisions of regional diversities and factional disputes. The Supreme Court's decisions in the 1980s against legislative vetoes and congressional agents in *Chadha* and *Bowsher* confirmed these historical structural restraints.[2]

19

Executive power gave the Framers greater reason for concern. Their numerous hostile comparisons at the Constitutional Convention of the presidency with a potential monarchy bring this home.[3] Their struggle against George III and colonial governors led them to abhor any re-creation of executive supremacy. To the Framers, the essence of monarchy was not that the head of state inherited office. They were familiar with both inherited and elective monarchies and distinguished both from the real problem, the doctrine of personal rule.

Personal rule meant rule by the head of state and ministers personally accountable only to him rather than by officials subject to law, to public accountability, and to checks and balances. Parliament had fought in particular with the personal rule doctrines of two Stuart monarchs. Charles I had attempted, in his period of personal rule after 1629, to govern by executive powers alone, without summoning Parliament to enact laws. Charles I looked at the House of Commons in 1629 the way John Sununu looked at the Congress in 1991: Each thought the chief executive, rather than struggling with an adversary legislature, would find himself better off governing without new laws. In the 1680s James II had asserted the power to suspend particular laws. James II looked at laws the way President Bush had in his Princeton Address: Each thought the chief executive, rather than engaging with the legislature by either vetoing or compromising on new laws, would find himself better off declaring particular provisions inoperative.

Whether the chief executive was Charles I after 1629 or George Bush after 1989, the resort to "personal rule" necessarily meant making less new law and policy than the chief executives who successfully pushed vigorous programs by engaging with the legislature. An executive who disengaged from the mechanisms of public action would inevitably make less new law. By turning instead to the internal mechanisms of the palace or White House, such an executive traded away establishing the most new law and policy in return for obtaining—he would hope—escape from democratic accountability. In fact, the chief executive with the weakest mandate, not the strongest, might experience the greatest temptation to govern outside the system. Charles I and George Bush each disengaged from major legislated changes in defense spending for lack of strength in the legislature. Each instead rejected the legislature's conditions on military spending as a means to personal rule, the one by refusing to convene Parliament at all and the other by declaring the conditions void. Neither had a strong mandate to draw on such as, for example, President Reagan for his program in 1981 of massive increases in military appropriations and spending. A chief executive with a "personal rule" approach could not implement a policy like President Reagan's requiring massive legislated appropriations. What such a chief executive instead hoped was to do whatever he could without the compromises, legislative conditions, and public accountability implicit in engaging with the legislature.

When Parliament brought Charles I's personal rule to bay in the English Civil War of the 1640s and dethroned James II in the Glorious Revolution of 1689, its struggles established the foundation for all subsequent Anglo-American democracy. That foundation consisted of the doctrines of supremacy of law over the power of any officer and the accountability to the public and to the legislature of all officers exercising lawful authority. The legislature took on the role of the "Grand Inquest of the Nation," with "Duty to inquire into every Step of public management, either Abroad or at Home, in order to see that nothing has been done amiss . . . ."[4] These concepts continued in America as the basis for government under the Constitution.[5]

No Presidential Power over the Laws, and Accountable Officers

Article I, section 1, which begins the Constitution (after the Preamble), conferred a monopoly of lawmaking power upon Congress with the words "All legislative Powers herein granted shall be vested in a Congress of the United States." Only the House and the Senate could shape a law. Although the president had his veto, it acted only upon whole bills and could not add or take away particular provisions or change the meaning of the bill. In light of President Bush's claims of power to treat provisions as void by his signing statements, it warrants notice that the Framers understood quite well the arguments for the president to have revisory power over new enactments. Understanding those arguments, the Framers rejected them. Presidents could bargain with Congress for changes, but with the decision to sign presidential power ended. Laws had power over the executive; the executive had no power to reshape laws.

Signing statements with purported legal impact did surface on occasion in the next two centuries, but not so very often until Attorney General Meese's tenure. As a commentator observed, "Before President Reagan, only a few presidents issued such statements."[6] No one asserted any particular presidential power accompanying signing. In contrast to the Bush Administration's systematic issuance of such statements, the scattered few statements before the 1970s almost all consisted simply of presidents using the occasion of signing a bill as an opportunity for issuing a public speech, without making any particular claims about presidential power to void or revise laws.

Once laws were enacted, the Framers bound the president to a system of execution of laws that made the laws themselves, not his own will, supreme. The Constitution gave to Congress the power to create offices and their incident authority. Hence, the federal departments and agencies all depended on the definition of their powers in the law.[7] Only the officers with authority by law, with Senate confirmation, and with the related checks by courts and congressional oversight would exercise authority. No president could act through some kind of personal guard or staff, unchecked by oversight or appropriations, like the personal rule of Charles I. Presidents would nominate the officers and might remove them, but the Supreme Court firmly established that the president could not use that leverage to command departmental officers contrary to the law.[8] The oversight of Congress joined judicial rulings in making officers accountable.

Through the end of World War II, the potential danger to the rule of accountability from vesting formal powers in White House staffs, like the staff of the Quayle Council, stayed well at bay. Presidents had no centralized budget office until the twentieth century, and even then that office rested comfortably in the Treasury Department, whose officials were accountable to Congress and to the law. As Arthur Schlesinger summed up, "Until recently Presidents had made do with very little in the way of personal staff. When [President] Hoover persuaded Congress to give him a third secretary, it was, Franklin Roosevelt used to say, the most positive accomplishment of his administration." As late as World War II, with a White House facing global challenges and managing an enormously fast-moving domestic sector, "President Roosevelt never had more than eleven White House assistants."[9]

Even in the realm of international relations—or what would today be called national security—the Framers saved key powers for Congress. They gave the power of regulating foreign commerce to Congress, which exercised it from earliest times to the Lend-Lease Act of World War II. The Framers vested Congress with the power to declare war and with the power of the purse.[10] Parliament had used that power of the purse to curb monarchical pretensions in foreign affairs, defense, or intelligence by refusing to fund them.[11]

The Framers championed most earnestly Congress's exercise of a power of the purse like Parliament's.[12] Although the Framers named the president commander in chief, this designation established only that the civilian executive would be supreme over all generals and admirals.[13] It did not free the military or him from needing Congress's declarations of war, appropriations, and other enactments making the decision and providing the means for the nation to go to war.

Until the Cold War era, the principle generally survived that only Congress did make war on the scale at issue with Iraq in 1990. The debate in late 1990 over President Bush's apparent intention not to seek congressional authorization for the war against Iraq awoke this classic issue. Presidential proponents have promoted "lists" over the years of 56, 125, or 200 incidents supposedly reflecting presidential war power before the Cold War. These incidents were mostly minor or distinguishable affairs, not wars.[14] Many were interventions in Latin America resembling President Reagan's Grenada intervention. The presidents justified their actions as mere landings or naval actions for self-defense or to protect American citizens. Wars, in contrast, were for the Congress to declare. War-hawk Congresses pushed reluctant presidents into the War of 1812 and the Spanish-American War. Congress ratified the start of the Civil War and decided on entry into World War I. Although President Franklin Roosevelt undertook controversial initiatives prior to America's entry into World War II, particularly in the Atlantic, he did not dare enter in 1941 before Congress declared war.[15]

Commentators have noted correctly that "[s]uccessive Presidents, Congresses, and courts agreed that the scope of assumed authorization extended no further than the protection of American citizens in certain circumstances and the defense of the American state." Congress authorized even the limited wars, such as the naval wars with Republican France in 1798 and with the Barbary pirates around 1803. Thus "with the sole exception of the protection of American citizens, no President ever claimed that congressional authorization [for war] could be assumed until President Truman did so in June 1950."[16]

THE TWO NEW POSTWAR CONDITIONS: THE COLD WAR AND DIVIDED GOVERNMENT

National Security Until Vietnam

The Cold War radically shifted authority on national security matters to the executive. In contrast to all the pre-1950 wars, Congress did not declare or specifically ratify the Korean War.[17] A decade and a half later, in 1964, Congress did adopt the Tonkin Gulf Resolution regarding Vietnam. Yet it adopted that resolution to authorize an air strike to respond after the Tonkin Gulf naval engagement, not with deliberate intent to authorize what became the massive American commitment to the Vietnam War on land the next year.[18] Presidents had seized the war power.

During the Cold War, presidents also displaced Congress from its traditional role in the twilight zone of limited war. Cold War presidents launched interventions and covert actions without clear congressional authorization.[19] Congress granted wide open statutory delegations of authority to the executive in the name of national security regarding foreign commerce and defense.[20]

With the president's new national security powers came another new Cold War development: White House directives and staffs that avoided traditional accountability. As Professor Koh noted, the national security charter—the National Security Act of 1947—had its roots and justification in the incipient Cold War.[21] The 1947 act created the National Security Council, consisting of the president and vice president and certain Cabinet members, with one staffer, the executive secretary. This isolated seedling grew into the large and powerful NSC staff that was headed by the national security adviser, who held office without Senate confirmation, without a specific mandate of law, and without consistent congressional oversight. In the case of Henry Kissinger, a national security adviser could virtually run the nation's foreign affairs.

Occasionally, the NSC staff exercised authority through a new species of presidential directive. These directives were called National Security Council policy papers in the Truman and Eisenhower administrations, National Security Action Memoranda in the Kennedy and Johnson administrations, National Security Decision Memoranda in the Nixon and Ford administrations, and Presidential Directives in the Carter Administration.[22] These directives took on the perilous role of secret law: They authorized action and specified the limits of the action, just as a public law or a public executive order would. This Cold War history provided the tools used by President Bush's NSC to manage the courtship of Saddam Hussein in 1989 and 1990 and to hold back congressional oversight of this courtship in 1991 and 1992.

National Security Since Vietnam

The Cold War rise of presidential power over foreign affairs and war did not go unchallenged by Congress. As the Vietnam War continued and grew, the country underwent the most pronounced reaction in its history against presidential power claims. With the enactment of the War Powers Resolution in 1973 over President Nixon's veto, Congress signified more than just the creation of a procedure that later presidents might evade or dispute. Congress also enacted particular restrictions, such as the Cooper-Church Amendment and its successors, which precluded further secret war in Laos and in Indochina generally (1970–1975); the Clark Amendment for Angola (1978); and the Boland Amendments for Nicaragua (1982–1988). These enactments marked a major statement that even in the midst of the Cold War, the public insisted on Congress's role in deciding on future wars.[23] Also, Congress began replacing the previous system of open-ended delegations of foreign affairs power with enactments typical of peacetime rather than wartime.[24]

Since the enactment of the War Powers Resolution, the public has given intensive scrutiny to each U.S. action with war overtones in debates that set the stage for January 1991 and Iraq.[25] Between Vietnam and 1990, like before 1950, presidents stayed below the level of initiation of wars absent congressional authorization.[26] Presidents did order many deployments of the armed forces without congressional authorization. They strained the War Powers Resolution's procedures or expressed disdain for the spirit of interbranch consultation. However, in sober moments both the White House and the Justice Department praised the War Powers Resolution and confirmed its constitutionality.[27] Of central importance, wars did not occur without congressional authorization.

Furthermore, the period during and after the Vietnam War brought major oversight exercises: release of the Pentagon Papers, the intelligence committee investigations of the mid-1970s, and the creation of a continuing system of congressional oversight by intelligence committees. Congress and the public developed a fuller view of how the NSC staff and its directives could make secret law and policy unless checked. After Henry Kissinger, the national security advisers of Presidents Ford, Carter, and Reagan never obtained, however much they aspired to, the power he had had.

Divided Government

A second novel condition, besides the Cold War, affected the separation of powers in the postwar era: divided government. In the first half of the twentieth century, it was a rank and temporary aberration to have a president of one party and a House or Senate of the other. From 1897 to 1954, such divided government occurred in only eight years, or 14 percent of the time. Before 1946, "[t]here had been only three previous instances during the twentieth century, all at the midterm and each accompanied by turnover of party control of the White House in the next election."[28]

Then, suddenly, the postwar era turned completely different. President Truman had two years of divided government; President Eisenhower, six years; Presidents Nixon and Ford, eight years; President Reagan, eight years; and President Bush, four years. Republican presidents faced Democratic chambers of Congress in the thirty-eight years from 1955 to 1992 a total of twenty-six years or 68 percent of the time, almost five times the rate of divided government from 1897 to 1954. The special exception that had been divided government before 1954 now had quintupled in frequency to become the regular rule through 1992.

Political scientists took some time to catch up with the new phenomenon. As one noted, "We look to Franklin Roosevelt and Lyndon Johnson for lessons of presidential leadership," with their same-party executive and Congress, "not to Dwight Eisenhower or even, despite his recent admirers, to Harry Truman and certainly not to Richard Nixon."[29] The Watergate-marked term of President Nixon had not established, by itself, that efforts to escape from checks and balances would necessarily come with divided government. Watergate, like Iran-contra, was a separate phenomenon, warranting separate discussion below.

On the contrary, looking back from the 1990s, political scientists studying divided government saw how presidents had used particular tools within the system, fully consistent with the Framers' vision. President Truman had appealed to the country over Congress's head, as President Reagan later did; such presidential appeals became a whole subject of study. President Eisenhower had bargained over legislation, and President Ford had depended on the veto. "Veto bargaining"—vetoes or threats against one version of a bill to get a better one—became another subject of study for an era of divided government.[30]

Domestic Affairs

The Supreme Court's seminal decision in 1952 in *Youngstown Sheet & Tube Co. v. Sawyer*[31] reflected vividly how little the president had escaped his classic relation to enacted law in domestic affairs. Even during the Korean War, the Supreme Court could, and did, find in *Youngstown* that the president could not act in domestic affairs—seize a steel plant as an antistrike measure in that case—absent a congressional enactment as authorization. The *Youngstown* opinions reiterated that the president could not make or revise the laws or instruct a department to act without law (apart from whatever temporary scope of emergency action might exist in anticipation of congressional ratification afterward).

Postwar presidents before President Reagan did establish some of the foundation for greater unaccountable White House power. In particular, President Nixon organized the Office of Management and Budget (OMB) and took other steps toward what was called an "administrative presidency." Even President Nixon did not yet exhibit the attitude toward new laws expressed by President Bush's signing statements. When Presidents Nixon, Ford, and Carter made any use of signing statements for purposes beyond mere speechifying, that use concerned mainly a single limited area of special constitutional dispute, the legislative veto. Legislative veto provisions were Congress's unique and, ultimately, unconstitutional attempt to obtain postenactment power. Presidents naturally countered this attempt with their own, if dubious, postenactment signing statements.[32] Presidents did not fight the issues that President Bush did, like civil rights, with such statements. Before President Reagan, such statements remained so insignificant that no one published even a single law review article or similar commentary on them.

Similarly, before the Reagan Administration there had been nothing comparable in influence to the Quayle Council. With the creation of the Environmental Protection Agency (EPA) in 1970 and the enactment of the Clean Air Act of 1970 and Clean Water Act of 1972, federal environmental regulation had taken on visible importance. The Nixon, Ford, and for that matter Carter administrations each had machinery for reviewing environmental regulation. None of these administrations created any special White House staff for regulatory review. As a leading commentator observes, before the Reagan Administration "[no] previous orders establish[ed] any formal mechanism for enforcement of [regulatory] review requirements."[33] Congress succeeded during the Ford Administration in forcing accountability onto the mechanism used for reviewing environmental regulations, namely, the Office of Management and Budget. It passed legislation subjecting the director and deputy director of the OMB to Senate confirmation. This legislation meant that OMB officials must make, and in fact have made, themselves available for congressional hearings and investigations.[34]

Thus, apart from some of the dangerous developments during President Nixon's Watergate period, the classic rule persisted, as stated by the Brownlow Commission of the 1930s, in proposing a White House Office as distinct from a statutory and accountable office. White House aides would have "no power to make decisions or issue instructions in their own right."[35] Only accountable officers could do so.

THE REAGAN ADMINISTRATION:
COMPARISON WITH THE SUCCESSOR

The Reagan Administration's early years warrant comparison with the years of the Bush Administration. Regarding separation of powers, one political scientist summed up three basic choices of strategy for presidents in divided governments: "They can bargain 'within the beltway,' accepting the cards that the electoral and constitutional systems have dealt them. They can attempt to expand the context . . . by appealing beyond the beltway to public opinion. Or they can seek to prosecute policy without the assent of the other party."[36] In 1981 and 1982, President Reagan made extensive use of public appeals. His personal style favored such appeals, and he wielded a conservative electoral mandate.

These factors and his desire to affect domestic tax and spending policy and defense spending all combined for a first term of public appeals followed by bargaining. He proposed and enacted a legislative program of cutting social assistance programs, raising military spending, and reducing upper-bracket and corporate taxes. In regard to this activist legislative program and accompanying public appeals, his approach contrasted with President Bush's reliance on a strategy of disengagement from 1989 on.

Similarly, President Reagan made appointments, like Interior Secretary James Watt and other anti-regulatory administrators, which asserted a conservative mandate in an open public challenge to Congress. In this he resembled President Andrew Jackson, who had destroyed the Bank of the United States in a great public struggle with Congress by appointing and removing Treasury secretaries until he found one who would execute the policy Jackson wished. Presidential struggles for control through appointments and removal enlivened the political landscape from President Taft's Ballenger-Pinchot affair to President Truman's firing of Douglas MacArthur. As required for such a struggle in the public arena, President Reagan supported Watt and his EPA administrator, Anne Gorsuch, in their subsequent public face-offs with congressional oversight. To this extent, his strategy contrasted with his successor's reliance upon unaccountable White House staff of the Council on Competitiveness to hamstring regulators by actions behind closed doors shielded from congressional oversight. The contrast was not total. President Reagan supplemented the open reliance on antiregulatory administrators with a closed-door White House staff antiregulatory effort, in which Vice President Bush and C. Boyden Gray played important roles.

In foreign affairs and war powers, during the early years of his administration President Reagan used both the mechanisms that engaged with the public and Congress and the mechanisms of the Cold War presidential prerogatives. He fought for public support and for victory in Congress on many issues from sale to Saudi Arabia of Airborne Warning and Control Systems (AWACS) to funding for his cherished "Star Wars" antimissile defenses. In 1983, he had accepted Senate Majority Leader Howard Baker's brilliantly engineered deal regarding the sending of the marines into Lebanon. He agreed in the end to the arrangement in which Congress followed the War Powers Resolution in adopting the Multilateral Force Resolution of 1983, and he as president received the limited authorization he needed from that resolution. The tragic American losses in the suicide bombing of Marine quarters in Beirut underlined that when the country faced such losses as a result of a decision to intervene in a war situation, the decision should not be made without public consent through Congress. However, the Reagan Administration flexed its Cold War presidential prerogatives in foreign affairs often even during the first term, such as in the covert actions of the Central Intelligence Agency under William Casey.

To some extent, the Reagan Administration's willingness to engage with the public and Congress, which always had its limits, diminished in the second term in ways that adumbrated the sovereign tendencies of the Bush Administration. In the international sphere, the administration conducted the Iran-contra debacle of 1985 and 1986, shunning notice to Congress of the arms-for-hostages deal with Iran, breaking the arms exports laws, secretly flouting the Boland Amendments in arming the contras, and covering up all these with lies to Congress. In the domestic sphere, Attorney General Edwin Meese III took the position that the president could declare provisions of laws unconstitutional rather than obey them. Meese also proclaimed the use of presidential signing statements to define the meaning of new laws. There were parallels between the 1985–1986 period and the excesses of the Nixon Administration. Many of the problems highlighted by Schlesinger in *The Imperial Presidency* in 1974 and Koh in *The National Security Constitution* in 1990 revolved around how White House staffs during the Nixon and Reagan administrations acted in similar illegality, using nongovernmental operatives and funding, from Cuban burglars and laundered cash in Watergate to North's operatives and diverted funds in Iran-contra.

In 1987 and 1988 President Reagan painfully repudiated much of what had taken place and carried through his last two years on a basis reminiscent, in a parallel but reversed way, of 1981 and 1982. As in his first two years, President Reagan's administration in his last two years moved forward on many policy questions through the regular system of the president and Congress resolving their differences in the public arena. Attorney General Meese lost much of his capability for pushing claims of presidential prerogative offensively and spent his energies on defending his past efforts.[37] With President Reagan in some respects a weakened lame duck and Congress having public support on its agenda, the substantive outcomes differed in orientation from 1981 and 1982. Congress enacted a major legislative reform agenda in 1987 and 1988 while it carried forward the massive oversight exercise of the Iran-contra investigation. For instance, it used the tool of conditions on defense appropriations and authorizations to try to push arms control, such as conditions to limit antisatellite missile testing. President Reagan reacted not by claiming some power to revise the laws but by public struggle and bargaining. This reaction meant that he had to accept losses; observers concluded in the end that "[a]fter eight years the executive's Thermidor to the Congress's 1970s revolution in defense policy can only be judged a total failure."[38]

Congress's oversight of the Reagan Administration's regulatory review systems, which were the precursor of the Quayle Council, similarly reflected how the system had continued to work. Congress had summoned OMB officials to face inquiries and changes in their charter, which the OMB, as a statutorily authorized and Senate-confirmed office, could not avoid. Faced with the prospect that Congress would enact further statutory impositions, the OMB in the late 1980s imposed disclosure requirements on itself to limit its use as a secret ex parte conduit for industry influence (the so-called Gramm procedures, after the OMB officer Wendy Gramm). Thus, for all the flaws of regulatory review it had receded considerably from what became the Quayle Council notion of empowering a White House staff to control regulation without congressional oversight or Senate-confirmed officers or congressionally sanctioned procedures against gross external influence.

Thus, whether as a "winner" in 1981 and 1982 or a "loser" in 1987 and 1988, President Reagan showed that a president and Congress of different parties could share a divided government. Through bargaining, public appeals, vetoes, struggles over accountable officers, and all the usual tools of the system of checks and balances, they would resolve or at least patch up temporarily their pending issues. The relations of presidents and Congress still involved serious problems. There was a legacy of unsolved issues and accumulating debt. There had been many excessive assertions of executive prerogative, a good deal of which went uncorrected even in the later years. Yet, still, during 1981 and 1982 and 1987 and 1988 the administration put much of its energies into engaging with Congress in the arenas of appeals to public opinion and legislating, in a manner not unfamiliar in the history of American government. As Walter Oleszek put it, while "[c]hances for gridlock increase . . . . for all its allegedly negative consequences, divided government produced a large number of policy successes in the 1980s."[39]

Moreover, just as Congress had responded to Vietnam and Watergate by enacting oversight framework laws that strengthened the separation of powers, so Congress might have been expected to respond to Iran-contra by enacting further reform laws.[40] With the Cold War approaching an end, the claims of the NSC staff to wartime powers might wither away like prior expansions of presidential power during and after wartime.[41]

In sum, the postwar period in general and the Reagan Administration in particular had laid a foundation for what transpired in the Bush Administration. Nonetheless, an optimist might not have foreseen the extent to which the Bush Administration would build upon that foundation a whole strategy for governing without Congress.

3

Striking Down or Revising Laws: Signing Statements in the Bush Presidency

The Bush Administration's separation of powers strategy centered on the White House Counsel, C. Boyden Gray, who used as his most treasured tool his newly exalted law-altering pen—the pen for presidential signing statements. Presidents traditionally influence how Congress shapes bills prior to enactment in many ways: by submitting their own proposals, lobbying Congress during consideration, and making veto threats. However, from 1789 to the 1980s, presidents recognized that after congressional passage the Constitution allowed them only one decision: whether to veto.[1]

Edwin Meese suggested the first real alternative: When President Reagan signed a bill he could simultaneously issue a "signing statement," which would declare provisions of the new law unconstitutional. At the time, this novel idea received intense criticism from Congress, the public, and the courts, and it appeared to be a temporary aberration. The strategy of the Bush Administration took this notion and expanded it into an extraordinary tool enabling White House staff to escape the system of checks and balances. A 1990 New York Times profile of Gray, one of the few such profiles before the struggle a year later over the civil rights bill, noted his support of the aggressive use of signing statements: "At the heart of Mr. Gray's public philosophy is his keenness to preserve Presidential prerogatives. Mr. Bush's method of signing bills with appended statements that he will not enforce certain provisions he regards as infringements on his authority is a technique Mr. Gray has championed."[2]

TWO LAWYERS FOR THE PRESIDENT: EDWIN MEESE AND C. BOYDEN GRAY

Edwin Meese

President Reagan began issuing a considerable number of signing statements upon the advice of Edwin Meese III, presidential counselor and later attorney general. For example, he signed a 1984 bill, the Competition in Contracting Act (CICA), which reformed federal procurement, but simultaneously declared key provisions of CICA to be unconstitutional. This was no mere matter of going on record, as in a public speech or message to Congress. Attorney General Meese backed up the president's declaration of CICA's invalidity with elaborate claims in public hearings and court submissions. They gave as the grounds that the president had the same constitutional role as the judiciary does under *Marbury v. Madison*, namely, that when the Justice Department objected to a law the president should have the power to invalidate the law and direct the government to treat it as a nullity rather than as a law. To implement the president's power, the OMB issued a governmentwide order directing all agencies not to obey the CICA but to "proceed with the procurement process as though no such provisions were contained in the act."[3]

The CICA statement illustrates the most potent part of the Meese innovation. But President Reagan also issued a few signing statements asserting power of a different kind: to revise the law being enacted. Only one of these had any particular importance. At passage of the Immigration Reform and Control Act of 1986, his signing statement watered down the law's important protection of lawful resident aliens against discrimination. The bill drafters wrote protection for them into the law; the president interpreted that protection out of the law. As a leading observer noted: "The implementation of the Act thus presents the danger of encroachment on both the Legislature and the courts inherent in the production of 'executive history' statements, and presents an action offensive to the doctrine of separation of powers."[4] In 1986, Attorney General Meese arranged for signing statements to be published in USCCAN, the report of legislative history often used by lawyers.[5] There, the statements joined the congressional committee reports as though they were part of the official record of the statute's shaping, even though they had been issued after completion of the shaping of the bill.

Notwithstanding the Reagan Administration's moves, the Meese claim of power through signing statements should have been no more than a temporary aberration. In a major legal battle lasting from 1985 to 1988, Attorney General Meese's pronouncements regarding the CICA received a total and devastating rebuff. The executive claim of power regarding CICA was assailed not only by the Congress and the public in 1985 but by the appellate courts as well in 1986 through 1988. The executive had to stage a humiliating retreat.[6] More generally, the Reagan Administration's assertion of power in signing statements drew well-reasoned scholarly criticism and little defense.[7]

Meanwhile, the Iran-contra affair shed light both on the Reagan White

House's extreme view of its own power to disregard laws and Bush's motivation during his own administration to claim that power in the form of signing statements rather than the way the Reagan White House did. When Congress limited U.S. government assistance for the Nicaraguan contras by the Boland Amendment after 1982, some of the White House staff viewed the Boland Amendment as not applying to them. President Reagan's own conservative supporters subsequently conceded that if the Reagan White House was willing to state its constitutional position openly, this was the time to use the tool of signing statements.[8] President Reagan could have signed the Boland Amendments into law during the key period of 1984 to 1986 with signing statements expressing the kind of views the NSC staff later expressed at Iran-contra congressional hearings—that the provisions were unconstitutional or did not apply to presidential staff. Instead of taking such a legal position in signing statements, the NSC staff, when it engaged in schemes like diversion of arms proceeds and foreign solicitation, covered up its activity by covert lawbreaking and deception.

The shadow that hung over George Bush from his own participation in and knowledge of Iran-contra affected the new president's personal style. It may have affected his willingness to use this tool of signing statements. The new president would choose to employ the formal-appearing mechanism of signing statements, regardless of their controversiality and dubious authority, rather than repeat what the Reagan White House had undergone in Iran-contra for not using such a tool.

By the end of the Reagan Administration, the setbacks regarding the CICA, Iran-contra, and Attorney General Meese's near-indictment by a succession of independent counsels took the force out of the earlier Meese moves. The extensive enactments of the Democratic Congress in 1987 and 1988 drew no significant signing statements.[9] Thus, despite the earlier fits and starts Meese's pretensions to lawmaking power through signing statements had not become deeply rooted before the Bush Presidency.

C. Boyden Gray

How did the White House counsel come to hold great power and to wield this extraordinary tool?

Gray's role in the Bush White House reflected both the president's personal style and political situation. The background of the White House counsel reflected the same kind of elite status that shaped George Bush. Like Bush, Gray grew up with wealth, as an heir to the R. J. Reynolds tobacco fortune in North Carolina, with a personal fortune of over $10 million. His first job in private practice was with the firm of Wilmer, Cutler &

Pickering in Washington, D.C., where colleagues describe his principal work as lobbying for business.

In 1981, George Bush, looking to fill the post of counsel to the vice president, found him through staff recommendations. Only then did they discover that their families both had had vacation homes in Kennebunkport, Maine, and Hope Sound, Florida, and that the two scions of wealth possessed numerous friends in common. In fact, their fathers—Prescott Bush, senator, and Gordon Gray, President Eisenhower's national security adviser—were members of the small, secretive, extraordinarily exclusive, all-white male Alibi Club in Washington. So were Bush and Gray themselves in the 1980s. This club, though it has only fifty members, has numbered over its history at least four CIA directors, four Supreme Court justices, three former secretaries of state, and three secretaries of war or defense. The two fathers not only clubbed together but often paired off to golf together, sometimes with young George Bush along. Young Clayton Boyden Gray had gone to St. Mark's School and Harvard College; young George Herbert Walker Bush had gone to Phillips Andover Academy and Yale College.[10] To put it mildly, they were a natural fit on Bush's elite side.

As the vice president's counsel, Gray had two tasks that held significance for the future. Vice President Bush headed a task force on regulatory reform and delegated most of the responsibility to Gray. Although the task force had a limited role, it stimulated Gray to later help create the Quayle Council.

Second, as counsel, Gray steered Vice President Bush through the worst scandal of his eight-year term, Iran-contra. When the story broke in 1986, Gray examined hundreds of boxes of records and devised the explanations by which Bush threaded through the numerous aspects of his troubled relations with the Iran-contra scandal.[11] Gray devised the clever approach of having the vice president tell his vague, thin story only once, early, to the sympathetic Tower Commission, and then avoid talking to the congressional inquiry.[12]

Even on election eve in 1992, Gray was still writing the defenses of Bush from Iran-contra charges. Gray himself decided at that time to withhold from the independent counsel Bush's Iran-contra diary entries that contradicted Gray's published account. Only after the 1992 election did he allow their release, when they showed that Bush—supposedly "out of the loop"—privately described himself in November 1986 as "one of the few people who knew fully the details" about the arms sales to Iran.[13] Gray devised the pardon of four convicted and two indicted Iran-contra figures that took place on Christmas eve 1992, just before the trial of former secretary of defense Casper Weinberger would have focused public scrutiny on the White House meetings in which Bush had supported the arms-for-hostages deal.

As White House counsel, Gray took over an office in which the prior counsel performed mundane tasks, such as checking White House fulfillment of ethics requirements and drafting routine proclamations. In the Reagan Administration two friends of the president, William French Smith and Edwin Meese, filled the lawyering role as successive attorneys general, but the White House counsels had relatively little access or power. They were notoriously cut out of the key matters: President Reagan's White House counsel never even knew of the Iran-contra matter.[14]

President Bush treated Gray from the outset as President Reagan had treated Meese from the outset: not just as the in-house lawyer but as a chief lieutenant: "When Bush became president, he gave his counsel three major responsibilities: making sure administration officials follow ethical rules, overseeing the selection of federal judges, and protecting the constitutional prerogatives of the presidency. Bush also asked Gray to work on new civil-rights and clean-air bills."[15] That constituted quite a level of power, with civil rights and clean air as the two most important legislative enactments of the Bush Administration apart from the budget. Protecting the constitutional prerogatives of the presidency, normally a job of the attorney general, became an open-ended mandate to get involved in foreign affairs, defense, regulatory review, and line-item veto proposals, among other matters.

Many insiders viewed Gray's power as very high. His predecessor as White House counsel, A. B. Culvahouse, said, "The President spends a lot of political capital on Boyden's advice on everything from quotas to clean air to the disability act. On the issues Boyden has chosen, he is awfully damned influential."[16] A conservative consultant said in 1990 that "the White House counsel's office has become the ex-officio policy shop in this Administration."[17] A White House adviser told the New York Times, "On domestic issues, it's basically him, [Richard] Darman and Sununu .... Basically nobody else gets to talk much to the President."[18]

As selector of judges, Gray played leading roles in two choices for Supreme Court Justice: David Souter and Clarence Thomas. One of the numerous junior attorneys in the White House counsel's office, Lee Liberman, had charge of the more vast project of filling hundreds of district and appellate court vacancies with ideologically approved choices. In President Bush's numerous vetoes and countless veto threats, Gray had a large role. For example, he "played a key role in encouraging Bush in 1990 to veto an intelligence authorization bill for intruding on presidential power."[19] Early on, he made a brief misstep in challenging publicly Secretary of State James Baker's accord with Congress on contra aid. The rebuke he drew seems mainly to have taught him to exercise power in the shadows rather than speaking on the record to the press.

This background frames the discussion of Gray's involvement with Bush's signing statements.

1989: PREVENTING CURBING OF IRAN-CONTRA ABUSES
Congress Proposes Reform

Traditionally, revelation of executive scandals and national crises led to legislative investigation and proposals to curb recurrences, from earliest crises through Pearl Harbor, Watergate, and the intelligence abuses revealed in the 1970s.[20] Foreign observers might look askance at America's dramatically public methods of cleaning house, but Americans have defended their willingness to uncover mistakes and respond with reform as a national strength.

Naturally, Congress expected to do the same in response to the Iran-contra scandal. In 1988, after the Iran-contra hearings of 1987, it laid the groundwork by preliminary consideration of reform bills for covert actions. However, President Bush and his White House counsel seized the initiative in 1989 to blunt such reform by using the newly broadened executive power of the signing statement. In effect, signing statements amounted to Gray's middle-period approach to legitimating what occurred in Iran-contra, after his explanations for Vice President Bush in the 1986–1988 investigations and before his arranging in 1992 for pardons of convicted or indicted participants. Understanding this moment requires a review of some of the pertinent Iran-contra abuses with attention to the special connection of the legislative reforms to Vice President Bush's own Iran-contra role.

The first focus of reform concerned leveraging, the practice of an administration evading prohibitions like the Boland Amendment by persuading foreign countries receiving American aid or arms sales to do what the administration itself was prohibited from doing. When the Boland Amendments cut off contra funding and the Reagan Administration secretly solicited other countries to fund the contras, Vice President Bush heard about the principal contributions directly from National Security Adviser Robert McFarlane.[21] Bush's active role in "leveraging" through Honduras in 1985 came out in the stipulated facts at the trial of Oliver North:

> On February 12, 1985, North proposed [that] . . . expedited military deliveries, economic funding, and other support should be offered as an incentive to Honduras for its continued support to the Nicaraguan Resistance. The memo stated that this part of the message should not be contained in a written document but should be delivered verbally by a discreet emissary . . . .

[Shortly thereafter,] when Vice President Bush met with President [Cordova Roberto] Suazo [of Honduras], Bush told Suazo that President Reagan had directed expedited delivery of U.S. military items to Honduras. Vice President Bush also informed Suazo that President Reagan had directed that currently withheld economic assistance for Honduras should be released; that the United States would provide from its own military stocks critical security assistance items that had been ordered by Honduran armed forces; and that several security programs underway for Honduran security forces would be enhanced.[22]

North's comment about setting the deal up "verbally" rather than "in a written document" reflects the standard pattern that such leveraging occurs with a minimum of proof available later (or in contemporaneous leaks) of quid pro quo.

Besides leveraging, two other Iran-contra problems became the focus of legislative reform: the trading of arms with terrorist nations and the lack of an independent inspector general at the CIA to curb abuses. With particular regard to these three problems, as *Congressional Quarterly Almanac* noted, "During the final days of the 1989 session, Congress approved three measures to close legal loopholes that became evident during the Iran-contra investigations."[23]

The president's familiar powers and tools could only soften somewhat such reform. Vetoing and veto bargaining had its limits, because even relatively pro-administration members of Congress supported reasonable reforms.[24] Nominating loyal subordinates, like former NSC deputy Robert Gates or former vice presidential aide Donald I. Gregg, had its limits, because even they, faced as Gates was with dramatic hearings about their own role in covering up the Iran-contra scandal, had to promise reform.[25]

The White House Defeats Reform

Therefore, Gray, in order to head off reform in general and Iran-contra reform in particular, needed a power outside the traditional relation of the president to lawmaking or execution. He needed a power invulnerable to public reaction expressed in override votes on vetoes, to oversight or confirmation hearings on agency officials like Gates and Gregg, or to other congressional tools such as conditions on appropriations. A White House angry about the shadow of Iran-contra but not wanting any more public arena fights than necessary found the perfect response in signing statements. In contrast with disputes over overrides or oversight, in which the political forces could hurt a president with such low support in Congress, the use of presidential statements outside the traditional process let the president increase his power while avoiding public and congressional reaction.

For example, to curb leveraging, the chairman of the House subcommittee on foreign aid appropriations, Representative David Obey (D-Wis.), in 1989 steered through his own prohibition, the "Obey Amendment," as section 582 of the annual foreign aid bill. Section 582(a) prohibited aid or arms sales "to any foreign government . . . in exchange for that foreign government or person undertaking any action which is, if carried out by the United States Government . . . expressly prohibited . . . ." President Bush vetoed the first version of the foreign aid bill over the two issues of leveraging and family planning. Congress then passed a second version, which compromised on family planning but not on leveraging. This sequence of presidential veto, and House compromise on one of two points, should have made this bill a classic example of the veto bargaining analyzed by political scientists studying divided postwar government.[26]

However, after Congress passed the second version of the foreign aid bill retaining the Obey Amendment, the president issued a signing statement that said:

> I have been most troubled by Section 582. . . . I intend to construe this section narrowly. I agree with the view expressed on the House and Senate floor that this section is intended only to prohibit "quid pro quo" transactions—that is, transactions in which U.S. funds are provided to a foreign nation on the *express condition* that the foreign nation provide specific assistance to a third country, which assistance U.S. officials are expressly prohibited from providing by U.S. law.[27]

President Bush took most of the force out of the Obey Amendment. Section 582 forbade providing any funds to foreign governments "in exchange" for taking actions prohibited to the U.S. government. It did not concern only the rare exchange with an explicit quid pro quo agreement, but all exchanges, including implicit agreements as well. The Iran-contra hearings and report had described the problem of implicit arrangements with "expectations of secret return favors" and "expectation[s] by the donor nations that they can expect something in return for their largesse."[28] Administration officials could readily conduct leveraging by soliciting aid for a prohibited object by an implicit understanding without any blatant "express condition."

For one example, the president's statement barred the provision from applying to the situation when, as vice president, he himself had delivered the aid message to President Suazo of Honduras while not stating express conditions. For another example, Secretary Weinberger had been told in 1985 of the Saudi contributions to the contras, and he returned the favor by helping the Saudis on arms sales. Weinberger was later indicted for denying his knowledge under oath, and the Weinberger trial would have explored further if not for President Bush's 1992 pardon. George Bush had gotten from Robert McFarlane, national security adviser in 1985, the same knowledge as Weinberger; Bush had withheld his knowledge even when McFarlane attempted suicide from compounded feelings of guilt. A transaction more suspiciously like leveraging would be hard to find, but as revised by the presidential signing statement, the Obey Amendment would not come near it.

President Bush's statement justified itself by this description of section 582's legislative history:

> As reflected both in Congressman [Mickey] Edwards' statements and in the explanatory colloquy between Senators Kasten and Rudman, a "quid pro quo" arrangement requires that both countries understand and agree that U.S. aid will not be provided if the foreign government does not provide the specific assistance. . . . My decision to sign this bill is predicated on these understandings of Section 582.

Gray had drafted this statement with a manipulation of legislative history, namely, having the president purport to attribute significance to "the explanatory colloquy between Senators Kasten and Rudman." Senators Robert Kasten (R-Wis.) and Warren Rudman (R-N.H.) had held, in fact, a colloquy on the Senate floor. However, their colloquy concerned an amendment that Senator Kasten himself withdrew when it faced rejection by Congress.[29]

The rejected version went nowhere. The Obey Amendment became law because Congress insisted on retaining it, even when it had to compromise on family planning, the other point of President Bush's veto of the first version of the bill.[30] Representative Obey had explained why Congress insisted on the Obey Amendment:

> [This bill] recognizes that both Houses of the Congress did not pass family planning language vetoed by the President by more than a handful of votes. And that means, because we have to have two-thirds vote in order to overcome the President's veto, it simply is not practical at this stage in the legislative process for us to pursue that issue again.
>
> The other issue on which the President vetoed the bill is what is known as leveraging. I happen to think that this is a crucial issue which relates to the integrity of constitutional processes in the American system of government.
>
> That is why even though we have dropped the language the President objected to on the question of population, we did not drop efforts to nail into this law the principle that taxpayer money for foreign aid ought to be expended for the purposes for which it is appropriated, and they ought *not* to

be expended *in any way to promote or entice* other governments to support policies which would be illegal if followed by the United States. . . .

We took an oath to uphold that Constitution, and that is why we have *insisted on retaining antileveraging language* in this bill. . . .

[N]o reasonable person can disagree with the proposition that the President is not above the law, that any administration is not above the law.[31]

In other words, after a presidential veto, the House had chosen to compromise on a different issue but to "nail into this law" the Obey Amendment by "retaining antileveraging language in this bill." That language barred not merely explicit quid pro quos but "any way to promote or entice other governments." Senate Republicans had proposed a substitute but had withdrawn it. They had left Representative Obey's language in place. Their colloquies could hardly accomplish what they had declined to do, namely, substitute their language for the actual provision. The president's declaration defending the view that the Obey Amendment concerned only "express," "quid pro quo" conditions simply obtained for the president what he was unwilling to obtain by a second veto (which he did not make) and did so by reciting the views of a senator unwilling to press an amendment (which he withdrew). It was as though the more evidence that the president and other opponents of the Obey Amendment had lost in the constitutional system of checks and balances, the more the president viewed himself as justified in revising the amendment—outside the system, using the new power.

Moreover, the circumstances made the president's signing statement all the more highly suspect. The Senate minority leader, Senator Robert Dole (R-Kan.), alluded to White House staff and its strategy during these particular floor debates.[32] As will be seen regarding the Civil Rights Act of 1991, Gray's strategy appeared to begin with the regular veto bargaining for whatever changes in the bill Congress would make. During this, Gray would have his congressional supporters plant in the Congressional Record an alternative account of what Congress was doing in passing the bill without the changes in the bill that Congress would not make. Merely in the record, they would mean very little. However, the president's signing statement, for both the Obey Amendment and the 1991 Civil Rights Act, then cited the view inserted in the Congressional Record, depicting that view as what the law actually meant. Through this coupled preplanting of what would normally be obvious as a losing view and post-reaping in a signing statement with the presidential stamp of power on it, the White House counsel harvested an entire law that supplants congressional legislating on a central and hotly contested issue.

Some may ask how a signing statement could have such effect. Because the Framers gave the president no revisory power, one would ordinarily assume that he cannot obtain one just by a statement and a claim of power. Further examples in this chapter will shed more light on this, but the revision of the Obey Amendment begins to indicate the complex reality. Once the president carried out this elaborate strategy for narrowing that key controversial provision, his view became likely to prevail, particularly in the context of foreign affairs, where the president traditionally had a large scope in the laws' execution anyway. The guarantors of correct interpretation of law common in some domestic contexts—court rulings—are very few and far between in foreign affairs. When they occur, they come too late and with extreme deference to the executive on the issue of whether to become involved at all. Most probably, the actual intent of Congress would never be heard about again once the president had imposed his view on the Obey Amendment. Congress had employed its best tools during a divided government—hearings, appeals to the public, debates on proposals, veto bargaining, renewed versions after a first veto— but the White House had defeated it by use of a new tool, outside the previous system, by which the White House could effectively nullify unwanted reforms.

Defeating Other Iran-Contra Reforms

A similar dismal fate at the White House counsel's office awaited the other two Iran-contra reform bills, one regarding the CIA and the other regarding terrorist nations. One bill had concerned the problem of abuse of the CIA in the absence of an independent inspector general. Vice President Bush, a former CIA director, had been immersed in the use of the CIA for the arms-for-hostages deal with Iran. He and his adviser Gregg, a former CIA officer, had been trapped in denials of knowledge of the contra resupply operation with its related CIA abuses.[33] The CIA had an inspector general office ostensibly to ferret out abuses, but the office had no statutory mandate, no independence, and hence little effect on the Iran-contra scandal.

Congress's Iran-contra report had stated:

> The Committees recommend that a system be developed so that the CIA has an independent statutory Inspector General confirmed by the Senate, like the Inspectors General of other agencies . . . .
>
> The CIA's internal investigation of the Iran-Contra Affair—conducted by the Office of the Inspector General—paralleled those of the Intelligence Committees and then the Iran Committees. It contributed to, and cooperated with, the Tower Board. Yet, the Office of the Inspector General

appears not to have had the manpower, resources or tenacity to acquire key facts uncovered by the other investigations.[34]

Two more years of experience, hearings, and reports further confirmed this. In that time, a single prosecution for false statements resulted from the CIA inspector general's inquiries into Iran-contra, and the Bush Administration scuttled even that.[35]

Accordingly, Congress enacted provisions for a statutory inspector general for the CIA as Title VIII of the Intelligence Authorization Act for Fiscal Year 1990. As with the Obey Amendment, the White House's approach began with the procedure familiar in postwar divided government: bargaining over a veto threat, actually vetoing a first version of a bill, and then having Congress decide what it would compromise on and what the second version of the bill would retain.[36] When President Bush signed the act, he released a three-page statement amounting to a full-length revision of the inspector general law.

The accompanying rhetoric about "resist[ing] any attempt by the Intelligence Committees to micromanage the CIA" and protecting the "deliberative processes of the executive branch" foreshadowed the themes of the 1991 Princeton Address. He bluntly declared that "I have repeatedly made clear that I am unpersuaded of the necessity for Title VIII of the Act . . . ."[37] Accordingly, "[i]n implementing Title VIII the operational policies of the existing Office of Inspector General will remain in force to the maximum extent possible." This meant retaining the practices enfeebling the inspector general (IG) as a check on abuse, including limiting the Intelligence Committees' access to IG reports such as reports about obstructed investigations, apparently retaining the system of IG staff rotation,[38] and rendering merely advisory the law's qualifications for the IG.

From the perspective of President Bush's own Iran-contra past, the particular interest consists of the signing statement's limits on the CIA IG telling the Intelligence Committees of obstruction. The November 1986 obstruction of the Intelligence Committee's attempts to find out about the CIA's role in Iran-contra fueled the subsequent scandal. Vice President Bush had attended the key presidential meetings on November 10, 12, and 24, 1986, after exposure of the scandal. There, as the indictment of Secretary Weinberger (before his pardon by Bush) explained, Attorney General Meese laid out the false story that would go to Congress's Intelligence Committees about the illegal missile shipment of November 1985 involving the CIA. Meese got everyone present, including Bush, to acquiesce in the false story denying U.S. involvement in (November 10 and 12)—or at least President Reagan's (November 24) knowledge of—that CIA-aided illegal shipment. The independent counsel publicly reported why "Vice

President Bush should have known the statement was false" denying President Reagan's knowledge.[39]

Moreover, two of the independent counsel's indictments charged perjury in inquiries about that shipment, the two pending indictments blocked by the 1992 Bush pardon. One was the indictment of Weinberger for denying he had contemporaneous knowledge of that shipment. The other was the indictment of the CIA official Dewey Clarridge for denying the CIA's role in that shipment.[40] From Iran-contra, President Bush and his White House counsel had evident reasons to prefer that Congress be kept in the dark about obstruction of investigations of the CIA. Those were ample reasons for the president, if he could, to draw the teeth of the reform law meant for Congress not to be kept in the dark. Court rulings are few and far between on the CIA's reporting duties to Congress. Hence, the actual intent of the CIA IG law, like the actual intent of the Obey Amendment, would probably never be heard about again once the president had imposed his view.

Finally, the very essence of the Iran-contra scandal was the sale of arms to a terrorist nation, Iran, for money and hostages. As explained in the congressional Iran-contra report, "Iran, which was considered a terrorist nation by the United States and which was the subject of a U.S. arms embargo, was not eligible for direct sales."[41] Secretary Weinberger had warned at the meetings attended by Vice President Bush in August 1985 and January 1986 that the trades were illegal. In 1993, former secretary of state George Shultz confirmed in his memoirs how Bush had supported the illegal trades at the meetings where Shultz and Weinberger had fought so hard against them, and how Shultz had reminded Bush of this at tense private encounters in late 1986 when Bush claimed publicly that he had been "out of the loop."[42] When Weinberger withheld his notes from the investigations, he covered up the contemporaneous documentary evidence of how Vice President Bush had been there to hear at those meetings but refused to listen, supporting the deals regardless of illegality.[43]

As follow-up, Congress enacted the Anti-Terrorism and Arms Export Amendments Act of 1989. The bill reflected a strong consensus across party and ideological lines, as shown by its title the Berman-Hyde Bill— named for Representatives Howard L. Berman (liberal D-Calif.) and Henry J. Hyde (conservative R-Ill.). As part of the price for that consensus, the bill still left leeway for the president to waive the ban on arms sales to terrorist nations. He just had to do so by a clear and aboveboard waiver with notice to Congress.

However, once again the White House counsel's narrowing of a bill followed the failure to use the legitimate tool of a veto: "Bush signed the bill into law, despite complaints from some of his lawyers that it posed an unconstitutional infringement on his powers to conduct foreign affairs."[44] Instead of the White House accepting its partial legislative defeats, upon the signing of the bill it again reached outside the system of checks and balances for a declaration by President Bush that radically revised key provisions:

> The new section 40(a)(5) prohibits the United States Government from "facilitating the acquisition of any munitions item" by a country designated by the Secretary of State under section 40(d). The new section 40(b)(1)(D) contains a parallel prohibition on actions by any U.S. person to facilitate such an acquisition. I shall interpret these provisions as placing *no limit* on our negotiations and communications with foreign governments.[45]

This revision undermined the provision almost completely, Congress again being in a context where there would be no court rulings, and after the president took this tack, the actual intent of Congress would probably never be heard of again. Congress enacted the law with a specific type of abuse in front of it: National Security Adviser Robert McFarlane's discussions could easily be described as "negotiations and communications with foreign governments." With "no limit" on such, the White House staff had just succeeded in taking a law meant to curb its prior abuses and revised the law to authorize the same type of abuses.

1990: VOIDING NUMEROUS PROVISIONS THROUGH THE ITEM VETO POWER

Defeating the Iran-contra reforms was only the 1989 warm-up exercise for the White House counsel. President Bush's Princeton Address in May 1991 included the following boast: "[O]n many occasions during my presidency, I have stated that statutory provisions that violate the Constitution have no binding legal force." What President Bush alluded to was nothing less than his having created a form of "line-item" veto in the face of judicial rulings utterly opposing that assertion of power.

Understanding the semi-sovereign nature of the Bush White House's claim of power requires a review of some interesting Anglo-American history. Chief executives have a long record of seeking personal rule by setting aside specific provisions of law. The Meese-backed CICA controversy in 1985 through 1988 revived study of that history. As a court noted, "During the reign of absolute British monarchs, the notion that the Executive, at the time the King, could decide for himself, without a decision of the courts, which laws should be obeyed was put to the test . . . ." That test of British monarchical power occurred in the late 1600s: "King James II attempted to claim such authority, but the English people would no longer tolerate such a claim, and their judicial system rejected it in the historic *Seven Bishops Case* of 1688."[46] The Framers embodied this rejection of sovereign prerogative in the "Faithful Execution" clause of the Constitution, modeled on the English Bill of Rights of 1689.[47]

A court explained that "[o]nce signed by the President . . . the bill becomes part of the law of the land and the President must 'take care that [it] be faithfully executed.'" For the President "[t]o construe this duty to faithfully execute the laws as implying the power to forbid their execution perverts the clear language of the 'take care' clause: 'To "execute" a statute . . . emphatically does not mean to kill it.'"[48] The Constitutional Convention further rejected any such power for the president when Elbridge Gerry persuasively argued "that the power of suspending might do all the mischief dreaded from the negative of useful laws (i.e., the President's veto), without answering the salutary purpose of checking unjust or unwise ones."[49]

The Constitution denied the president the power of "line-item veto" or the power to revise bills, as an appellate court explained during the CICA controversy:

> Art. I, § 7 is explicit that the President must either sign or veto a bill presented to him. . . . Art. I, § 7 does not empower the President to revise a bill, either before or after signing. It does not empower the President to employ a so-called "line-item veto" and excise or sever provisions of a bill with which he disagrees. The only constitutionally prescribed means for the President to effectuate his objections to a bill is to veto it and to state those objections upon returning the bill to Congress. The "line item veto" does not exist in the federal Constitution, and the executive branch cannot bring a de facto "line item veto" into existence by promulgating orders to suspend parts of statutes which the President has signed into law.[50]

President Bush's program of signing statements directly contradicted these judicial exegeses of the Constitution, particularly when he boasted in the Princeton Address of the "many occasions" of his declaring that provisions of the laws had "no binding legal force." In 1990 came President Bush's demonstrations of his claimed power to pick out long lists of items on individual bills and either declare them unconstitutional or construe them into meaninglessness on assorted constitutional grounds. President Bush's treatment of nine individual items in the 1990 foreign aid authorization was previously mentioned. In an even bigger example he challenged no fewer than eleven provisions of the 1990 defense authorization bill, which amounted almost to a complete overhaul of the parts of the bill he disliked.

During the Reagan and Bush administrations, the vastly enlarged defense budget provoked extensive controversy in Congress. President Reagan and Congress had fought over, and resolved, numerous conditions that Congress had placed on expenditures, as it invoked the "power of the purse" in defense matters.[51] Such controversies were as old as the "ship money" dispute during the period of personal rule of Charles I in 1628 to 1640 and as fresh as the congressional cutoffs for spending on the Indochina War in 1974, on Angola in 1978, and on the contras in the 1980s. In these defense bill controversies, President Reagan used his veto threat for influence and President Bush continued to use this classic tool of divided government. Additionally, President Reagan used his ability, during consideration of the defense bill, to work out an array of compromises. These compromises altered congressional proposals of conditions from initial forms objectionable to the president into more acceptable forms. Although Iran-contra showed that, on occasion, the Reagan White House would break the law and the Constitution to defy appropriation bill restrictions such as the Boland Amendment, this was the exception rather than the rule. President Reagan had enough of a public mandate, enough support in Congress from often sympathetic Armed Services Committees in both the Senate and the House, and enough military programs for which he wanted and needed Congress's help to engage with Congress in a practical matter of give and take on the vast majority of issues regarding military spending bills.

During the consideration of the 1990 defense authorization bill, President Bush continued to use all the appropriate presidential means to adjust defense bill conditions including veto threats. However, President Bush refused to rely on engaging with Congress or making appeals to the public and instead resorted to a new method to defeat such conditions. Because of the public's anger that American defense spending shielded Japan while Japan refused to share that costly burden or to contribute with adequate speed to Desert Shield, Congress sought to impose conditions on military spending in defense of Japan. Exercising his traditional powers of influence and compromise, the president had lobbied successfully to soften provisions regarding Japanese burden sharing, making some into "sense of Congress" provisions and putting a waiver provision in another.

After all the debate, negotiation, voting, and ultimate decision to sign rather than to veto, however, President Bush did not accept that the outcome was the will of the democratic process. Instead, his signing statement claimed the power to dispense with or alter a long list of provisions. Atop the list came his postenactment changes, on asserted constitutional grounds, in the provisions already compromised at his request regarding

Japanese and European burden sharing, despite compromises already reached during the enactment process. These provisions, his signing statement declared, he would treat as "precatory"—that is, merely expressing a wish—"rather than mandatory," whatever the actual language of the law. President Bush's signing statement said:

> Several provisions might be construed to impinge on the President's authority as Commander in Chief and as the head of the executive branch. Thus, section 1455 purports to impose a limit on the number of military personnel stationed in Japan, and section 406 purports to do the same with respect to military personnel stationed in Europe.
>
> I am particularly concerned about those provisions that derogate from the President's authority under the Constitution to conduct U.S. foreign policy, including negotiations with other countries. One such provision is section 1455, which purports to require the President to begin negotiations with Japan on an agreement under which Japan would offset U.S. costs associated with the presence of our military personnel in Japan.[52]

Here was Congress acting on the basis of the public will and its long-standing constitutional authority, shaping the funding arrangements for an expensive overseas deployment yet still allowing the president much freedom of action. On the House floor, the burden-sharing provision (referred to as the Bonior Amendment for its sponsor, Representative David E. Bonior [D-Mich.]) passed 370-53, with even its opponents saying, "It's a vote on the depth of feeling that people have that our allies should contribute more."[53] The debate and vote appeared to have effect: "Two days after the House approved the Bonior amendment, Japan quadrupled to $4 billion the amount it pledged to support the multilateral campaign against Iraq."[54] President Bush nevertheless invoked his asserted power as commander in chief at this most dubious point—against a signed act of Congress regarding funding—and in the line-item fashion by nullifying particular provisions of an enacted law.[55]

Similarly, the president invoked supposed supremacy over the laws by asserting the last word on the matter of violating the Antiballistic Missile (ABM) treaty. President Bush said:

> I note also that section 221 contains criteria for conducting Strategic Defense Initiative research and development that might be construed as a constraint on the President's authority to interpret treaties. I sign this Act with the understanding that the Congress did not intend that obligation of funds for the ground-based interceptors and sensor identified in the conference report on H.R. 4739 be dependent on a determination at this time that these systems are deployable under the ABM Treaty.[56]

This rather detailed assault struck at a provision, section 221(b) (2), which simply limited the authorization to what the ABM Treaty allowed.[57] President Reagan, in his fervor for the "Star Wars" (Strategic Defense Initiative [SDI]) antimissile program, had asserted the power to violate the ABM Treaty's authoritative interpretation given to the Senate during ratification. Congress had defeated that assertion of power.[58] Despite the seeming resolution of the issue, here was President Bush claiming power to spend on SDI without obeying a provision of law he disliked.[59]

The president also rewrote statutory provisions intended to restrain exports of technology for weapons of mass destruction including missiles. In November 1990, when the president signed this bill, the nation had been awakening to Iraq's buildup of missile technology—a buildup manifested two months later in the Scud firings that would kill civilians in Israel and American troops in barracks in Saudi Arabia. In the bill, Congress had amended, pursuant to its plenary power over foreign commerce, the Export Administration Act and the Arms Export Control Act. The amendments concerned a new multilateral initiative, the Missile Technology Control Regime (MTCR), to prevent further spread of missile technology.

Congress strongly encouraged the MTCR and agreements like it with non-MTCR countries. Section 1702 gave a broad delegation of authority to the secretary of state for making agreements—agreements that would take effect without Senate treaty ratification or affirmation by further law.[60] The provision gave the State Department mere "responsibility" to negotiate, with the carrot that if the State Department was satisfied with its resulting agreements, it could give non-MTCR countries the favorable treatment of MTCR adherents.

Yet even this supportive broad delegation of authority, in the context of Congress's plenary power over foreign commerce, set off an assault by the White House counsel on the provision's constitutionality. Again, President Bush explained that he would treat the provision as "precatory"— merely expressing a wish—regardless of the actual language of the law. He said:

> I am particularly concerned about those provisions that derogate from the President's authority under the Constitution to conduct U.S. foreign policy, including negotiations with other countries . . . . Another [such provision] is section 1702, which could be construed as requiring the Secretary of State to negotiate with foreign countries regarding restricting the export of certain goods and technology.[61]

Here Congress was giving a highly supportive grant of advance authority; here the president was so affronted at a provision that "could be construed as requiring the Secretary of State to negotiate" that he reached for a form of assertion of power outside the constitutional process. Previous presidents had dealt with such provisions through their many ways of engaging with the public and Congress.

Two final assertions of presidential power, still in this same statement, had particularly chilling overtones in another context: presidential claims of unbridled power over classified programs. Congress had passed two seemingly unobjectionable sets of provisions on this subject. First, section 1461, entitled "Congressional Oversight of Special Access Programs," and section 1482(a), which also dealt with "special access program[s]," curbed new programs for which the restricted information ("special access") limited public accountability and created a breeding ground for abuses.[62] Second, a classified annex to the defense authorization bill provided money for classified programs. Section 1409 made that annex the law.[63]

President Bush knew firsthand the need for oversight, as he had been CIA director in 1976 during Congress's investigations (the Church and Pike committees) of intelligence abuses from spying on Martin Luther King, Jr., to assassination plots. Yet President Bush chose to escalate the disputes into a war against oversight, as later expressed in his Princeton Address. His signing statement declared:

> [C]ertain reporting provisions raise national security concerns. Sections 1461 and 1482 purport to require prior notice to the Congress regarding initiation of, or classification changes in, special access programs. I shall construe these provisions consistent with my constitutional authority to protect sensitive national security information.
>
> In addition, section 1409(a) refers to a classified annex that was prepared to accompany the conference report on this Act and states that the annex "shall have the force and effect of law as if enacted into law." The Congress has thus stated in the statute that the annex has not been enacted into law, but it nonetheless urges that the annex be treated as if it were law. I will certainly take into account the Congress' wishes in this regard, but will do so mindful of the fact that, according to the terms of the statute, the provisions of the annex are not law.[64]

Since the establishment in the 1970s of the Intelligence Committees, the annual intelligence authorization bill, and that bill's "Classified Annex," the system of such annexes had served to bring law to a part of the government that might otherwise be lawless. Now, President Bush insisted that the law be merely "the Congress's wishes" and "not law." Because the Bush Administration had been picking an increasingly serious dispute with Congress on this matter, "[i]n a letter, Senate Appropriations Chairman Robert C. Byrd, D-W.Va., complained that defense and intelligence agencies had 'ignored or challenged' congressional directions regarding funds appropriated for some secret programs."[65]

President Bush had not employed either his lobbying or his vetoing powers in this dispute. Rather, outside of the system of checks and balances, he had weighed in to free the intelligence community both from any limits on its proliferating special access (i.e., restricted information) programs and from the budget limits in the Classified Annex. It was a sad but natural continuation of his 1989 signing statements to further undercut the intelligence oversight so plainly necessitated by Iran-contra.

1991: REVISING THE INTENT OF CONGRESS IN THE CIVIL RIGHTS ACT

A Technique Develops for Defusing Civil Rights

President Bush's challenge to the intent of the 1991 Civil Rights Act received at the time, and will undoubtedly continue to receive, widespread attention from its great significance for civil rights law. His approach to the 1991 law reflected a culmination of the twin origins of his administration's general strategy: political forces and personal style. The nation elected in 1988, and reinforced in 1990, a Congress with a mandate to enact civil rights laws. President Bush had not campaigned against civil rights laws in 1988 or 1990 and so he had not received any mandate against such laws. Rather, he had made enough gestures toward minorities to have "the highest sustained poll ratings among blacks of any Republican president in 30 years," achieving in April 1990 an approval rating of 56 percent among blacks.[66] When it came to the crucial point in late 1991, he did not have the desire to kill the civil rights bill by a high-visibility veto override fight, and he did not appear to have a likelihood of success in one.

George Bush's personal style traditionally involved flexible tactics on civil rights because of his party's conservative wing. His career as a Texas Republican, running successfully for the House in 1966 and 1968 and unsuccessfully for the Senate in 1964 and 1970, had inevitably forced him to face the civil rights debate of that time. In 1964, he found it expedient to join those critics of the civil rights bill who denounced it with the language of "constitutional" objection for cover:

> Bush's opposition to the bill put him in the company of segregationists. . . . [with a] position against the fair employment practices and public accommodations sections of the bill, which he described as "unconstitutional." . . .

. . . . "I favor keeping government close to the people, States' rights in the constitutional concept," Bush was quoted as saying in *The Dallas Morning News*.[67]

Both political forces and personal style thus pushed him to seek a way not to veto the 1991 civil rights bill but to have some legal contentions outside the public arena that would defuse the bill.

For almost three years, the White House had honed a set of extraordinary tools for bending or breaking newly enacted laws before employing them against this crucial statute. To understand those tools requires recalling two streams of Bush Administration signing statements: those employing a strategy using thinly based constitutional arguments and those dealing specifically with civil rights. The maneuvers of the signing statement for the 1991 act will then become clear.

Aside from the crude tool of voiding provisions as flat-out unconstitutional, the Bush Presidency found another, tactically more flexible tool for using postenactment assertions about constitutional issues. The crude tool had the potential for explosive confrontation with Congress and ultimately with the courts. It is doomed to failure when the underlying constitutional theory about the particular provision is too weak.

In contrast, a weak constitutional argument that could not accomplish much by itself can accomplish much more when used in a strategy to "avoid" constitutional "problems" by revising the meaning of the statute. This technique plays upon real or fancied ambiguity in the statute. A White House counsel determined to find such ambiguity can nearly always find it by distorting the broad weave of statutory wording, case law, and legislative history, particularly when the counsel has manufactured some legislative history precisely for use in this fashion. Effectively used not for striking down provisions but for bending them in a preferred direction, this tactic allows the president to put his personal views above the enacted law.

The signing statement for the Clean Air Act Amendments of 1990 allowed the White House counsel to practice a full-length set of maneuvers along this line, providing a warm-up for the Civil Rights Act of 1991. As background, Congress has used citizen suit provisions in the federal clean air and clean water laws as a potent tool. Such provisions empower both the national environmental groups like the Natural Resources Defense Council and the Sierra Club and many local groups as well to sue polluters directly and to embarrass the Justice Department for neglecting such suits. Because the Reagan and Bush administrations had no taste for such vigorous enforcement, they have sought to find threshold barriers against such suits. These looked-for threshold barriers parallel, in the context of suits against private polluters, the barriers of the "standing" doctrine raised in environmental suits directly against government agencies.

This Reagan Administration effort culminated in its Supreme Court brief in 1987 in *Gwaltney of Smithfield, Ltd. v. Chesapeake Bay Foundation, Inc.*[68] In that case, a local citizen environmental group sued Gwaltney on the basis of past discharges into Chesapeake Bay before the company installed new equipment. The Clean Water Act allowed citizen suits against those alleged "to be in violation" of the act. Gwaltney said that the citizen group could not assert standing based on a company's formerly being in violation but only based on the company's currently being in violation.[69] In the Supreme Court, the Reagan Administration filed a brief also urging this as a standing barrier of constitutional dimension and embellished it with various notions of executive power.[70]

The Supreme Court disdained to give the slightest attention to the Reagan Administration's strained constitutional argument. Rather, the court simply told Congress how to rephrase such a provision to ensure that citizen groups could sue based on past violations. It concluded that "Congress could have phrased its requirement in language that looked to the past ('to have violated'), but it did not choose this readily available option."[71]

When Congress amended the Clean Air Act in 1990, an act *in pari materia* on citizen suit issues with the Clean Water Act, it followed the court's advice on how to "phrase[] its requirement" to broaden citizen suit opportunities. The act's "Past Violations" section provided: "Section 304(a) of the Clean Air Act is amended by inserting immediately before 'to be in violation' in paragraphs (1) and (3) '*to have violated* (if there is evidence that the alleged violation has been repeated) or'" . . . .[72] By the traditional rules of checks and balances, that statement should have laid to rest the standing barrier.

Instead, when President Bush signed the bill, he issued a declaration taking considerable trouble, in view of the magnitude of the bill's other changes, to revise this particular section. Presumably this action reflected White House Counsel Gray's own well-known opposition to strictness in air pollution laws.[73] President Bush stated:

> In addition, there are certain aspects of the bill's enforcement provisions that raise constitutional questions. I note that in providing for citizen suits for civil penalties, the Congress has *codified* the Supreme Court's interpretation of such provisions in the Gwaltney case. As the Constitution requires, litigants must show, at a minimum, intermittent, rather than purely past, violations of the statute in order to bring suit. This requirement respects the con-

stitutional limitations on the judicial power and avoids an intrusion into the law-enforcement responsibilities of the executive branch.[74]

The Bush Administration had a weak constitutional argument, not even accepted by the moderate justices in contexts much more appealing to them.[75] Yet the White House counsel used this weak constitutional argument as a basis for reinterpreting the law as a so-called codification of barriers to suit, exactly opposite of what Congress intended.

Turning from the general power to its particular application to civil rights, the Bush Administration made frequent use of this extraordinary tool to deal with this precise issue. The special value of this power—a power of acting without accountability—was made to order for civil rights as a subject most unpleasant for the Bush Administration to tackle in an open public arena. Even the Bush Administration's fervent supporters recognized the frequent use of the signing statement mechanism on this issue. Terry Eastland's enthusiastic review of the Bush Presidency's signing statements noted the following:

> Most significantly, Bush has used signing statements to register constitutional reservations. . . . Some are based on constitutional provisions that do not implicate his powers but which, of course, he is sworn to uphold. No fewer than six times, for example, has Bush said that a preference based on race or sex is in apparent conflict with the Fourteenth Amendment's equal protection clause.[76]

An example is the 1991 minority set-aside of 10 percent of the funds for the Superconducting Super Collider.[77] No objection appears to have been voiced to this provision on the floor of the House or Senate. In fact, the year before, President Bush had signed the parallel 1990 provision without a murmur. Yet, the 1991 provision elicited this presidential response, which slipped a vague direction to disobey the law and two comments about supposed "constitutional concerns" into a bland background.

> Section 304 . . . of the Act raise[s] constitutional concerns. Section 304 would direct the Secretary of Energy, "to the fullest extent possible," to ensure that 10 percent of the funds for the Superconducting Super Collider go to various institutions that are defined by their racial composition. To the extent that important governmental objectives are not clearly identified as the basis for such designations, they may raise constitutional concerns. I therefore direct the Secretary, as part of his obligation to implement section 304 "to the fullest extent possible," to administer the section in a constitutional manner. [78]

By the Supreme Court's tests in this context, President Bush's asserted concern was peculiarly feeble. In its decisions upholding minority preferences for broadcasting licenses and federal contracting, the Supreme Court majority had reviewed and upheld precisely the same type of statutory mechanism as for the Supercollider.[79] This provision had a full justification.[80] Thus, the president took an unpersuasive constitutional argument, which could not accomplish anything on its own, and used it for the tool of directing that the law be disobeyed in accordance with his personal desires. This and other examples of opposition to civil rights earned the label for Gray's staff as "the best and the rightest."[81]

The 1991 Bill Reaches Passage

Years of such previous tactics and ideological prejudices came together in the strategy of the White House counsel regarding the Civil Rights Act of 1991. Because the signing statement for that act relies upon an elaborate use—a misuse—of legislative history, the prelude to the act requires a brief legal and political review.

The Supreme Court had issued a string of decisions overruling its prior rules, in effect since Chief Justice Warren Burger's seminal opinion in *Griggs v. Duke Power Co.*[82] in 1971. Its new decisions made it harder for minorities to win employment discrimination cases. Above all, the 1989 *Wards Cove* decision increased the requirements for minorities to prove that employment practices that had weeded them out had "discriminatory impact."[83] *Wards Cove* changed the preceding regime in three key respects: burden of proof, "business necessity," and "cumulation."[84] Congress took up a bill to restore the law to its status before the new Supreme Court decisions, which President Bush labeled "quotas legislation." The president gave responsibility for the issue to Gray for the following reason, journalists explained:

> [Bush] turned to longtime counsel C. Boyden Gray to take charge of the administration's foot-dragging negotiations with Congress in 1990 and 1991 on a civil rights bill. (Gray was also a master of circumlocution. As one aide put it, "When a law degree was deployed, it was usually deployed to bollix something up, to come up with a convoluted reason for something we couldn't do. It was never a positive thing." But the effect was the same: to deflect flak from the right-minded president.)[85]

Gray put out, as the explanation for why restoring the *Griggs* law would constitute quotas, that employers would institute quotas under the new bill rather than litigate. Business did not see the matter that way, regarding the law as less likely to generate new litigation than any of Gray's alternatives. So eager were all sides to reach an agreement that even Sununu, a conservative on the issue, reached a seven-point agreement with Senator Edward Kennedy (D-Mass.) in 1990. But Gray rejected Sununu's settlement as unacceptable. In October 1990 President Bush vetoed Congress's bill, and the Senate fell one vote short of overriding the veto.[86]

A year of confrontation ensued. Gray principally distinguished himself by chastising business leaders for trying to negotiate a compromise. He called them "naive" to their faces until they recognized that he did not want a bill and was stalling.[87] However, by October 1991 the fierce battle over the Clarence Thomas nomination to the Supreme Court had used up the administration's capital in the Senate. Simultaneously, David Duke had gained visibility in the November 1991 runoff for Louisiana governor, as a former high officer of the Ku Klux Klan and an American Nazi. The campaign had focused media attention on the downside of the race issue, particularly when Duke aped the president's phraseology about quotas. Senator John C. Danforth (R-Mo.), who had guided the Thomas nomination, and other Republicans encouraging a compromise on the bill met privately with President Bush after Thomas's swearing-in on the White House lawn on October 18. The president got the warning that Republican senators would not support him in a repeat veto override battle for the civil rights bill. After the meeting, the president "'strongly expressed' to White House counsel C. Boyden Gray and others that he wanted a bill to sign."[88] This action marked the culmination of the political forces from the 1988 and 1990 elections that had put George Bush in the White House without a clear mandate for a legislative program.

Gray immediately began an elaborate maneuver to take back, through a signing statement, what he could no longer hold back by veto. On October 24, a "compromise was crafted chiefly by Sens. Edward M. Kennedy, D-Mass., and John C. Danforth, R-Mo., and White House Counsel C. Boyden Gray and Chief of Staff John H. Sununu."[89] The compromise had two aspects. Explicit language in section 105 of the law addressed the three *Wards Cove* aspects of burden of proof, business necessity, and cumulation. In addition, Senator Danforth provided an interpretive memorandum on section 105, setting forth a position joined by both sides—by Senators Edward Kennedy (D-Mass.), Orrin Hatch (R-Utah), and Robert Dole (R-Kans.).[90]

The White House counsel felt defensive enough to publish an opinion editorial subsequently with his version of what now started to unfold, entitled "Civil Rights: We Won, They Capitulated." In this, he noted that:

"[i]n its most critical component, [this Danforth] proposal included *exclusive legislative history* that would supply the definition of 'business necessity' . . . 90 percent of the negotiations centered on the legislative history rather than on the statute itself."[91]

Notwithstanding the understood exclusive nature of the legislative history, in the week of October 26 both sides—the administration through Minority Leader Dole and the other side through Senator Kennedy—quickly added additional statements on the Senate floor. Gray commented about the other side's Senate statement in terms that would apply equally to his own sides' statement: "Had we been sandbagged? Had the agreement so laboriously negotiated ever been meant to stick? . . . On these fundamental issues the president won a clean victory . . .[that] will survive the current round of fictions . . . ." He spoke perhaps more revealingly than he wished in describing the tactics used as "sandbagg[ing]," not "stick[ing]" to an "agreement so laboriously negotiated," and particularly his term "fictions." For in the next round, he did exactly what he was claiming had been done by the civil rights bill proponents.

To handle the new problem posed by the two sides' Senate floor statements of the week of October 26, more negotiations ensued, and at Senator Danforth's motion on October 29 the Senate amended the bill to define what legislative history could, and could not, be relied upon for interpreting section 105. In this new subsection of section 105, the law declared: "No statements other than the interpretive memorandum appearing at Vol. 137 Congressional Record S 15276 (daily ed. Oct. 25, 1991) shall be considered legislative history in construing or applying, any provision of this Act that relates to Wards Cove—Business necessity/cumulation/alternative business practice."[92] Thus, Congress preserved an agreed-upon legislative history, the Danforth Memorandum, now marked by the language of the law as the exclusive legislative history. By the White House counsel's own public account, he had agreed to this as the exclusive legislative history.[93]

The Most Controversial Signing Statement

On this basis, the bill passed both chambers by November 7 and went to the White House for signing on November 21. An insightful Washington Post article put the signing statement prepared by Gray in context thusly: "Gray has frequently written such statements of White House interpretation—often at odds with congressional intent—as attachments to controversial legislation. He has been consistently more averse than Bush to affirmative action and preferences for minorities."[94] What Gray attempted at this point provoked its own firestorm. He floated not only a signing statement but also a draft executive order that would have rolled back the government's major mechanism for sponsoring affirmative action, the minority hiring goals for government contractors. This step had been too radical even for Edwin Meese, who had suggested it but backed down when other Reagan Cabinet members warned that it would rouse a storm of protest.[95] With Sununu about to be driven from office on travel abuse charges (his letter of resignation came on December 2), the draft executive order had to be disavowed, as reported: "Bush declared on Nov. 21 that he supports affirmative action, in the wake of an uproar over a draft [executive order] directing the government to end affirmative action. The draft was prepared under the direction of Counsel to the President C. Boyden Gray."[96]

However, although President Bush pulled the executive order, he extensively undermined the 1991 act in the final signing statement. As an essayist noted about the Bush Administration and civil rights, "Bush sought to quell criticism by reaffirming support for affirmative action. But his [signing] statement did no such thing."[97] It amounted to nothing less than turning the law upside down on its most central and controversial points. His statement begins with a thesis that turns the Civil Rights Act into a codifier, rather than an overruler, of even the *Wards Cove* decision, which it was enacted to reverse. President Bush's statement begins:

> Until now, the law of disparate impact has been developed by the Supreme Court in a series of cases stretching from the *Griggs* decision in 1971 to the *Watson* and *Wards Cove* decisions in 1988 and 1989. [These] . . . have explained the safeguards against quotas and preferential treatment that have been included in the jurisprudence of disparate impact. S. 1745 *codifies* this theory of discrimination . . . .(emphasis added)[98]

The presidential declaration thus took the 1991 act as one that "codifies this theory of discrimination" in the *Wards Cove* decision and its parallel predecessor *Watson*. An observer reading about the years of congressional and public civil rights debate preceding the 1991 act might well be amazed to hear that the act "codifies" those decisions. Had Congress fought the president for years, taking a veto in the process and coming to the point of overriding another veto, to codify the decisions it had wanted to overrule? This tactic followed prior uses of this method, as in the statement for the Clean Air Act of 1990, which Gray also declared to "codify" a Supreme Court decision (*Gwaltney*) when Congress most plainly acted to change the result.

The presidential statement continued:

> [This bill] includ[es] a compromise provision that overturns *Wards Cove* by shifting the burden of persuasion on the "business necessity" defense. This change in the burden of proof means it is especially important to ensure that all the legislation's other safeguards against unfair application of disparate impact law are carefully observed. These highly technical matters are addressed in detail in the analyses of S. 1745 introduced by Senator Dole on behalf of himself and several other Senators *and of the Administration* (137 Cong. Rec. S 15472-S15478 [daily ed. Nov. 5, 1991]; 137 Cong. Rec. S 1953 [daily ed. Nov. 5, 1991]). These documents will be treated as *authoritative interpretive guidance* by all officials in the executive branch with respect to the law of disparate impact as well as the other matters covered in the documents.

As previously described regarding the Obey Amendment, the White House counsel had developed an elaborate procedure. First, members sympathetic to the administration position, albeit lacking the votes to win, would preplant legislative history. Although those members would lose in Congress, their legislative history would be deemed authoritative in a postenactment presidential signing statement. This strategy would revise the law beyond what the executive could obtain within the lawmaking process by traditional methods—vetoes, veto threats, bargaining, and public debate.

For the 1991 Civil Rights Act, the White House counsel took that basic system and went much further. His signing statement went blithely against the provision, section 105(b) of the act, which made the exclusive legislative history the agreed-upon joint statement by Senator Danforth and others. Far from being a minor gloss or triviality, this section, according to Gray himself (in his piece "Civil Rights: We Won, They Capitulated"), was an absolutely vital provision, reached in "[t]ense meetings" of the principals themselves on the critical two days when, absent such an agreement, "it seemed at points that there might be no civil rights bill at all." The agreement, in Gray's own words, "directed the courts to ignore any legislative history . . . apart from the two sentences originally agreed to." Now the president cited, relied upon, and incorporated at full length the entire alternative legislative history set forth for his own side by Senator Dole. Presumably, those who had reached the agreement with Gray might well ask, using his own words, "Had we been sandbagged? Had the agreement so laboriously negotiated ever been meant to stick?"[99]

Moreover, the signing statement announced itself as a vehicle for governmentwide "authoritative" direction. It prescribes *"authoritative interpretive guidance* by all officials in the executive branch with respect to

the law of disparate impact as well as the other matters covered in the documents." Elsewhere in this analysis, other such examples of
govermentwide authoritative directives will receive discussion. Here, it
suffices to note that the signing statement, which in so many other incar-
nations might be a mere public comment, an occasion to go "on record,"
or some other statement with weight no more formal than speechifying at
presidential ceremonies, now became "authoritative" as to controversial
areas of national law. As the Washington Post said of this section of the
signing statement:

> [T]he statement also directs the federal government to use the interpretation
> of the new civil rights act written by the White House and placed in the leg-
> islative record by Sen. Robert J. Dole (R-Kan.) in applying the law. That in-
> terpretation, supported only by conservative senators, is widely viewed as
> favoring business over minority and female employees attempting to charge
> job discrimination.[100]

The 1991 Civil Rights Act represented the last major legislative enactment of President Bush's term. Observers totaled up a long list of bills that
did not pass: health care, antirecession job packages, "tax restructuring,
education reform, campaign finance, striker replacement legislation and a
crime bill." Roger H. Davidson commented about 1992, "Once Bush's
popularity plummeted, there was even less incentive for Congress to
work with him."[101] When Congress did pass bills, including middle-class
tax relief, the president vetoed them.

The end of major legislative enactments did not exhaust the tools in the
Bush Administration's strategy, however. There were tools for dealing
with other active matters, such as congressional investigations and foreign affairs. In particular, there was a tool for dealing with previously enacted legislation on the environment, health, and safety regulation. It is to
that tool that the analysis turns next.

4

The Quayle Council: "No Fingerprints" on Regulation

QUAYLE'S ROLE

Overview

In the Bush Administration's general strategy for governing without Congress, a special place goes to the president's Council on Competitiveness, known by its chair as the "Quayle Council." Of course, Bush's choice of Senator Dan Quayle as candidate for vice president elicited widespread ridicule. This remained a constant—from the 1988 comment in the vice presidential candidate debate of his opponent, Senator Lloyd Bentsen, of "You're no Jack Kennedy" (after Quayle had compared himself to President Kennedy, whom Bentsen had known) to Quayle's attempt in 1992 to correct a student by insisting on a misspelling of "potato."

Whatever reactions the name "Quayle" alone tended to draw, the Quayle Council was no joke. In 1992, the Washington Post summarized a "six-month examination of the council's work" thusly:

> Vice President Dan Quayle, a self-proclaimed "zealot when it comes to de-regulation," has made his chairmanship of the President's Council on Competitiveness a command post for a war against government regulation of American business. . . .
>
> Seven congressional committees are investigating the council's activities. But the council's real role is much larger than even its critics imagine.
>
> A six-month examination of the council's work by The Washington Post shows that Quayle and his small council staff . . . have intervened in dozens of unpublicized controversies over important federal regulations, leaving what vice presidential aides call "no fingerprints" on the results of its interventions.[1]

In terms of how it operated, the Quayle Council bore a significant connection to other aspects of the presidential strategy discussed in other chapters. Like the president with signing statements, the Quayle Council diminished the effect of duly enacted acts of Congress after Congress passed them and even though the president had used up all his legitimate authority in the enactment process to extract concessions by lobbying or veto threats. The Quayle Council, too, acted in a way that precludes public accountability. When newly enacted legislation, notably the Clean Air Act of 1990, would require the administration to implement environmental policies, the administration did not choose to accept the result after fighting openly by lobbying during bill consideration or by veto bargaining. It did not choose to respond directly during execution by appointing an EPA administrator, like Anne Gorsuch or James Watt during the Reagan Administration, who would be an open, visible, accountable opposition to environmental regulation. Looking at two of the most important domestic enactments during the Bush Administration, one can see that the Bush Administration blunted the Civil Rights Act of 1991 by the president's signing statement and that the Bush Administration blunted the Clean Air Act of 1990 by extensive intervention of the Quayle Council staff.

There is a second connection between the Quayle Council and signing statements. As President Bush employed the White House counsel's office for signing statements, so he employed that office for the Quayle Council. The White House counsel chaired the key Quayle Council working group on deregulation, which supervised new regulations on a government-wide basis. This position matured further after the presidential order of a moratorium on regulations in 1992, so that the White House counsel formally cochaired the moratorium working group that the president had given greater power over regulation.

This hands-on operational role clashed with the traditional informal advisory role appropriate for the unaccountable White House staff. In other words, the White House counsel did not merely provide legal advice to the Quayle Council or give advice for presidential actions. Rather, through the Quayle Council the White House counsel occupied an additional position of formal power while still remaining shielded from Senate confirmation, limits in enactments, or oversight hearings. In turn, the White House counsel's office helped protect the Quayle Council from public accountability, blocking congressional oversight under a theory of executive privilege. Thus, through the Quayle Council, as through presidential declarations invalidating or revising provisions in new laws, the White House counsel created an extraordinary vehicle for his own action.

Vice President Quayle conceded that the Council sought not to be publicly accountable. As the Washington Post noted from an interview with Vice President Quayle:

"We've had sometimes more visibility than I really want," Quayle said of the publicity surrounding the council. He said he would prefer that most of their interventions, like that on aircraft noise, leave no fingerprints. . . .

It is the use of informal, back channels outside public or congressional purview—designed partly to thwart publicity and partly to hold down the temperature of disputes within the government—that critics say denies the protections of open government.[2]

A particularly troubling aspect of the Quayle Council was its functioning, in an atmosphere colored by charges of conflicts of interest and campaign contributions, as a conduit for business influence exerted off the record. Quayle made no secret of his effective campaign fund-raising in business circles. As the Washington Post noted from its investigation, "Quayle and the president derive immense political benefit from business and big-donor Republican circles because of the council's deregulatory activities."[3] Numerous observers from a variety of camps agreed. A partly admiring piece in Time appeared under the title "Need Friends in High Places? For Industries Trying to Skirt the Law, Dan Quayle's Council on Competitiveness Is a Good Place to Start."[4] One study concluded that "the industry associations that successfully enlisted the council in their cause contributed approximately $3.5 million in the past three years to the Bush-Quayle campaign."[5]

The executive director who built the council staff into a powerful force, Allan B. Hubbard, crystallized the ethical issue of regulatory review in the hands of White House staff with political and fund-raising missions. Hubbard was a multimillionaire owner of an Indiana chemical manufacturing company with numerous other business interests, thus having a personal antiregulation stake. Moreover, he had an extensive history of ties to Quayle and Bush in campaign managing and fund-raising.[6] After a long period of legally dubious activity, he finally had Quayle provide him with a formal waiver of the conflict-of-interest law. This action raised questions about both the legality of his conflicted activity up to the date of the waiver and the propriety (though no longer potential criminality) of his continuing the conflicted activity that necessitated waiving that basic ethical law.

The issues concerning Hubbard ended only when he left the executive directorship in 1992 to become Vice President Quayle's own campaign manager. If anything, that move confirmed the Quayle Council's function as a mechanism for trading influence for funds. As campaign manager, Hubbard was visibly positioned to raise funds from the business interests for which he had done antiregulatory favors as Quayle Council director.

This book provides the first overall history of the Quayle Council with an emphasis on its legal status and aspects.[7] After a background from prior administrations, this discussion will start with the obscure authorization of the Quayle Council in 1989, which began a period in which the council lay moribund. It continues with the actual activation of the Quayle Council in 1990. Only in 1991, when the Bush Administration turned back to domestic matters, did the Quayle Council have wide-scale impact. This influence culminated with the moratorium on regulation in 1992.

Prior Administrations

As previously discussed, although the Nixon, Carter, and Ford administrations had regulatory review, systematic executive review awaited the Reagan Administration. Two executive orders, executive order 12291 in 1981 and executive order 12498 in 1984, established a systematic review machinery centered in the Office of Management and Budget and specifically in its Office of Information and Regulatory Affairs (OIRA). Pursuant to those executive orders, the Environmental Protection Agency, the Occupational Health and Safety Administration, the Food and Drug Administration, and other regulatory agencies had to clear proposals for major regulations with OIRA, which applied cost-benefit analysis to them.

Frequently, congressional hearings charged that the OIRA used its review power to delay, diminish, or simply block regulation.[8] The very fact that those hearings took place reflected that the Reagan Administration regulatory review system had not escaped congressional accountability. Moreover, House members threatened to cut off appropriations that sustained regulatory review and senators, notably Senator (later Vice President) Albert Gore, Jr. (D-Tenn.), threatened to enact limiting legislation. In 1986, faced with these threats, the OMB adopted the "Gramm procedures," subjecting itself to at least a minimal level of public scrutiny.[9]

Moreover, judicial decisions also scrutinized the OMB's regulatory role. The Supreme Court banned cost-benefit analysis for regulations in which Congress, on health and safety grounds, did not accept such criteria. Lower courts said OIRA review was no excuse for delaying statutorily mandated regulations. These court decisions called into question some of how OIRA proceeded, but no court decision seriously disabled the regulatory review process. In some sense, the congressional oversight and judicial review both reformed the OIRA process somewhat and gave it whatever level of legitimacy could thereby accrue.

At the end of the Reagan Administration, regulatory review had remained a comparatively accountable operation. Still, the Reagan Administration had laid something of a foundation for what followed by its Presidential Task Force on Regulatory Relief, chaired by Vice President George Bush and directed by the vice president's counsel, C. Boyden Gray. Some press accounts criticized this task force in action.[10]

1989–1990: CREATION, DORMANCY, AND ACTIVATION

Creation and Dormancy

Initially, when the Bush Administration began, it did not seek to change significantly the regulatory review system inherited from the Reagan Administration. Executive orders 12291 and 12498 remained in effect, and the OIRA proceeded pursuant to them. In April 1989, President Bush did announce a Council on Competitiveness, the Quayle Council, as the successor to his own Vice Presidential Task Force. The vice president's office offered this description of the council's creation:

> The establishment of the Council was announced in a White House press briefing of April 4, 1989. As characterized in the briefing, the Council was to "review regulatory issues and such other matters as may be referred by the President and bear on competitiveness of the United States economy" and it was noted that formation of the Council had been proposed by the President in his February 9 budget message.[11]

The council's emergence was merely a gesture without creation of any special machinery. No staff were assigned and no procedures were created to give the Quayle Council any significance. Vice President Quayle's office did make its own announcement of the council's establishment in a press release dated April 12, 1989. The Quayle Council itself claimed at that time a grant of authority regarding executive orders 12291 and 12498 but there was no evidence to support that claim.[12]

During its first year, the council apparently neither met nor had any staff. Quite the contrary, the National Journal described its initial year thusly: "[t]he council initially seemed to be little more than a facade that allowed the Administration to at least give a passing bow to the increasingly contentious debate over U.S. global competitiveness. It had no full-time staff and no real structure until Hubbard was brought on board in July 1990 . . . ."[13] According to the press, "The council was relatively inactive until mid-1990, when Bush and the business community perceived backsliding from the Reagan administration's deregulatory victories."[14]

Activation in 1990

One account tells colorfully how the Quayle Council, after having neither significance nor activity in 1989 and 1990, became activated:

> Bush created the panel in 1989 but gave it new powers a year later, when he began hearing complaints from friends that his government was reregulating industries that the Reagan Administration had sought to deregulate. Not long afterward, the President appeared before aides one morning waving a newspaper clipping about reregulation and asking, "What's going on here?" Bush, who headed a task force on regulatory relief as Vice President, asked Quayle to review new regulations to make sure that costs would not outweigh benefits. Lacking a high-profile White House role at the time, Quayle jumped in with both feet.[15]

As this account reflects, although the Quayle Council had claimed power starting in 1989, it was a year later that the president actually "asked Quayle to review new regulations."

As a formal matter, the 1990 empowering of the Quayle Council occurred as follows. A June 13, 1990, "Memorandum for the Cabinet and Agency Heads," listing "Subject: Federal Regulation," from the secretary of the Cabinet, Ede Holiday, told the Cabinet departments:

> At last week's Cabinet Meeting the President said that, after discussing the matter with Vice President Quayle, he had decided to ask the Council on Competitiveness, chaired by the Vice President, to assume responsibilities previously exercised by the Task Force on Regulatory Relief. . . .
> Attached is the President's official announcement of this assignment for the Council on Competitiveness.

The announcement attached to the Ede Holiday memorandum was a statement by the White House press secretary, dated June 15, 1990:

> The President today designated the Council on Competitiveness, chaired by Vice President Quayle, as the appropriate council to review issues raised in conjunction with the regulatory program under Executive Order 12498. The President has also directed the Council on Competitiveness to exercise the same authority over regulatory issues as did the Presidential Task Force on Regulatory Relief under Executive Order 12291, which established the Administration's regulatory review process.

Why does it matter that the Quayle Council had no actual activity in 1989 when it became the instrument, nominally, of executive orders 12291 and 12498? Why does it matter that, in fact, the Quayle Council's activity started in mid-1990, based not on the executive orders, which had been in effect all along and carried out by the OIRA, but on new White House memoranda without any formal status like an executive order? It matters because the Quayle Council shortly began to revolutionize the authority structure behind regulation. Had the Quayle Council's role in this revolution rested on a new executive order, that executive order—an ordinary and relatively open and accountable instrument of authority—would have received intensive public, congressional, and judicial scrutiny. Instead, the Quayle Council actually drew its authority from the president's oral command as implemented by internal White House staff memoranda that did not even surface publicly for a long time.

Subsequently, the Quayle Council sought to tie itself to the structure during the Reagan years by the executive orders. However, in 1989 and 1990, while those executive orders applied fully, the Quayle Council did nothing. Its real power came not from the previous system of regulatory review pursuant to executive order but from the major change accomplished in an invisible and unaccountable fashion by internal White House staff memoranda.

Moreover, not the president himself, but two other White House staffs—the Cabinet secretariat and the press office—specified and defined the parameters (to the extent anything and anyone did) of the Quayle Council's power. All the authority was thus informal and shaped by the staff, in contrast to authority from laws or executive orders. When the charges later began that the real power of the Quayle Council came from Vice President Quayle's ability to reap business fund-raising by political interference with administration, it became useful to synthesize more of a legitimate pedigree for the council. Then, the systematic and documented but after-the-fact defense of the council, as Senator Pete Domenici (R-N.M.) ably presented it, would become that it "was created on March 31, 1989," that it "exercises the same authorities given . . . [by] Executive Order 12291 . . . and Executive Order 12498," and that it was a legitimate part of the advisory structure for the president.[16]

This vagueness in the council's mandate served the administration strategy well. From the outset of its active phase, the Quayle Council lacked the kind of charter for which there can be a public accounting about the extent of its power and its obedience to limits. Furthermore, the June 13 memorandum included the following statement regarding what the president was said to have requested of the Cabinet: "In particular, he has asked that your staff work closely in cooperation with OMB's Office of Information and Regulatory Affairs (OIRA), *White House Counsel's Office* and the Council on Competitiveness at every step in the regulatory process. . . ." (emphasis added).

In other words, the informal method of activating the hitherto quiescent Quayle Council had the built-in purpose and effect of providing the White House counsel's office with a large part of its new power. In that light, it does not appear that the vagueness and informality characterizing the June 1990 authorization of the Quayle Council resulted from lack of lawyering. Rather, it seems to have resulted from the White House counsel trading a vague and informal mandate giving expansive opportunities to another White House staff (the Quayle Council's) for a share of power given back to his own White House counsel's office. In sum, by internal and invisible documentation, the White House counsel conferred power on the vice president's staff and received back a share of that power. Nowhere did a law or other legitimate procedure for the people to consent to such a new ruling authority play any part.

On June 28, 1990, the Quayle Council held its first meeting ever, and a press release announced the appointment of Allan Hubbard as its executive director. The press has described Hubbard's strategy for asserting authority:

One of Hubbard's first moves as executive director was to ask OMB's Office of Information and Regulatory Affairs for a list of issues on which the agencies had been dragging their feet.

Hubbard and [the council's deputy director, David M.] McIntosh began applying the heat to agency lawyers in phone calls or meetings to resolve these issues. Hubbard met personally with the number two officials in many agencies and departments, calling on Quayle to talk to the appropriate Cabinet secretaries when Hubbard was not satisfied.

Word quickly spread through the business community that the Competitiveness Council was ready and able to help on regulatory matters, and its agenda filled up.[17]

First Major Actions

Two Quayle Council actions symbolized the vice president's growing role: the municipal incinerator rule and the vice president's governmentwide directive to come forth with proposals against regulation.

The municipal incinerator rule signified that by December 1990 the council could itself kill a significant regulation. Its December 19 press release announced that it had reviewed the EPA's standards for municipal incinerators ("draft Air Pollutant Emission Standards and Guidelines for Municipal Waste Combustors"). The EPA had proposed that cities not burn recyclable refuse. Instead, the EPA should require municipal incinerators to engage in recycling ("source separation"). Initially, the proposal won favor not merely in the environmental and recycling community but also from skeptical analysts in the OMB's budget operation.[18] This proposal fit President Bush's campaign promise that he would be the "environmental president," but now he had begun seeking a method, without opening his administration to public accountability for breaking such promises, to realign himself with the antienvironmental political forces on his party's right wing.

Before the meeting, the press had noted that "the EPA recycling rule is the first major regulatory action to come before the council and as such is being billed as a test case. . . . As a result, the handling of the recycling rule 'will be a key signal to the rest of the administration on how the council system will work,' said an administration official who opposes EPA's rule."[19]

The Wall Street Journal reported the next day: "A White House council headed by Vice President Quayle used its muscle to kill a government proposal for trash recycling just days before it was to go into effect . . . . This was the first time that Mr. Quayle's obscure panel, which was created to stop rules that stifle industry, has intervened to block a regulation."[20]

The Quayle Council's press release for that December meeting said: "The Council reached the consensus that the mandatory requirement for source separation was not consistent with several of the Administration's regulatory principles."[21] It explained that the council "reached the consensus" that the proposal "violated the principle of Federalism, embodied in the Federalism Executive Order (E.O. 12612), which requires agencies to avoid Federal regulations in areas traditionally reserved for state and local government." Environmentalists called the notion of "some pristine, constitutionally hallowed role for localities in handling garbage" a "silly" one in light of the 1976 Resource Conservation and Recovery Act governing recycling of solid waste.[22]

Moreover, the executive order on federalism of 1987 had previously been largely a dead letter. The Supreme Court's decisions on federalism had marched away from imposing any such federalism principles as a matter of law.[23] With no statutory authorization or confirmation and no judicial support, the executive order consisted largely of Attorney General Meese's platitudes issued in October 1987 in his term's twilight. Now, those platitudes came to life as a potent legal barrier by which a president without the support in Congress to change the environmental laws could nevertheless hamstring them. Those federalism platitudes now took effect through a legal judgment made by a White House staff group behind closed doors with no public participation, which could not receive judicial review or meaningful congressional oversight.

Ironically, even the lobbyists who won in that Quayle Council meeting expressed uneasiness. Barbara Paley, a lobbyist against the recycling rule on behalf of localities, afterward expressed misgivings about the process:

> It's nice that we got it, but I guess that there may be times when we will be concerned about an organization like the competitiveness council, which nobody knows a whole lot about and nobody knows who does what to whom there. We don't think that you should have to go around the back door to groups that are not out there in the open and who do not function in a substantive area to achieve this kind of objective.[24]

The killing of the recycling rule received scrutiny in the first congressional hearing on the Quayle Council. On March 21, 1991, the House Subcommittee on Health and the Environment held a hearing on implementation of the Clean Air Act. The Environment Subcommittee chairman, Henry Waxman (D-Calif.), defended the soundness of the council-killed recycling rule, obtained testimony from the EPA, and released the report of a staff investigation of the Quayle Council's action. He then stated regarding the Quayle Council:

> What is particularly abhorrent about such intervention is the complete absence of public accountability. Most Americans have never even heard of the Council on Competitiveness. We asked Mr. Quayle to send a representative to today's hearing to tell the subcommittee about the Council and its actions,

but he refused to do so. We then asked Mr. Quayle to have the Council respond to a series of very basic written questions, on matters such as the Council's membership and the rules that guide its actions. But the council has furnished no response.

The other noteworthy step in 1990 involved another in the series of governmentwide White House directives that further created a systematic mechanism for exercising power outside the channels of accountability, like laws, executive orders, or even OMB circulars, but without any clear or formal legal precision. At a September 27 meeting, according to the Quayle Council's press release, "[t]he Vice President requested that each Cabinet member propose 3 or 4 deregulatory initiatives in their areas by the end of October." Following this up, Vice President Quayle initiated memoranda to each agency like the one to the EPA, an October 24 memorandum on the Council on Competitiveness:

MEMORANDUM FOR ADMINISTRATOR REILLY

Thank you for your participation in the Council's work. I would like to ask your personal involvement on one question, in particular. To follow up on the President's request that the Council work to remove the burden of excessive regulations, I am asking all agency heads to propose a few de-regulatory initiatives in their area that can be implemented through administrative action, and, if necessary, one or two legislative proposals. I would appreciate you or someone from your staff contacting Al Hubbard within the next few weeks with your suggestions.

Such memoranda then received circulation inside the agencies, thus harnessing the whole government, in effect, to expand the agenda of the Quayle Council.

Thus, by the end of 1990 the Quayle Council had established itself. It did so by the verbal support of President Bush, personal involvement of Vice President Quayle, and activist White House staff work but very little in the way of legal formality, clarity, or limitation on its authority. It established a method of operation involving meetings by the Quayle Council staff with interest groups of potential political campaign value and informal contacts by that White House staff with regulatory agencies. Backing up the staff, the council held occasional meetings at which it pressured officials such as the EPA administrator to kill rules.

1991: MAJOR INTERVENTIONS, CONGRESSIONAL OVERSIGHT

Whereas 1990 had been the year of the Quayle Council's ascendance to power, 1991 became the year of the Quayle Council massively exercising that power. Once the Quayle Council staff attained power, it took on two particular tasks that symbolized the height of President Bush's effort to weaken the environmental laws without dealing with Congress: the Clean Air Act and the Wetlands Delineation Manual. Thereafter came the season of press and congressional attention.

Clean Air Regulations

President Bush signed the Clean Air Act on November 15, 1990. During Congress's consideration of the act, it had rejected numerous administration proposals for standards that would allow higher air pollution levels. In particular, when the House and Senate conferees met to strike the crucial final terms, President Bush submitted his own version. However, it came too late. "[B]y the time the administration sent the conferees a counterproposal on the bill Sept. 26, it was too late to make much of a difference. . . . Congress felt free, in part, to opt for the stronger controls because of the skepticism that Bush would veto the bill over its price tag in the waning days of an election-year session."[25] Because Bush's own proposals and veto bargaining had initially influenced the Clean Air Act, this later loss of power over it reflected the shifting and subtle interplay of presidential-congressional interaction in a divided government.

When President Bush signed the Clean Air Act, he issued a signing statement of which one aspect was previously discussed: how he sought to block citizen suits regarding a polluting facility's problems from the past. President Bush's pronouncements on the bill also sought to blunt the act in other major respects. Rather than simply allow implementation of the compromises struck in the bill between the preferences of the president and those of congressional environmentalists, the presidential statement sought to revise the law as though the president's September 26 proposal or his other preferences had magically triumphed.

Thus, President Bush had largely failed to persuade Congress to subordinate health factors to considerations of polluters' costs through cost-benefit balancing and so-called market mechanisms. President Bush's weak support in Congress in 1989 had grown even weaker in 1990. He had not relied upon the mechanisms for putting his own personal popularity on the line either during Congress's shaping of this key 1990 enactment or in the midterm 1990 congressional election. Instead, when he signed the act on November 15 with the congressional enacting process and the midterm electoral process both behind him, he now declared he would have the act "implement[ed]," in the form he preferred: "In all, these path-breaking features allow us to implement the legislation in a way that achieves my environmental goals at an acceptable cost. The result will be the dawning of a new era in regulatory policy, one that relies on the market to reconcile the environment and the economy . . . ." President Bush directed that the law be interpreted in its implementation contrary to the congressional rejection of proposals to reduce enforcement on cost grounds: "To address the serious concerns raised by the cost of this legislation, I am directing Bill Reilly, Administrator of the Environmental Protection Agency, to implement this bill in the most cost-effective manner possible. This means ensuring that plants can continue to use emission trading and netting to the maximum extent allowed by law. . . ."

President Bush also included a thinly veiled instruction to underestimate the risks to health when regulating: "This Administration will also pursue the use of more realistic assumptions when estimating risk. These implementation strategies will help keep unnecessary costs . . . down, while ensuring [implementation] . . . in the most efficient manner possible."[26]

The Quayle Council provided a mechanism for the president to propitiate and to reward his industry supporters without relying upon the president's weak support in Congress. President Bush's pronouncements on the newly signed bill drafted by the White House counsel's office prepared the way for the second stage of having this other White House staff, at the Quayle Council, complete the revision. As early as the council's September 27, 1990, meeting, it had announced this approach:

EARLY INTERAGENCY REVIEW OF THE
MOST IMPORTANT EPA RULES

In the important area of environmental regulation, the Environmental Protection Agency (EPA) has been working with OMB and the Council to establish early interagency review of the most important EPA regulations, especially when there is tight statutory or judicially imposed deadlines. The Council, OMB, and EPA reaffirm the cost-benefit principles of regulatory review under Executive Order No. 12291.[27]

The Quayle Council established six working groups, including the Working Group on Deregulation. In the words of the council's staff, "The Vice President has asked these working groups to make recommendations to the Council regarding particular policy and regulatory issues that arise in their respective areas."[28] These working groups created a structure allowing delegation of power to smaller groups consisting of White House staff, the agency officials with statutory responsibility to execute the law, and other agency officials without that responsibility. The mix allowed maximum pressure by the antiregulatory officials upon the agency officials who have the responsibility while remaining within the White House framework assertedly immune from judicial review and congressional oversight. Through the Working Group on Deregulation, the president could transfer power away from the accountable head of the EPA surrounded by legal and political reasons to carry out the law and instead confer the power on trusted White House staff lieutenants of known antiregulatory views but no public or congressional accountability.

Implementation of the Clean Air Act was expected to require approximately fifty-five new major regulations. The Quayle Council staff began systematic review, with the EPA, of all the Clean Air Act regulations. As Hubbard told a House committee by letter, he "chaired biweekly [working group] meetings with EPA, other agencies, and representatives from other offices in the Executive Office of the President interested in the Clean Air Act Amendments to determine the status of regulations being developed by EPA and reviewed by OMB."[29]

The Quayle Council focused on two particularly significant rules: the permit rule and the WEPCO (Wisconsin Electric Power Company) rule. In the Clean Air Act's system, general overall requirements such as industrywide regulations became translated into specific duties for individual sources, like chemical plants and oil refineries, through their inclusion in the permits issued to those sources. Thus, the permit rule governed how strictly the overall regulations and principles would either apply or be watered down when it came to obedience by specific sources of pollution. President Bush's November 15, 1990, signing statement of the Clean Air Act had singled out the permit rule. The president insisted "that the permit program [be] phased in over time in an orderly, nondisruptive manner."[30] This vague formulation meant that even where Congress in enacting the Clean Air Act had insisted on strictness in permits and had rejected presidential proposals for relaxing pollution prohibitions in permits, the president anticipated sufficient laxity at the permit stage to be "nondisruptive."

The EPA published the draft rule for public comment in late April 1991. As for the 1991 draft, it faithfully followed the key instructions of an April 6, 1991, memorandum from the Quayle Council's then-deputy director, David McIntosh, to the EPA's assistant administrator for air and radiation regulation, William Rosenberg. Those Quayle Council directions, which McIntosh admitted were "from White House Counsel's office, the Office of Policy Development, and OIRA," included more than one hundred changes in the EPA's own original permit proposal. In effect, these changes took the president's signing statement for the act and substituted that for the act itself where it mattered most, in the implementation of the act.

The Quayle Council's changes included unleashing a so-called minor permit amendment procedure to allow unlimited rewriting of permits by polluters. This procedure violated the statutory provisions requiring, for all permit revisions, nothing less than public notice, an opportunity for public comment and a public hearing, and an opportunity for judicial review.[31] Also, the Quayle Council staff widened the statutory provision for "operational flexibility," which explicitly allowed only those variations possible "without requiring a permit revision," to allow the permits themselves to be revised. This widening of the provision denied any opportunity for objection by state pollution-control authorities, whom the law and the public expect, by control of permits, to achieve the pollution reductions necessary for clean air.[32]

Another Quayle Council staff change implemented one of Gray's personal enthusiasms, trading in emission rights. As noted earlier, the signing statement for the Clean Air Act had promoted such "market mechanisms" even beyond what the president had been willing to bargain for them in the legislative process. Gray now used the working group's rewriting of the regulation to provide, in contravention to the statute, that such trading could authorize pollution sources to violate the law written into their own permits.[33] In effect, the White House had exercised the sovereign prerogative to grant dispensation from obedience to the law.

The White House Staff: Evasion of Oversight

The House Subcommittee on Health and the Environment held a hearing on May 1, 1991, that focused in part on the changes in the draft permit rule. The subcommittee chairman asked Vice President Quayle to have the Quayle Council staff appear if he himself would not appear. The request was refused. Instead of submitting to oversight, the Quayle Council, after its May 6 meeting, simply released the unenlightening statement that "[t]he Council supported EPA's recent proposed rule establishing requirements for State permitting plans under the Clean Air Act."[34]

That Clean Air hearing occurred less than two weeks before President Bush's Princeton Address on May 10, 1991. The refusal to submit to congressional accountability crystallized how the Bush White House implemented the major strategic themes expressed in that address. Accordingly, a brief note about "executive privilege" is appropriate.

During two centuries of congressional oversight, presidents claimed, from time to time, the power to withhold executive agency documents or employee testimony. However, the specific issue of White House staff rarely arose because until the term of President Franklin D. Roosevelt, there were hardly more than three "White House staff" at any time, as the term would be used today. Presidents did all their work with employees of executive departments. In the era starting with President Roosevelt, congressional committees still typically found they could do without summoning White House staff. Necessary explanations could be extracted from agency officials.

The unresolved issues about White House staff began surfacing during the Nixon Administration. White House staff held the key to the ITT scandal, which involved ITT's use of influence at the White House to fix its antitrust case. President Nixon's national security adviser, Henry Kissinger, who possessed unparalleled control over foreign affairs, held the key to oversight on such matters. Of course, regarding Watergate such White House staff as H. R. Haldeman, John Ehrlichman, John Dean, and their subordinates had the essential knowledge of the matter. In all these areas, the Nixon Administration started by claiming that a form of blanket executive privilege cloaked White House staff. In all these areas, struggles broke out between Congress and the White House, and Congress succeeded in extracting the requisite evidence regarding ITT, Kissinger, and Watergate.[35]

These Nixon Administration struggles left a mixed legacy. On the one hand, Congress could still often conduct oversight by questioning agency officials rather than White House staff, as the White House requested. On the other hand, if a congressional committee needed White House staff evidence, it could call upon the legal and political tools that had eventually extracted evidence from the Nixon White House.

The system worked as long as White House staff stayed in the roles of advisers or managers of the president's appearances. It broke down if White House staff became the wielders of authority for which accountability would be demanded. Thus, in 1985 and 1986 the issue surfaced again when press reports linked White House staff—the NSC staff, specifically Oliver North—to contra aid, violating the Boland Amendment. Initially, the White House tried to divert the inquiries of the House Intelligence Committee and a subcommittee of the House Foreign Affairs Committee.

Nonetheless, these committees questioned successive national security advisers in writing and brought National Security Adviser Robert McFarlane and Oliver North before them for questioning in October 1985 and August 1986. When the Iran-contra scandal broke, the House and Senate intelligence committees brought the next national security adviser, John M. Poindexter, before them for questioning. North subsequently admitted lying in his appearance and McFarlane and Poindexter respectively pled guilty, and were convicted at trial, for lying. President Bush's December 1992 pardon extended to such charges.[36]

The May 1, 1991, Clean Air hearing and President Bush's May 10, 1991, Princeton Address again brought to a head the problem of the president giving power to a White House staff and then denying Congress the opportunity to question that staff at a hearing. In his speech, President Bush claimed the right to act with "secrecy" and not "unnecessarily" to keep Congress "in the dark," and he indicated his disdain for congressional oversight that "confuses" the public. The Bush Administration strategy had prepared to carry out this approach by using White House staff, such as the Quayle Council staff, for activity that they would attempt to cloak with executive privilege when faced with a congressional demand for accountability. Congress, looking at why the Clean Air Act was being systematically deprived of meaning, ran directly into that strategy as a barrier.

All that happened at this moment was that the House Clean Air hearing relied on Quayle Council documents that it had obtained, and it issued a public denunciation of Vice President Quayle for not allowing his staff to appear for questioning. The subcommittee chairman stated:

> The subcommittee is today releasing an April 6 memo from the Office of the Vice President demonstrating how he has sabotaged the most important rulemaking to date under the new Clean Air Act. . . .
>
> One particularly abhorrent aspect of this process is the complete absence of public accountability. Most Americans have never even heard of the Vice President's Council on Competitiveness, but now the Council is presuming to rewrite the Clean Air Act and savage EPA's regulations . . . . We asked Mr. Quayle to come himself or to send a representative to today's hearing to tell the Subcommittee about the Council and its position on the permit proposal, but he declined to do so.[37]

Besides what the Quayle Council was doing to the permit rule, its systematic revision of the Clean Air Act produced a similar effect on the "WEPCO rulemaking," a rulemaking proceeding named after a case concerning Wisconsin Electric Power Company. This WEPCO rulemaking concerned the Clean Air Act's "new source" requirements and renovation of existing facilities. Existing electric utility plants produce most of the nation's sulfur dioxide air pollution and much of the nitrogen oxides. Environmentalists had long recognized that curbing such pollution required that strict standards be met not only by the utilities building new facilities but also by those utilities renovating existing facilities.

However, the Bush Administration favored relaxing such utilities' pollution requirements in the WEPCO proceeding, and in 1990, during the Clean Air Act conference, the administration made proposals to Congress reflecting that position. Congress rejected these proposals. President Bush responded, in his signing statement for the act, by reinterpreting the new law to mean "that the Administration's proposed policy on WEPCO [be] implemented to the extent allowed by law as quickly as possible." This was going to be yet another case in which a congressional enactment *rejecting* an administration position would be taken as *codifying* it.[38]

When the EPA at first followed the act as enacted, industry sought to water down the requirements, and the Council of Economic Advisers weighed in on industry's side. By law, the council served as a purely advisory White House organ on fiscal and monetary matters. It had no charter to intervene in rulemaking or to force environmental agencies to relax particular regulations. The Council of Economic Advisers, like the White House counsel, now took the opportunities offered by the vague and unlimited mandate of the Quayle Council to develop hands-on operational power over regulations while still remaining cloaked in White House unaccountability. On this WEPCO rule for utility renovations, a July 1991 hearing by the House Subcommittee on Health and the Environment traced a paper trail from the industry group (the Edison Electric Institute) and the Council of Economic Advisers to the final WEPCO rule, which relaxed the Clean Air Act's requirements.[39]

As the Quayle Council waded into the major environmental issue of clean air, it also promulgated yet another governmentwide directive expanding its mandate. On March 2, 1991, the vice president sent a "Memorandum for heads of Executive Departments and Agencies," entitled "Subject: Regulatory Review Process." It provided a murky recitation, with vaguely expansive overtones, of the regulatory review process within the White House and its own role in this. At its clearest point, it expanded the review beyond regulations to "include all agency policy guidance that affects the public": "Such policy guidance includes not only regulations that are published for notice and comment, but also strategy statements, guidelines, policy manuals, grant and loan procedures, Advance Notices of Proposed Rule Making, press releases and other documents announcing or implementing regulatory policy that affects the public." Like prior and subsequent governmentwide directives from the Quayle Council, the March 1991 directive asserted maximum power without providing any clarity about how it was authorized to exercise that power or what its limits were.

One of the functions of the March 1991 directive may simply have been to further shore up regulatory review during a period when the OIRA suffered a major blow to its legitimacy. As one of the signs of President Bush's need for mechanisms to govern without Congress, the Senate continued to refuse to confirm any director for the OIRA. The OIRA had not had a director since 1989. In 1990, the White House counsel's intervention had killed a compromise legislative proposal to reauthorize the OIRA. In the absence of a reauthorization, the Senate let the administration's nomination of James F. Blumstein as OIRA director lapse without action at the end of 1990.[40] Thus, the March 1991 Quayle Council directive signified a measure of support for OIRA—even without its having a legitimately confirmed head—so long as it continued to serve the Quayle Council. As the president shifted away from his 1988 campaign promise to be the "environmental president," the Quayle Council helped him with conservatives in his own party who wanted more from regulatory review than the president could obtain in public or legislative arenas.[41]

Besides the Clean Air Act, the other major demonstration in 1991 of the Quayle Council's power to intervene in environmental regulation concerned wetlands. Wetlands are ecologically fragile areas that are vital for wildlife, flood control, and filtering out potential contaminants of waterways. Environmental concerns mounted in the 1980s over the gradual elimination of wetlands through filling in and other actions. In a key 1988 campaign pledge repeated in the 1989 budget submission to Congress, President Bush promised "no net loss" of wetlands.

The EPA and the Army Corps of Engineers, pursuant to section 404 of the Clean Water Act, control federal permits required for developers to fill in wetlands. In 1991, the wetlands issue took shape as a controversy over impending revision of the 1989 EPA manual of guidelines for defining wetlands requiring protection. An interagency scientific team had been developing data consistent with the prior definition of wetlands. A wetland was defined, in simplified form, by the number of days per year it was saturated with water. The lower the number of days, the larger the number of acres deemed wetlands and thereby protected from elimination. The 1989 manual had used the figure of seven days of saturation per year, protecting large areas and thereby burdening President Bush's effort to fulfill his "no net loss" pledge.

Into this process came the Quayle Council, with the press describing the start of Vice President Quayle's intervention thusly:

> On his political swings around the country, Quayle said, he heard frequent complaints that the federal government was unnecessarily restricting the use of wetlands for real estate development and other business ventures. . . .
> Last May [1991], an official said, Quayle told the [Quayle] council's executive director, "Hubbard, we need to do something about wetlands." EPA Administrator William K. Reilly protested against the intervention . . . but Quayle received Bush's approval to become involved.[42]

In place of seven days of saturation per year, "EPA Administrator William Reilly started negotiations on the revised manual at 10 days; the Quayle Council countered with 21."[43] With its antiregulatory approach, the Quayle Council supplanted the agency-level technically qualified environmental teams and transformed the issue by the White House's pressuring on behalf of complaining commercial interests.

After the Quayle Council met on April 6, 1991, it issued this press release noting its new dominance of the issue:

> OIRA and Council to review Wetlands Delineation Manual. The Vice President announced that the proposed revisions to the Wetland Delineation Manual

would be going to OIRA for review. This manual is the interagency policy that defines what land is considered to be "wetland" for government programs. The Vice President reaffirmed the President's goal of "no net loss" of wetlands as a balanced policy that both protects environmentally important wetlands and allows legitimate land use, such as farming, housing development, and the construction of roads, airports, and energy facilities.[44]

In a famous exchange, Reilly and Quayle almost reached a deal on the eve of a July 10 Senate subcommittee hearing, but the Quayle Council staff prevented it by an extreme antiwetlands stance. The Washington Post described the events as a "near fiasco":

> On the night before Reilly was to testify to the Senate, he, Quayle and Hubbard engaged in a round-robin series of telephone conversations trying to broker a deal. Each time Reilly thought he had Quayle's agreement, Hubbard called Reilly to say he had misunderstood. When their final agreement was presented at a White House senior staff meeting the next morning, Darman and Chief of Staff John H. Sununu erupted, and a last-minute call was made to Reilly—in his car on the way to the hearing—to tell him the deal was off.[45]

Here, President Bush's personal style, with its preference for elite maneuvering behind the scenes, coincided with his political situation, which disfavored open decisions in the legislative arena.

The full Quayle Council met on July 29. Vice President Quayle "began the session by expressing astonishment that vast areas of his home state of Indiana could have been classified as wetlands under the original definition in the manual, when he knew those areas were farmland."[46] He is quoted as suggesting, as a possible wetlands definition, "How about if we say when it's wet, it's wet?"[47] Using the leverage gained at the meeting, the next day Quayle and Hubbard again pressured Reilly. Reilly acquiesced the next day to their figures, fifteen days of standing water and twenty-one days of surface saturation as the minimum for a wetland, an approach "which significantly narrowed the definition of wetlands in a way experts have said would halve the amount of protected acreage."[48] On August 9, President Bush announced the outcome, which was formally published in the Federal Register as a draft regulation on August 14.

In November 1991, the White House backed down. The press linked this to other contemporaneous White House firestorms. It was the eve of Chief of Staff John Sununu's departure. Sununu, as a White House chief of staff who rejected seeking action in Congress, exemplified the Bush Administration strategy. A year earlier, he had said: "Frankly, this President doesn't need another single piece of legislation, unless it's absolutely right. There's not a single piece of legislation that need be passed in the two years for this President. In fact, if Congress wants to come together, adjourn, and leave, it's all right with us."[49]

As Professor James P. Pfiffner noted, the dumping of Sununu reflected both a long-term phenomenon and a response to the situation at that moment in late 1991. From the long-term perspective, it illustrated a common fate of chiefs of staff in divided postwar governments: "There have been four domineering chiefs of staff in the modern presidency; Sherman Adams for Eisenhower, H. R. Haldeman for Nixon, Donald Regan for Reagan, and John Sununu for Bush. *Each* of these domineering chiefs of staff has resigned in disgrace after doing considerable harm to his President." At that moment in 1991, Sununu's "firing came at a low point in the Bush Administration; the economy was doing poorly, the President was sliding in public opinion polls from his huge popularity after the Gulf War, and the Administration seemed to be in disarray."[50] Sununu's departure exposed the emerging failure of the Bush Administration's strategy. Avoiding public and legislative struggle not only did nothing about national problems for which the president received blame, but it also displayed a president not willing to grapple with those problems in any visible public arena.

The Quayle Council's August wetlands coup had brought on a stormy public debate in congressional hearings and in the press, with widespread popular reaction in defense of wetlands and against the proposal.[51] Agency field studies between August and November showed that the Quayle Council's twenty-one-day figure would have lifted protection for nearly half of the nation's wetlands. With Sununu leaving and with the president also backing away in that same period from the White House counsel's most extreme draft proposal on the Civil Rights Act, the Quayle Council also had to give in for the moment on this particular issue. The New York Times noted that the November announcement on the wetlands issue came from a Quayle spokesman because "Mr. Quayle's council . . . had revised the guidelines proposed by four Federal agencies." That Quayle spokesman pledged "that the amount of wetlands counted in 1988, an estimated 100 million acres, would be the basis for the new rules."[52]

Congressional Scrutiny

Although the Quayle Council appeared to lose the round relating to wetlands, its growing power, symbolized by its intervention into the most important of all national environmental controversies, brought it into the limelight. Congressional efforts at scrutiny had begun before with hearings of the House Subcommittee on Health and the Environment conducted in March, May, and July 1991. A spate of press coverage followed in July.[53] In August, Vice President Quayle gained nationwide attention for his industry-supported proposals to hamper plaintiffs' lawyers in areas such as products liability, with a coating of generalized anti-lawyer rhetoric to win popular support.

Meanwhile, oversight efforts by the Senate Committee on Governmental Affairs received diversion and avoidance. Senate interrogatory letters in April and May failed to elicit a response until October, when the Quayle Council sent a letter listing the dates of the Quayle Council meetings in 1990 (three) and 1991 (six) and the names of the council's working groups (six).[54] Otherwise, the response letter just reiterated prior statements or uttered generalities. On November 15, the Senate committee summoned the head of the OIRA to a hearing, the frustrating essence of which the Washington Post summarized in its headline "Competitiveness Council Suspected of Unduly Influencing Regulators: Secrecy Foils Senate Panel's Attempt to Probe Vice President's Group."[55] The Senate committee followed this hearing by approving on November 22 a bill to require a public record of the OIRA's communications on rulemaking.[56]

By the end of 1991, Quayle Council staff estimated their level of intervention as approximately fifty significant rulemakings per year. Two oversight controversies marked the year's end. The charges against the council's staff director, Allan B. Hubbard, that he had a conflict of interest because of his personal holdings in a chemical company began to take a serious toll. At a December 1991 hearing of the House Subcommittee on Health and the Environment on the Clean Air Act, Hubbard refused to show up. Instead, he had the White House counsel's office bless his position, based on the waiver he had received from Vice President Quayle for conflicts of interest.[57] Eventually he simply left his post to become Quayle's campaign manager.

An even more interesting controversy in terms of the separation of powers concerned the first congressional subpoena for documents dealing with the Quayle Council. A Quayle Council working group had developed a new set of drug approval policies for the Food and Drug Administration. These policies watered down the FDA's requirements for pharmaceutical companies to establish the efficacy of drugs. When the House Government Operations Committee's Subcommittee on Human Resources and Intergovernmental Relations, which oversees the FDA, commenced an inquiry, initially the Quayle Council staff directed the FDA to withhold documents concerning the Quayle Council.

The subcommittee responded with a subpoena to the FDA in November 1991. In a tense confrontation, the White House counsel's office threatened that the president would claim executive privilege. However, the result would have been contempt of Congress charges, for which the administration had little stomach. Moreover, the confrontation came during the same period as Sununu's departure and the firestorm over the signing statement for the Civil Rights Act of 1991. The White House decided to give in. As the subcommittee chairman, Representative Ted Weiss (D-N.Y.) subsequently told the House during a debate on the Quayle Council:

> The White House has interfered with our investigation of the FDA and the Council on Competitiveness by ordering FDA to withhold several hundred documents from the subcommittee. In November we issued a subpoena for these documents. Only after the subpoena was served did we receive all of the documents we requested from FDA. So do not tell us how forthcoming they are and how public their information is.[58]

The Washington Post reported the outcome contemporaneously:

> In its bouts with the White House, Congress appears to have won a short, opening round in its efforts to unlock the mystery of Vice President Quayle's Council on Competitiveness.
>
> At about 10 P.M. Thursday, after days of negotiations, the Food and Drug Administration turned over a 20-inch stack of documents to the House subcommittee on human resources and intergovernmental relations. The FDA had previously claimed some of the documents were part of the White House deliberative process and not subject to disclosure.[59]

In March 1992, the subcommittee held hearings based on the documents, illuminating much about the methods used by the Quayle Council to cut back on FDA regulation of pharmaceutical safety and efficacy.[60]

1992: REGULATORY MORATORIUM, POWER-OF-PURSE BATTLE

Regulatory Moratorium

As 1992 began and President Bush turned his full attention to reelection, he apparently decided to take an even harder stance against environmental regulations, but not to do so in an accountable way through legislative proposals or through changing the heads of the EPA and other agencies. Instead, he turned over massive new powers to the Quayle Council staff by announcing in his State of the Union Address in January 1992 an unprecedented regulatory moratorium. Although he did not hint in that speech about the Quayle Council's role, it soon developed that the Quayle Council would supervise the moratorium. Moreover, the president implemented the moratorium by yet another vague governmentwide directive that further expanded the Quayle Council's powers. In so doing, President Bush created a system that he subsequently extended.

On January 28, 1992, President Bush issued his memorandum entitled "Subject: Reducing the Burden of Government Regulation." It told federal agencies to stop regulatory action: "[t]o the maximum extent permitted by law, and subject to the exceptions listed below, your agency should refrain from issuing any proposed or final rule during the 90-day review period." It conferred the supervisory authority over that moratorium and over agency-reporting requirements as follows (with the emphasis added): "The 90-day review, and the preparation of [those] reports . . . will be coordinated by a working group of the Council on Competitiveness, chaired by the Chairman of the Council of Economic Advisers *and the Counsel to the President.*" Although still occupying a position without Senate confirmation, without statutory mandate or limitations, and without appearing at congressional hearings, the White House counsel now enjoyed a new position and power as chair of the working group.

For example, President Bush's memorandum vaguely told agency heads that it exempted from the moratorium "regulations that you determine, after consultation with the working group of the Council on Competitiveness described below, will foster economic growth." Because the White House counsel, as chair of the working group, could describe whatever he liked as fostering economic growth, he now became the czar of exemptions from the moratorium. Although Gray did not submit himself to accountability by congressional hearings, he gave public interviews on the moratorium, where he admitted the large role of politics in the matter. He said of the moratorium: "Is that political? I suppose . . . [it] means a better election-year climate."[61]

President Bush also made permanent changes, not limited to the ninety-day period, that he intended to strengthen the Quayle Council's role. The January 1992 directive installed a permanent network of officers throughout the federal government to report to the Quayle Council. It told agency heads:

> You should designate, in consultation with the Council on Competitiveness, a senior official to serve as your agency's permanent regulatory oversight official. This person will be responsible for conducting the review, for implementing the resulting proposals, and for ensuring that future regulatory actions conform to the standards set forth in this memorandum and in applicable Executive orders.

This Quayle Council network of "permanent regulatory oversight officials" throughout the government contrasted vividly with the historic system of accountable agency action. These officials in the agencies themselves would extend many of the unaccountable aspects previously limited to White House staff. They did not receive their office or authority from laws but from White House memoranda. They did not receive their appointments from Senate confirmation, or even from formal president commissioning, but from choice "in consultation with the Council on Competitiveness," meaning, in practice, by direction of the White House staff.

When the ninety-day time period for the moratorium expired, President Bush extended the moratorium in a set of widely publicized remarks. In a public speech, he began by saying he "want[ed] to salute the three generals in the war for regulatory reform: Our Vice President, Dan Quayle, Boyden Gray, and Dr. Michael Boskin." The memorandum that he issued to extend the moratorium another 120 days ended with another recognition of the Quayle Council's working group headed by the White House Counsel: "In implementing your reforms and in preparing the reports described in paragraph 3, you and your agency's regulatory oversight official should continue coordinating with the Competitiveness Council's Working Group on Regulatory Reform."[62]

Thus, the moratorium reinforced the dramatic evolution of the Quayle Council. By statute, decisions on regulations lay with the Cabinet departments and agencies, accountable to law and the Congress. Step by step, White House staff had created an entire system for themselves to control regulations, established by vague presidential and vice presidential memoranda. Between 1990 and 1992, the White House staff had developed a permanent network throughout the government of officials they would choose. This network would implement criteria they would promulgate and preferences they would express, which would supplant the statutorily created and accountable system. Not even a council of accountable or elected officials but rather a mere "working group" of White House staff headed this governmentwide network.

The Rio Treaty and Other "Victories"

Other administration boosts for the Quayle Council staff followed the moratorium on regulation. Most tangibly, the council played a key role in perhaps the administration's most visible action against international environmental efforts. At the so-called Earth Summit in Rio de Janeiro in June 1992, other nations pressed the United States to join the multilateral convention on "biodiversity" designed to preserve species from extinction. EPA Administrator Reilly, head of the U.S. delegation in Rio, cabled the White House with a request that the treaty, with minor changes, be signed. This context of foreign affairs negotiation had elicited President Bush's Princeton Address passages about how "[i]t is the president who is responsible for guiding and directing the nation's foreign policy . . . [and] performing this duty with 'secrecy and dispatch,' when necessary." President Bush exercised that responsibility as follows. The Washington Post reported:

> The White House Council on Competitiveness, headed by Vice President Quayle, has been outspoken against the [biodiversity] treaty. The decision to reject Reilly's 11th-hour effort was made by White House domestic policy counsel Clayton Yeutter, after consulting with *competitiveness council staffers and White House counsel C. Boyden Gray*, according to administration sources in Washington [emphasis added].[63]

Critics of the Quayle Council provided further details of how it blocked the treaty:

> The most recent example of the council's backdoor maneuvering surfaced at the Earth Summit in Rio, where Competitiveness Council staff succeeded in averting U.S. support for the biodiversity treaty supported by other participating nations. Lobbied heavily by biotechnology groups, such as the Industrial Biotechnology Assn. and Genentech, council staff were highly critical of the treaty. Meanwhile, press accounts reported that John Cohrssen, a council staffer, leaked the draft agreement in order to raise the ire of biotechnology companies and sink the treaty.[64]

Of the Quayle Council's various regulatory victories in 1992, its impact on Clean Air Act regulations received the greatest attention. The council stopped the implementation of regulations designed to address the global problem of the ozone hole. Initially, the EPA sought to promulgate regulations for phasing out the chemicals depleting the ozone, chlorofluorocarbons. Then, as a Washington Post columnist reported in February 1992, "Regulations on [chlorofluorocarbons] required by Congress more than a year ago . . . have disappeared into the regulatory black hole of the Quayle Council."[65] More attention came in June, when permit regulations, previously described at length at the draft stage, became final. This time, the dispute between Quayle and the EPA went all the way to the president, who sided against the EPA. The press reported that "Bush sided with the position taken by the Council on Competitiveness, chaired by Vice President Quayle" on the major question of public notification when industries changed their emissions permits.[66]

Power of the Purse Versus Executive Prerogative

After years of attempted oversight and legislative proposals, in 1992 Congress finally confronted the executive prerogative claims of the Quayle Council by flexing its own power of the purse. In March, the House Appropriations Subcommittee that has jurisdiction over White

House funds demanded and obtained from the White House a formal statement of the council's mission. This statement eschewed all mention of the various memoranda and other informal documents that had actually erected the council's power. Apart from generalities and platitudes that were by then standard, the White House continued the fiction that power had existed all along, pursuant to the old Reagan Administration executive orders, ignoring the actual mid-1990 activation of the council:

> The Vice President is the Chairman of the President's Council on Competitiveness. The regulatory review functions of the Council are authorized by Executive Order 12291 of February 17, 1981; and Executive Order 12498 of January 4, 1985. Generally, the Council serves as a deliberative forum for discussing regulatory proposals, most of which involve the interests of more than one Executive Branch agency or department. The Council provides an arena in which the representatives of concerned agencies and senior Administration officials can clarify relevant policy issues and ensure proper coordination between a given regulatory activity and the Administration's overall agenda.[67]

In June, the House Appropriations Committee cut from the White House appropriation bill $86,000, the salaries for two Quayle Council staffers. The Appropriations Committee's report explained: "The Council on Competitiveness acts in secret, refuses to disclose from whom it has heard, refuses to disclose all regulations in which it has intervened, and refuses to detail the actual facts and evidence upon which its decisions are based." In defunding the Quayle Council, the Appropriations Committee placed stress upon its resistance to congressional oversight: "The Committee is also very concerned about the Council's refusal to cooperate with congressional committees conducting legitimate inquiries about its activities."[68]

Shortly thereafter, that appropriation bill came to the House floor. In a major confrontation, the House voted on July 1, 1992, to retain the funding cutoff. The sponsor of the provision, Representative David E. Skaggs (D-Colo.), emphasized the Quayle Council's resistance to oversight and contrasted it with the OMB's activity under the regulatory review executive orders:

> The heart of this problem is that the Council operates in secret, not letting the American people or Congress learn even the most basic facts about its activities. . . . The Council refuses to testify before Congress. The Council refuses to provide Congress with requested information on its activities . . . .
>
> OMB testifies before Congress on its regulatory affairs activities. The Council on Competitiveness refuses to do so, and won't even answer questions submitted to it by congressional committees. . . .[69]

In the end, the House voted 236-183, largely on party lines, to make the cut.

Later that month OMB director Richard Darman responded by defending the Quayle Council as "a core function of the president" and threatened a presidential veto because of the funding cutoff.[70] When the Senate took up the White House appropriation in September, Senator John Glenn (D-Ohio), chairman of the Senate committee that had attempted oversight of the Quayle Council, offered an amendment to cut off the council's funding. However, in the face of the veto threat he withdrew the amendment. As the manager of the appropriations bill said in thanking him for withdrawing the amendment, "The White House has said that it will veto this bill if the Council's activities are restricted or defunded. Do we want to bog down this appropriations bill and the entire process . . . ?"[71]

As the 1992 election approached, public attention on the Quayle Council issue focused on its evident role serving the political interests of the president's campaign. During the primaries, Gray had used his power over regulations for plain campaign purposes. In March, on the eve of the Michigan primary, he demanded release of a regulatory decision sought by the automobile industry.[72] By September, a survey of petitions to the Quayle Council over the prior six months showed its rewarding of campaign donors.[73] An October study for the Wall Street Journal, on the eve of the election, explained: "[M]any of those who seek the Council's help also supply the GOP with large contributions, many of them in the form of 'soft money'—contributions for 'party-building' efforts like get-out-the-vote drives, which aren't limited by federal election laws."[74]

Thus, right up to the November election the Quayle Council served the Bush Administration's political need to reward major campaign-funding donors among large corporations. Without this special help, the president's fund-raising would have slowed down from his low standing in the polls and the economic slowdown's curbing of contributions generally.[75] However, exit polls after the election suggested that whatever filtered out on this issue may have alienated some segments of the electorate. The Quayle Council certainly did not salvage Vice President Quayle's own image. Of the voters who considered "choice of Vice President" one of the qualities that mattered most in deciding how to vote, 63 percent favored Clinton and only 25 percent favored Bush for having chosen Quayle. On the issue side, of the voters who considered the environment one of the issues that mattered most in deciding how to vote, 74 percent favored Clinton and a minuscule 14 percent favored Bush.[76]

The Quayle Council represented an administration's strategy for exercising great power outside the channels of checks and balances. It served both the president's personal style and his political situation. A president much more personally comfortable with elite deal making than with public appeals and struggles turned over the resolving of environmental issues of the highest importance, from the ozone hole to biodiversity, to an internal unaccountable forum. That same president's political situation placed him at the end of the line of development of postwar divided government without a mandate or legislative support, deeply desirous of a means to govern without Congress. This mechanism also allowed the harnessing of the government's regulatory power to his campaign fundraising from interested industries in a circumvention of a host of ethics laws and policies. For all its advantages, the Quayle Council not only could not deal with the problems requiring legislative action but did not even afford the president the appearance to the public of trying to deal with those problems.

5

National Security Directives and the Cover-up of the Courtship of Saddam Hussein

OVERVIEW: IRAQ AND THE WHITE HOUSE SECRECY SYSTEM

In 1992, the fourth year of the Bush Administration, the Washington Post first gave an account of the 1989 mechanism of the Iraq policy of the Bush White House. "When President Bush soon after taking office ordered a fresh appraisal of U.S. relations with Iraq and Iran, his aides responded in June 1989 with the draft of a now-famous directive that became the basis of what critics today say has been the greatest foreign policy failure of his presidency."[1] It had taken until 1992—after literally years of congressional investigations—for the public to be able to learn how a White House national security directive in 1989 established the misguided policy of courting Saddam Hussein of Iraq. For years the White House's role had been hidden, and to some extent it continued to be hidden even at the end of the Bush Presidency.

The White House hid its role in 1989 and 1990 behind the apparatus of secrecy left over from the Cold War: National Security Directives and national security committees. Using the Cold War machinery, President Bush established the national policy toward Iraq the way a sovereign would—as an act of personal will—not by methods accountable to Congress or the public. President Bush's Iraq policy epitomizes his foreign policy strategy for governing without Congress. A president with a personal style of elite dealmaking acted out that style by a course of dealing with Saddam Hussein that amounted to aiding, arming, and attempting to appease him while circumventing likely congressional opposition to this course.

With neither an electoral mandate nor much support in Congress, President Bush had to direct the government's policy through channels that largely precluded debate in Congress or in the public. The Cold War had receded, and with it the original basis for the postwar White House to exercise unilateral power in foreign affairs. Nevertheless, a president desiring, for reasons of both his political situation and his personal style, not to face the reaction of the public and Congress to his policy, found his means for avoiding such accountability in the White House staff's extraordinary tools of power.

Even in 1991 and 1992, after the error of the earlier policy had been exposed by the Kuwait invasion and the war with Iraq, by far the largest U.S. armed conflict since the Vietnam War, the NSC staff could attempt and, in significant measure, succeed in covering up its role or at least delaying and blurring exposure. After the invasion and the war, the country might have been expected to look back critically at the earlier course of action. At the White House's request, examination by Congress waited until early 1991, after the war ended. Then, in 1991 and 1992, Congress attempted a series of investigations. Yet even at that late time the Bush Administration's national security staff seemed largely able to dodge or defer a full accounting of its role in 1989 and 1990.

NSC Directives Until Iran-Contra

Chapter 2 described the genesis of the White House national security system. To manage the Cold War, the National Security Act of 1947 created a NSC staff that subsequently grew to grand dimensions. During presidencies from Truman to Carter, the NSC staff made some limited use of directives to confer the authority and directions for action with any accompanying limitations. Such directives functioned as secret law—as powerful as law but withheld from Congress as part of an implicit Cold War understanding that left national security in part to an unchecked White House process.[2]

In the Reagan Administration, the desire for greater administration control of foreign policy in a government in which, on some foreign policy issues, the president and Congress differed sharply led to increased importance for the NSC's system of directives. By estimates of the General Accounting Office and former officials, the Carter Administration had issued only about 54 NSC directives whereas the Reagan Administration issued over 300.[3] Christopher C. Shoemaker, a military officer who served on the NSC staff during both the Carter and Reagan administrations, described the turn from the later administration's perspective:

> Like the Carter NSC, the Reagan NSC had a system of . . . decision documents (called National Security Decision Directives, or NSDDs) . . . . but were vastly different in their actual use. Recognizing the problems of the Brzezinski system where PDs [Carter Administration presidential direc-

tives] were issued too infrequently, the Reagan NSC was quite liberal in the use of NSDDs—more than 300 were signed during the Reagan years.[4]

In contrast to the relatively sparing use of directives during the Carter Administration, the hundreds of secret directives used "liberally" (in Shoemaker's unintentionally ironic term) during the Reagan Administration had major implications leading up to the Iran-contra affair. Constantine Menges, a loyal member of the Reagan NSC staff, described the role of NSDDs in his published memoirs. He described them as White House barriers to what he termed "end runs" of the policy regarding the Nicaraguan contras. By this he referred to action, with which the NSC staff disagreed but which departmental officials carried out because their Senate confirmation and responsibility to answer at congressional hearings made them accountable to the public. Menges explained how the NSC staff reined in such departmental officials by using NSC directives and meetings shaded from oversight:

> On Central America alone there were, I believe, seven attempts to end run clear, written policy decisions of the president. An important reason why I knew that President Reagan really meant what he said in his public speeches and in his top-secret National Security Decision Directives is that when these end runs were made known to him and when he heard the sometimes heated debate at NSC meetings he *always* held to his policy.[5]

Menges described his own use of NSDDs, as an NSC staff member, to direct the State Department at NSC committee meetings on contra policy:

> [Assistant Secretary of State for Interamerican Affairs Langhorne] Motley felt defensive about getting into a debate with me because I had the annoying habit of bringing along copies of the president's National Security Decision Directives or excerpts from his major public statements. I'd show them to Motley and the other subcabinet members in order to document and clarify the president's foreign policy, which we were *all* supposed to be implementing.[6]

Several critical congressional studies of NSDDs, even before Iran-contra, occurred during the Reagan Administration.[7] That the Reagan Administration had the ability to conduct such oversight reflected that the Reagan Administration, although eager to use the directives and somewhat secretive about them, did not manifest the extremes of secretiveness about directives shown later by its successor administration. At least during the Reagan Administration Congress obtained a fair number of whole or partial NSDDs, and it could track the numbering of NSDDs (and thereby the total number of these). As reflected in the three years it took for the Bush NSC to release its Iraq directive, during the Bush Administration the NSC concealed everything about directives that it could.[8]

The 1947 act gave George Bush as vice president from 1981 to 1989 a position on the NSC, and as he witnessed how the NSC made foreign policy in isolation from public and legislative processes, he apparently found a fit with his own personal style. Public appeals and consultations with Congress on controversial foreign policy issues held comparatively little interest for Bush, who liked the NSC's workings. The vice president's Iran-contra diary notes, when released in 1993 after his general Iran-contra pardon, showed his attitude toward the NSC system at that system's nadir. On November 10, 1986, after initial exposure of the scandal, as Secretary of State George Shultz warned Bush about the scandal's depths and the particular problems of the NSC staff, Bush recorded in his diary that "[t]he idea that the NSC is a loose cannon is being debated out there now, and of course, as we know it isn't a loose cannon."

Even while congressional investigation neared in late November 1986 and the NSC staff was devising criminal obstruction, on November 20 Bush wrote with continued longing for the NSC system: "I suggested to the President that the only thing he could do was call a Monday meeting which he decided to do to get the key NSC players together and to get them all to lay it on the table and to just simply say, 'we're going to hammer this thing out and what are you upset about, Poindexter?'"

Bush looked favorably on NSDDs and similar NSC staff instruments even when they stood revealed as an unaccountable means of policy beyond the control of even the president. He wrote in his diary in mid-November 1986 that "[President Reagan is] awfully good in his reactions, but on the facts of when the findings were found and the NSDD signed . . . there's no reason that he should know this, and he doesn't know it." By late December 1986, as the public reaction became apparent, Bush had settled on his own position, which was that the Iran-contra problems at the NSC simply required the NSC staff to be more formal: "It should have been coordinated and reported," and the solution is to "formalize [the] process of the NSC staff."[9]

After Iran-Contra

Ultimately, the Iran-contra affair brought to a head the concern about the hundreds of Reagan Administration NSDDs. In August 1988, Congress held a hearing specifically on the subject of the NSDDs.[10] The hearing record included a report by the General Accounting Office of its examination of 247 directives that had been publicly released since the 1947 act. Representative Lee Hamilton (D-Ind.) gave strong testimony at the hearing, drawing on his experience both as chairman of the House Iran-contra committee and previously as chairman of the House Intelligence Committee during Iran-contra's initial cover-up. He pointed to the importance of the directives: "NSDD's have increased in number, scope, importance, and authority. They were originally position papers, but in recent years these directives have been used to initiate and to determine policy. As of January 1, 1988, President Reagan had issued nearly 300 NSDDs."[11] He then described the congressional experience with the directives as a barrier to oversight:

> I might say that I think all of us have had the experience of listening to testimony by executive branch officials who are articulating policy of the Federal Government, and have had those officials refer to an NSDD as the basis of that policy. We don't know what that NSDD is and we cannot evaluate the official's comments without reference to it, but it is not available to us.

Chairman Hamilton then discussed Congress's "irregular" access to the directives, which was the pattern prior to the even more closed Bush Administration: "The use of secret NSDD's to create policy infringes on Congress' constitutional prerogatives by inhibiting effective oversight and limiting Congress' policymaking role. NSDD's are revealed to Congress only under irregular, arbitrary, or even accidental, circumstances, if at all. Even the Intelligence Committees do not usually receive copies of NSDD's." Furthermore, Chairman Hamilton explained the impact of the directives on the system of checks on executive power:

> The widespread use of these directives can alter the tenuous balance of power between the Congress and the President. The secrecy and uncertain legality of NSDD's give the President extraordinary power to formulate or to alter policy without the knowledge of Congress. The President can amend current NSDD's at will. If Congress cedes to the President the right to withhold information from it, the balance of decisionmaking power shifts dramatically toward the President.[12]

It was hardly necessary to describe how such directives enhanced the power of the White House's national security staff. The Iran-contra matter showed, regarding the similar documents of covert action findings, not only that the NSC staff decided when to create these documents, what they should say, and how to use them but also that President Reagan often had little idea whether he had signed them, which ones he had signed, and to what in them he had agreed. Not until the national security adviser, John M. Poindexter, testified before the Iran-contra congressional committees did the public—or even President Reagan (by his own account)—learn that the president had signed an explicit arms-for-hostages retroactive finding in December 1985, let alone that Admiral Poindexter had torn up the document later in an act of obstruction of congressional oversight for which he was tried and convicted.[13]

Besides the directive, the NSC staff had another instrument of authority that they could wield without even the nominal involvement of the president, namely, the system of NSC committees and subcommittees. The Quayle Council staff effectively arrogated power by its "working group" system, because the full council's formal Cabinet-level members, headed by the vice president, met only at limited times and often preferred to keep their fingerprints off controversial actions. Such a working group system shows how White House staffs control action by holding frequent meetings that resolve most matters with second-level officials in the departments.

Similarly, the National Security Council, headed by the president, can meet only at limited times. White House staff can most effectively exercise power, with the least accountability, if they sit on a system of working groups or committees to exercise power between such formal meetings of Cabinet-level officials. These working groups or committees move authority down from the presidential or Cabinet level to the level of White House staff while seeking to keep the decisions insulated from accountability to Congress, the public, and the courts. The NSC's counsel and the White House counsel convened a series of governmentwide meetings in 1991 to coordinate the resistance to congressional oversight of the Iraq matter, yet they refused to appear at a congressional hearing on those meetings to discuss what they had done.

Two developments at the end of the Reagan Administration and the beginning of the Bush Administration might have been expected to ease up the secrecy system of the White House staff. The Iran-contra scandal, by massively discrediting the NSC staff under National Security Advisers McFarlane and Poindexter, might have been expected to reduce the staff's power or at least to confine it within the bounds of accountability to the public through Congress. Second, the relaxation of the Cold War under Soviet Premier Mikhail Gorbachev and the impending termination of the Cold War as the Soviet Union collapsed might have been expected to reduce the need for the quasi-wartime NSC system that originated in 1947 precisely to deal with the Cold War.

Despite the Iran-contra scandal and the end of the Cold War, the Bush Administration not only preserved the national security staff secrecy system but even intensified it. President Bush started his series of National Security Directives, or NSDs, to fulfill the task of NSDD's during the Reagan Administration. He quickly authorized a series of NSC committees, allowing the NSC staff its coveted hands-on power. Moreover, the NSC staff soon put forth positions, in correspondence with congressional oversight committees, amounting to a further tightening of the secrecy of these directives. As described earlier, even during the secrecy-oriented Reagan NSC, the administration only "irregularly" withheld directives from Congress, so Congress had been able to hold hearings on a few of the most controversial directives. Now the NSC sought to deny Congress the means even to do that.

1989–1990: THE QUIET COURTSHIP
OF SADDAM HUSSEIN

A Moment for Reconsideration of Iraq Policy

The start of the Bush Administration and of the 101st Congress in January 1989 came at a moment when critical developments concerning Iraq offered a major policy choice. In August 1988, at the end of the Reagan Administration, the Iran-Iraq war had stopped with a cease-fire. Until then, that war had provided the driving justification for the Reagan Administration's "tilt" toward Iraq, for if Iraq's resistance in the war to Iran crumbled, the United States had concern over projection of Iranian power beyond Iraq into the rest of the Middle East. The cease-fire in 1988 freed the United States to reconsider its relationship with Iraq.

Meanwhile, the effective end of the war led to two further developments regarding Iraq that offered serious reason for such reconsideration. In August and September 1988 Iraq engaged in massive use of chemical weapons against its own Kurdish civilian population. A critical Senate report in October 1988, "Chemical Weapons Use in Kurdistan: Iraq's Final Offensive," estimated that "the Kurdish death toll could be in the hundreds of thousands."[14] In itself, this use of chemical weapons constituted an outrageous violation of human rights and international law. More broadly, it brought forcefully to public attention the menace of Iraq's drive for weapons of mass destruction—chemical, biological, and nuclear.[15] The 100th Congress in 1988 did not work out the procedural problems for enacting sanctions, but it came close. Absent presidential resistance, the 101st Congress starting in January 1989 could move to legislate controls and/or sanctions against nations like Iraq that acquired and used chemical weapons.

Additionally, the end of the Iran-Iraq war left Iraq in an exposed financial condition. During the war, massive loans from the Persian Gulf states, particularly Kuwait, had buoyed Iraq.[16] When Iraq received no loan forgiveness at the war's end, "[b]y the end of 1988, Iraq's cash-flow problem became so serious that it defaulted on loan payments to the United States, Canada, Australia, and Britain. Western banks began to turn down Iraqi requests for credit."[17] Iraq's squeezed, credit-hungry postwar condition thus offered the United States a key choice between courting Iraq and pressuring it by sanctions.

Congress Supports Sanctions

During 1989, Congress evinced a clear choice to be strict with Iraq on the issues of chemical warfare and financial relations. Strikingly, this congressional choice occurred on a bipartisan basis, with members at opposite ends of the ideological and partisan spectrum agreeing on the need for such a policy. In January 1989, Senator Claiborne Pell (D-R.I.), the liberal chairman of the Foreign Relations Committee, and Senator Jesse Helms (R-N.C.), the conservative ranking Republican on the committee, joined forces in hearings and in legislative proposals to curb the spread of chemical weapons. They started a process leading toward House and Senate adoption of a tough chemical weapons bill. However, they met delays because of NSC-driven policies of which they, like the rest of Congress, were kept largely in the dark.

Congress's consideration of the matter started with briskness and dispatch in early 1989. In January, Senators Pell and Helms heard testimony from CIA director William Webster that "[d]espite the current cease-fire with Iran, Iraq continues to produce and stockpile chemical weapons. Moreover, it is expanding its chemical weapons capability and is taking further steps to make its program entirely independent of foreign assistance."[18] Senator Helms noted that not only did he support legislation imposing sanctions and curbing suppliers of technology to chemical weapons–wielding nations, but "I have every reason to believe that in the end the Congress and the administration will see the wisdom of both approaches."[19]

The drumbeat of congressional concern about this subject continued throughout 1989. In February, the House Armed Services Committee heard administration testimony of an Iraqi thrust toward the technology of Scud missiles, chemical warfare, and nuclear weapons.[20] Observers described the committee as "shocked," this being "the first time a high-ranking American intelligence official had gone on record to warn about Iraq's nuclear activities since the destruction of the Osirak reactor in June 1981."[21] Unbeknownst to Congress, this warning revealed only a hint of what the administration knew. At this same time, the Department of Energy suppressed internal warnings about Iraq's nuclear program. But Congress did not learn about these warnings until 1991 and could not secure declassification and open revelation until spring 1992.[22] The administration also had internal knowledge of Iraq's network for obtaining advanced weapons and the technology to produce them.[23] Another Senate Committee held hearings on chemical weapons proliferation throughout spring 1989. By October, the Senate Foreign Relations Committee had reported out the "Pell-Helms" chemical weapons sanctions bill, and by November the House had passed a similar bill.[24]

Congress made even greater progress on the companion issue of restricting financial relations with Iraq. On August 4, 1989, a surprise development revealed the desperate measures to which Iraq had resorted to obtain U.S. loans. Acting on a tip, federal law enforcement authorities raided the Atlanta office of a foreign bank, the Banca Nazionale del Lavoro (BNL), and quickly learned of what turned out to be $4 billion in unauthorized loans to Iraq. This revelation added further fuel to all the other reasons for not extending credit to Iraq. The Export-Import Bank, which had suspended credit for exports to Iraq earlier in the 1980s, had resumed in 1987. In 1989, after the federal authorities raided the BNL, the Senate Foreign Aid Appropriations Subcommittee reported in its annual bill a provision by Chairman Daniel Inouye (D-Hawaii), section 512, barring Export-Import credits for Iraq.[25] With a modification, Congress enacted that provision into law in November 1989.

National Security Directive 26: Adoption

Meanwhile, the White House national security staff had been preparing to lead national policy on Iraq in the direction opposite from that of Congress—away from sanctions regarding weapons of mass destruction or financial chicanery and toward courtship. It has been suggested that even during his vice presidential term, George Bush already had developed and implemented a pro-Iraq attitude.[26] The origin of this outlook was similar to that of his support of China: It derived from a friendship prior to his presidential term, which he implemented as president without regard to actions that alienated the American public and Congress (like the Tienanmen Square massacre or the Saddam Hussein speeches of 1990). There is an intriguing but unproven hypothesis that relates Vice President Bush's support of the 1986 Iran-contra deals of exchanging antiaircraft missiles for hostages to his pro-Iraq stance: While America publicly took the position of helping neither side in the Iran-Iraq war, Vice President Bush neatly flipped to the opposite position of telling both sides he supported that side. Specifically, the suggestion is that on his Middle Eastern trip in 1986 he encouraged, through diplomatic intermediaries, the Iraqi air campaign that made Iran eager to complete the deals for those antiaircraft missiles.[27] If this were so, then Vice President Bush undermined U.S. policy and credibility; he would thereafter have to resist oversight of his involvement regarding his siding with both Iran and Iraq, as the unraveling of his claims regarding either one might ruinously unravel his claims regarding the other. In any event, by the 1988 Bush campaign the pattern had been set. As a Wall Street Journal reporter later noted, "Rich-

ard Fairbanks, who headed the Bush campaign's Middle East policy team
. . . was until recently also Iraq's registered agent in Washington."[28]

Immediately after the Bush Administration took office, the NSC staff
member with responsibility for the region, Richard N. Haass, "in February 1989 wrote the criteria for an interagency review of U.S. policy toward
Iraq that led to the directive [NSD-26] Bush later signed," according to the
Washington Post.[29] The same newspaper reports how the secretive NSC
committee system shaped NSD-26 without a hint to Congress, which during this period conducted hearings and enacted bills supporting sanctions
for Iraq. This "1989 national security directive['s] . . . final outlines were
decided at a meeting of the administration's 'deputies committee' on
April 12. The committee was composed of senior officials from State, Defense and Commerce, under the chairmanship of then-deputy national security adviser and current CIA Director Robert M. Gates."[30] Thus, the apparatus of NSC staff–initiated directives and NSC committees, particularly its "deputies committee," served a critical function of allowing
NSC staff to secretly set the policy. "Bush met with the National Security
Council to approve completion of NSDD 26 on June 26, 1989 . . . ."[31]

NSD-26 remained classified until May 1992 in a display of the secretiveness of the NSC system. Long before then, on the basis of leaks the press
had reported aspects of NSD-26 but Congress could not discuss these in
the open without a struggle with the Bush Administration about classification. In a 1991 article in the Washington Post Magazine, "Missed Signals
in the Middle East: Why Was the Administration Blindsided by Iraq's Invasion of Kuwait?" the press had focused on the role of the directive in the
Bush Administration's Iraq policy:

> "Access to the Persian Gulf and the key friendly states in the area is vital to
> U.S. national security," said National Security Directive 26, signed by Bush
> in October 1989, as the basis for U.S. policy . . . .
> Regarding Iraq, an important and potentially rich country with the
> world's second-largest proven oil reserves, the underlying premise was that
> Baghdad had emerged from the war prepared to play a more constructive
> international role. The central assumption of U.S. policy was that normal re-
> lations with Iraq would serve long-term American interests and promote
> stability in the Persian Gulf and the Middle East generally. . . .[32]

When the Bush Administration finally declassified NSD-26, the New
York Times published an account of it—"'89 Bush Order Says Ply Iraq
with Aid"—that explained both what the directive said and its significance:

> A secret policy directive on the Persian Gulf region signed by President Bush
> in October 1989 said the United States should offer economic and political

incentives to President Saddam Hussein of Iraq as a way of moderating his behavior and increasing American influence in his country . . . .

The directive served as the operative guide for American policy until Iraq invaded Kuwait in August 1990.[33]

National Security Directive 26: Impact

Just as the Reagan White House, as Constantine Menges recalls, used NSDDs to force departmental officials into support for contras, so the Bush Administration used NSD-26 to force departmental officials into support for Iraq. The directives compelled the agency officials into actions they would normally avoid out of concern about congressional oversight and public skepticism. Yet, the directive itself remained a hidden, extraordinary tool.

The Bush Administration made immediate and intensive use of NSD-26 on several fronts to defeat the thrust of congressional hearings and legislation regarding sanctions and instead to promote a courtship policy toward Iraq. On October 6,1989, Tariq Aziz, the Iraqi foreign minister, met Secretary of State James Baker in Washington. Aziz "complained of a propaganda campaign in the U.S.—particularly by the Congress. He noted congressional moves to legislate economic and political sanctions."[34] At the moment of the approval of NSD-26, the State Department could respond authoritatively to undermine the congressional actions. Published State Department records describe Baker's response to Aziz: "Regarding Aziz['s] point on congressional criticism. The Secretary noted that the administration never supported sanctions in Iraq and that he personally had so testified. The Secretary added that congressional actions were limited to Iraqi use of CW [chemical warfare] during the war. Our position continues to be that we need to look forward, not backward."[35]

At that moment in October 1989, there was obvious reason for the administration to pull back on agricultural loan credits for Iraq through the Commodity Credit Corporation (CCC) program: the BNL scandal, other Western nations' refusals to extend credit to Iraq, and the congressional expressions of concern regarding Iraq. Moreover, subsequent congressional investigations brought to light that information from the Justice Department's BNL case, which worked its way to the State Department, showed that the Iraqis were using loans for their weapons program, including their nuclear program. Nevertheless, the administration pushed on with a program of supporting loans to Iraq based on NSD-26.

A later report by Attorney General Barr in connection with whether to have an independent counsel investigate these matters conceded that "it appears that as of late October and November 1989, the State Department was supporting the extension of further CCC [Commodity Credit Corporation] guarantees to Iraq in accord with NSD-26, in which President Bush mandated pursuit of improved economic and political ties with Iraq."[36] Specifically, according to the attorney general's report, "Secretary Baker apparently did call Secretary [of Agriculture Clayton] Yeutter on October 31, 1989, to urge him to approve additional CC[C] loan guarantees for Iraq."[37] The CCC guarantees loans for sales of agricultural goods to Iraq; over time it became clear that Iraq found ways to buy weapons technology when it received loans of any kind, including agricultural loans.

After the call to Secretary Yeutter, the action shifted to the advisory committee for the loans, where the NSD was also used. According to documents in the Congressional Record, the State Department invoked NSD-26 on November 8, 1989, in talking points for a meeting of the advisory council regarding the loans: "In NSD-26, the President mandated that we seek to improve and expand our relationship with Iraq. At present, trade is central to that relationship and credits guaranteed by CCC finance a large part of that trade."[38] When the Treasury Department wanted a documenting letter, the State Department wrote it, urging "a full, billion-dollar program of Commodity Credit Corporation GSM-102 export credit guarantees in FY 90, with adequate safeguards, for Iraq. In addition to the near-term benefits for agricultural sales, the CCC program is important to our efforts to improve and expand our relationship with Iraq, as ordered by the President in NSD-26."[39] Soon thereafter, the administration extended to Iraq the coveted installment of $500 million in CCC credits.[40]

Finally, the Export-Import Bank experienced much reluctance to extend credit for the benefit of Saddam Hussein. An internal memo entitled "Mythology About Iraq" systematically demolished every argument for Iraq as a reliable partner. The bank's "Iraq Country Review Update" not only further blasted Iraq's creditworthiness but also expressed an awareness that the BNL loans had been used for Iraq's war machine: "The BNL incident has revealed the extent of Iraqi efforts to attract Western financial support for Iraq's military industrialization program."[41]

Nevertheless, President Bush pushed through credits for Iraq. When the foreign aid appropriation bill came to the Senate floor in September 1989 with the Inouye provision as a barrier against Iraq, Senator John Heinz (R-Penn.) had obtained an amendment that President Bush could waive the restriction on Export-Import Bank credits if he found that the provision's "application is not in the national interest." As the amendment mover commented, "It has to do with the Eximbank in Iraq."[42] On January 17, 1990, President Bush issued a formal public waiver order invoking that amendment. In Presidential Determination No. 90-7, "Application of Export-Import Bank Restrictions in Connection with Iraq," President Bush stated:

> By virtue of the authority vested in me by Section 512 of the Foreign Operations, Export Financing, and Related Programs Appropriations Act, 1990 (P.L. 101-167), I hereby determine that, with respect to Iraq, application of

the prohibition contained in that section to the Export-Import Bank or its agents is not in the national interest of the United States.

You [the Secretary of State] are directed to report this Determination to the Congress and to have it published in the Federal Register.[43]

The grant of a half-billion dollars of CCC credits, extension of Export-Import Bank guarantees, and discussions by Secretary Baker with Tariq Aziz had negated Congress's year-long signals to Saddam Hussein about American attitudes toward Iraq's postwar course. Yet the National Security Directive that set the administration policy remained secret. The NSC staff thereby denied Congress the means to hold the administration accountable.

1990: SANCTIONS THWARTED BY THE NSC COMMITTEE

In spring 1990, Saddam Hussein largely dropped the pretense that he sought peaceful and amicable relations with the United States by a series of bellicose statements and actions flatly negating the NSC's premises in NSD-26. Congress reacted to Saddam Hussein's aggressive statements and actions by a stronger push toward sanctions. However, NSD-26 remained in effect, and the administration hobbled Congress by a vigorous resistance. The White House national security staff orchestrated this policy through its committees, which used the tools of the Cold War secrecy system, much as the NSC staff in 1984 through 1986 had used similar tools in its Iran-contra actions.

In terms of congressional consideration, the year started with a House Foreign Affairs Subcommittee hearing on February 28, 1990, that was highly critical of Iraq.[44] At the hearing, the subcommittee pressed the assistant secretary of state for Near East and South Asia, John Kelly, on such matters as Iraqi development of chemical, biological, and nuclear weapons; Iraqi missile development; and allegations that Iraqi political assassins were using diplomatic cover in New York.

More intense congressional oversight followed Saddam Hussein's April 1 speech, in which he threatened to "burn half of Israel" with chemical weapons. The House subcommittee held a series of hearings in which the Bush Administration's spokesman, Assistant Secretary of State Kelly, again opposed sanctions. At an April 4 hearing, Representative Tom Lantos (D-Calif.) made what was later seen as a prophetic statement, ironically describing Saddam Hussein's threats as "welcome": "Mr. Chairman, I feel that Dictator Saddam Hussein of Iraq has injected a welcome tone of realism into the dialogue . . . . I find that much of recent discussion about the area had an Alice in Wonderland quality by treating Iraq as a very favored entity with all kinds of credits and grants and loans and what have you . . . ."[45]

On April 26, Assistant Secretary Kelly testified:

> Mr. Chairman, this brings me to the question of sanctions. I am well aware there is strong sentiment on this committee and in the Congress for trade sanctions against Iraq. . . . While we do not rule out appropriate responses to recent actions by the Government of Iraq, we are not prepared to see economic and trade sanctions legislatively imposed at this point . . . . [W]e are hopeful that the Government of Iraq will move quickly to bring U.S.-Iraq relations back to a more positive level.[46]

Also, Assistant Secretary Kelly minimized Iraq's efforts to develop nuclear weapons, taking a position quite at odds with the information that the Energy Department had internally suppressed the year before:

> We do not believe Iraq is close to possessing a nuclear weapon. . . . Iraq has a peaceful nuclear program under the International Atomic Energy Agency Safeguards. There is no certainty as to how far along the Iraqis are toward a nuclear weapon . . . . If we and the other western nations are successful in denying them equipment, it would be a longer period of time, perhaps a decade.[47]

The assistant secretary neither discussed NSD-26 nor offered any insight into the administration proceedings that occurred at that time in the NSC Committee.

Congress continued to push, in a bipartisan and bicameral way, for sanctions against Iraq, even in the face of administration resistance. In May 1990, the House Republican Research Committee—which, like Senator Helms, normally did not move in sync with Democratic thinking—issued a report as critical of Iraq as the corresponding Democratic spokesmen. The Republican Research Committee's Task Force on Terrorism and Unconventional Warfare released a report section, "Chemical Weapons in the Third World: Iraq's Expanding Chemical Arsenal," chronicling Iraq's use of chemical weapons throughout the Iran-Iraq war and giving a detailed account of Iraq's production capabilities. The report put its precise history and recounting of Iraqi sophistication and aggressiveness in the context of Saddam Hussein's April speech about burning half of Israel. It noted that "[u]sing an Iraqi idiom, Saddam Hussein actually stated clearly Iraq's ability to destroy the entire state of Israel with chemical weapons."[48]

On May 17, 1990, the Senate considered a bill containing most of the provisions of the "Pell-Helms" proposal of the previous year that would impose sanctions on suppliers of countries using chemical or biological weapons. The Senate enacted this bill on a bipartisan basis in the face of continued administration opposition, which still did not admit the existence of NSD-26, that "the Senate bill remained unacceptable to Bush, according to a State Department official."[49] Eventually, Congress passed a version of that Senate bill in October 1990, but President Bush pocket vetoed it in November 1990. He opposed sanctions legislation as an interference with his foreign policymaking even at a time when American troops faced an Iraqi army armed with chemical weapons.

In May 1990, key House Republicans introduced a bill that would have prohibited U.S. assistance to Iraq and imposed other sanctions unless Iraq opened suspected production sites for its nuclear, chemical, and biological weapons.[50] The drumbeat of sanctions proposals continued in June when sanctions bills were introduced by key senators, including Senator Inouye, author of the Iraq sanctions provision enacted (with the administration's waiver provision) on his subcommittee's appropriation bill the previous year.[51]

The Eve of the Kuwait Invasion

Congress's penultimate showdown on Iraq sanctions came on July 27, 1990. It occurred in the shadow of Saddam Hussein's massing of troops on the Kuwait border, as the participants in Senate and House floor debates noted. A leading columnist, Charles Krauthammer, had labeled Saddam Hussein a "nightmare from the 1930s" in a July 27 column that was reprinted in the Congressional Record and repeatedly cited during the July 27 debate on adding Iraq sanctions to the pending farm authorization bill. Krauthammer had noted that "Hussein has a million-man army left over from the war he started with Iran . . . . Whether Hussein will in fact use his weapons against Kuwait will depend purely upon whether or not he feels that he needs to occupy Kuwait in order to turn it into a vassal state."[52]

Senator William S. Cohen (R-Maine), principal sponsor of the Iraq sanctions amendment, noted that "what Mr. Saddam Hus[sein] has in mind [is] exactly what he had his 30,000 or 40,000 storm troopers headed for the Kuwaiti border for."[53] The sanctions amendment passed the Senate. However, in the House intense resistance by the Bush Administration succeeded, even at this eleventh hour, in effectively gutting the sanctions amendment. At first, the House passed a sanctions amendment, but then it took up a modifying amendment to allow the administration to avoid sanctions and passed it by the close vote of 208-191. The modifying amendment was defended as "the option that really ought to be available to the President of the United States through the Secretary of Agriculture." As another sanctions opponent had stated, "I do not think that we should be meddling here in the House quite as much as we do in foreign policy. I think the President should have more discretion than we sometimes give him."[54]

Congressional supporters of sanctions struggled on. On July 30, Senator John Glenn made a floor speech describing "Brazilian-Iraqi nuclear cooperation" and how "Brazil is actively assisting Iraq in the missile area as well."[55] On August 1, the House Foreign Affairs Committee marked up chemical warfare export controls legislation. However, by then such signals could have no effect. On August 2, after the Bush Administration had given him no reason to anticipate potent American opposition, Saddam Hussein occupied Kuwait.

It should be noted, as described, that several times the Bush Administration had secured majority support in Congress against sanctions. Numerous members could be found to speak against sanctions; there is no suggestion to the contrary here. Although President Bush lacked as much support in Congress as other presidents, he still had considerable support in 1990 when Congress took up the issue, such as on July 27. In other words, the Bush Presidency's approach did not completely avoid engaging with Congress, nor did Congress always stand up to the Bush Administration even when it had before it for a vote one of the issues in the separation of powers that divided the branches of government.

Nonetheless, even when Congress did have the opportunity to fight over an issue such as Iraq sanctions, the Bush Administration's strategy of working through the NSC system gave the president a major advantage. NSC secrecy limited the occasions and the focuses of criticism. Whereas Congress held its debate with full administration participation, the administration, by keeping its NSD-26 and its NSC Committee meetings secret, avoided Congress and the public knowing fully the administration policy and its implementation. The NSC system prevented the possibility that Congress would confront the White House meaningfully on Iraq.

NSC Thwarting of Sanctions

What had the Bush Administration been doing out of Congress's eye during this period? The administration had given out through public testimony only some veiled descriptions of its position while not putting the NSC process on the line. Meanwhile, the administration had made its decisions to resist Congress's thrust for sanctions through two NSC Committee meetings in April and May 1990. To Saddam Hussein, the administration continued to express a policy of courtship through the meeting of Ambassador April Glaspie and Saddam on July 25 on the eve of invasion.

The administration's policy for the year had started on January 17, 1990, with President Bush's personal waiver of Iraq sanctions regarding the Export-Import Bank's activities, a step taken despite internal Ex-Im Bank warnings.[56] On February 11, Assistant Secretary of State Kelly and Ambassador Glaspie met with Saddam Hussein. According to media reports, Kelly "reassured the Iraqi that the Bush administration was determined to strengthen ties to Baghdad, despite continued efforts on Capitol Hill to impose sanctions on Iraq."[57] It was Kelly who testified before Congress in the next two months without mentioning NSD-26 or the rest of the NSC directions on Iraq.

After Saddam Hussein's April 1 speech in which he threatened to burn half of Israel and after the ensuing redoubled thrust of congressional proposals for sanctions, the administration found itself besieged in its anti-sanctions position. On April 16, the NSC committee system held the first of its two key meetings on Iraq, described as an "NSC/Deputies Committee meeting of April 16."[58] Deputy National Security Adviser Robert Gates chaired this meeting, with such top officials (under the Cabinet level) in attendance as Undersecretary of State Robert Kimmitt, Undersecretary of Commerce Dennis Kloske, and Undersecretary of Defense Paul Wolfowitz.[59] The undersecretary of commerce, Dennis Kloske, firmly pressed a view favoring sanctions, as he testified during the congressional investigations in 1991: "All I can tell you is that as far as the position of the Department of Commerce beginning in April of 1990, we made our position very clear that we should either impose economic sanctions on Iraq or alternatively curtail the flow of technology to Iraq, and/or greatly expand and enhance the missile technology control regime."[60]

At the NSC Committee, the Commerce Department's support of sanctions did not prevail. As Undersecretary Kloske testified in 1991, "The consensus at the time was that it would be far more useful and diplomatic, if you will, to pursue a diplomatic line with Iraq, that the imposition of further controls would send a very powerful signal to Iraq, which was judged at the time to be counterproductive."[61] This decision apparently came down from President Bush through the NSC staff, a way that made it difficult to hold the president accountable later. Representative Sam Gejdenson (D-Conn.) noted at a hearing the following year what Undersecretary of Commerce Kloske had told committee staff: "Mr. [Richard] Ha[ass]," the NSC official with responsibility for the Middle East, "said the President opposed restrictions on U.S. exports to Iraq."[62] In other words, the president's direction came to the April meeting through the NSC staff. The cover of NSC secrecy concealed that the president's own direction was at odds with both congressional and departmental reactions to the developments in Iraq. In this way, the NSC staff fought off the Commerce Department's effort to agree with the congressional proposals of sanctions, without any accountability to Congress for squelching the proposal, because the squelching occurred within the secret NSC Committee. Moreover, as long as President Bush refused to return Iraq to the official list of terrorist nations, the Commerce Department had limited authority to control trade with Iraq.

The April 16, 1990, meeting did not conclude the matter. Before the next meeting, on May 29, options papers were prepared. A paper prepared by the State Department after the meeting showed a continuing awareness of congressional proposals for sanctions by discussing "the sanctions legislation on the Hill" and how, regarding dual-use technology, "Congress is considering new controls to ban such sales to all states in the region, including Iraq."[63] In the same vein, one media report said about the April 16 NSC meeting that "[the] State [Department] continued to oppose the drive in Congress to cut off these [CCC and Export-Import] benefits through legislation, on grounds that this would tie the administration's hands when and if the time came to renew them."[64] However, under the NSC aegis the policy review process occurred so secretively that even the extensive 1991 and 1992 congressional and press investigations could not sort out the conflicting accounts of the State Department's position.[65] Following the May 1990 NSC meeting, the administration adhered to its opposition to sanctions against Iraq.

By July 1990, Iraq had made major military preparations on the border of Kuwait. A key exchange took place in Baghdad between the United States and Iraq. According to media reports, on July 24 the State Department gave instructions, in a cable over Secretary Baker's signature to the American ambassador to Iraq, April Glaspie, to say that the United States had "no position" on the Iraq-Kuwait border dispute.[66] On July 25, Saddam Hussein summoned Glaspie to a meeting. According to the transcript later released by Iraq, Glaspie explained in that meeting, consistent with those instructions, that "we have no opinion on the Arab-Arab conflicts, like your border disagreement with Kuwait."[67]

In the context of the administration's intense resistance to sanctions, such comments told Saddam Hussein to ignore what Congress had attempted to signal by proposing sanctions. Back in 1989, the policy driven by NSD-26 had overpowered the earlier congressional attempts to impose sanctions; now, in 1990, the policy driven by NSC Committee meetings had overpowered the later congressional reactions to Saddam Hussein's increasingly aggressive stance. As the Washington Post concluded:

[I]t literally took Iraq's lightning invasion of Kuwait in August 1990 to dash all hope of fulfilling the mandate of Bush's National Security . . . Directive (NSDD 26). . . .

Only after the invasion did the administration do what some legislators had been urging for months: halt billions of dollars in exports to Iraq . . . press other nations to halt their robust sale of military equipment to Iraq . . . and begin to scrutinize Baghdad's aggressive effort to accumulate weapons of mass destruction.[68]

1991: THE WHITE HOUSE STALLS OVERSIGHT

The Start of White House "Coordination"

From the period immediately after the Kuwait invasion of August 1990 until some months after the Desert Shield and Desert Storm operations, the administration and Congress largely agreed to defer oversight regarding the administration's 1989–1990 Iraq policy. In late 1990 and early 1991, President Bush and Congress focused on what military steps to take regarding Iraq, and Congress allowed President Bush to proceed without the embarrassment of oversight.

To be sure, several provocative actions tested Congress's patience during late 1990 and early 1991. Unleashed by the Kuwait invasion and the end of administration favorability toward Iraq, the House and Senate adopted a tough measure against weapons proliferation, the fruit of the earlier Pell-Helms proposal.[69] On November 16, President Bush pocket vetoed this bill, providing the ultimate statement of his opposition to working with Congress in this area.[70] During this period, the seeds of future oversight were planted. In September, the media published Iraq's transcript of April Glaspie's July 25 meeting with Saddam Hussein. In October, a subcommittee of the House Government Operations Committee conducted a hearing, followed by a further investigation, on the misguided licensing in 1985 through 1990 of militarily useful goods and technologies for Iraq. The administration gave falsified records to that subcommittee.

Also in September and October 1990, the House Banking Committee held oversight hearings and voted for subpoenas on the BNL matter, with follow-up that soon ran up against active Justice Department resistance. In particular, in September the attorney general wrote the Banking Committee to object to the investigation. The attorney general called the BNL case "a sensitive case with national security overtones." This invocation of that key phrase—national security—amounted to a playing of the trump card against oversight (during the fall 1990 build-up period), although without justification.

Even the Justice Department's own investigation—conducted for the department after the 1992 election by retired Judge Frederick B. Lacey—apologized for "[t]he unfortunate use of the words 'national security' [which] may have led Representative [Henry] Gonzalez to conclude that DOJ sought to obstruct Congressional inquiry." That term, Lacey delicately admitted, was "overstate[d]." In fact, the attorney general had conjured that "unfortunate," "overstate[d]" term of "national security" just for the administration's desire to block the congressional inquiry, not for reasons of national security. Reaching for a justification, the Lacey Report harkened back to the root of all inquiry blocking, namely, NSD-26, which had still not exhausted its potency even in December 1992. His report concluded: "Thornburgh's concern with national security was to be expected. President Bush issued NSD-26 less than one year earlier. That security directive called for the normalization of relations between the United States and Iraq."[71] On this basis, Congress muted these matters during the late 1990 buildup of American forces in Saudi Arabia and the early 1991 combat with Iraq. By February 27, 1991, when President Bush announced a cease-fire with Iraq, it became inevitable that the deferred congressional oversight would begin in earnest.

Moreover, in February 1991 the Justice Department finally announced the long-deferred indictment of officials of the Banca Nazionale del Lavoro for their part in the illegal loans of $4 billion to Iraq. This indictment removed the caution about oversight of a case previously in the sensitive preindictment phase. Unbeknownst to Congress, at that moment the NSC and the White House counsel reached out to block such oversight under the guise of "coordinating" the administration response. In April 1991, the counsel for the National Security Council, Nicholas Rostow, convened meetings of departmental general counsels to discuss the matter.

Two contemporaneous memoranda reflected these meetings. One, by the Agriculture Department counsel who had attended the meeting, described how the White House counsel and the NSC counsel used these meetings to direct the legal apparatus of the entire administration:

> The NSC's legal adviser . . . called an inter-agency meeting to discuss the Administration's response to numerous requests for Iraq-related documents. Boyden Gray attended the meeting, as did the Assistant Attorney General for the Office of Legal Counsel and the legal and congressional officers for State, Treasury, Commerce, and Energy Departments as well as the CIA, NSA and Joint Chiefs of Staff. Each agency reported on document requests it had received.[72]

In this effort, the White House employed several techniques for stalling and stonewalling the congressional inquiries. The first was to suggest broad availability of executive privilege without actually claiming it in a forthright manner that would lead to public scrutiny and congressional testing of the claim. Rather, as shown on the second memorandum on the subject, a directive from the NSC, the White House instructed that "Department General Counsels should review and inventory all requests to determine which, if any, raise issues of executive privilege (deliberative process, foreign relations, national security, etc.)."[73] Agencies should offer the congressional inquiries, at first, only nonresponsive "[a]lternatives to providing documents . . . (e.g. briefings)." To delay any access to documents, any such access would first have to "be circulated to this group for clearance," meaning that the NSC and the other departments could interpose delays between each department and the congressional committee with jurisdiction over that department. "[A]gencies should not act unilaterally."[74]

Most tellingly, the NSC directed that various conditions be imposed to stymie oversight. The NSC memorandum directed that an agency "recommendation to provide access should be restricted to members only." In other words, the documents would be shown only to busy committee chairmen and other members, not to the congressional investigators with the time, facilities, and context to analyze fully the documents. The memorandum also indicated that "no document should be retained": Congressional committees could not take away copies, thereby being unable to dispute with the administration its claims for keeping the documents non-public. To nail this down, if a member took notes, these "should be marked for classification by the department or agency in question." The Justice Department official went beyond this, ultimately suggesting in the meetings "editing out the deliberat[ive] or advisory portions of potentially privileged documents"—having the administration under investigation decide for itself what the investigation would see.

Falsified Documents

The Bush Administration's strategy for governing without Congress made its way by this White House directive and the related meetings and discussions down to the departments. In this way, President Bush's personal and political reasons for avoiding congressional oversight overrode the departments' own awareness of their constitutional requirement to be accountable. The Bush White House would not accept the kind of accountability that had historically followed major misjudgments or crises. In particular, explosive resistance to oversight took place at the Commerce Department. Throughout the period before Iraq's invasion of Kuwait, there had been a long history of disputes within the administration over licensing defense-related items for export to Iraq. The Department of Defense had sometimes opposed such licensing; the State Department had favored it; President Bush, through the NSC, had communicated his orders as to the policy recorded in NSD-26; and the Commerce Department had carried out the licensing.

Prior to the invasion, the NSC staff had presided over the settling of interagency disputes, one of the White House staff's chief sources of authority. This role became a source of vulnerability to oversight, for the involvement of so many agencies, and the keeping of records at the Commerce Department, created opportunities for Congress to pin down the

NSC staff involvement. In particular, the White House needed to curb the Commerce Department from revealing in an early or stark way how far the NSC Committee had gone in implementing President Bush's NSD-26 courtship policy.

Representative Doug Barnard, Jr. (D-Ga.), chaired the subcommittee of the House Committee on Government Operations with oversight jurisdiction over the export licensing system. On September 17, 1990, he convened a hearing on how the United States had licensed for sale to Iraq materials usable for nuclear, biological, and missile-related equipment. Former Assistant Secretary of Defense Richard Perle and his former deputy, Stephen Bryen, gave blunt testimony about the Defense Department's opposition to such licensing and the refusal of other departments to heed that opposition.[75]

Shortly after the hearing, the subcommittee sought from the Commerce Department all export license applications (and dispositions) for exports to Iraq in 1985 through 1990. First the subcommittee made a request, and then it voted to subpoena the data. By a follow-up letter, the subcommittee also requested information concerning the interagency review process for those applications.[76] These demands covered approval of $1.5 billion in dual-use exports for Iraq.

What led subsequently to major criminal investigation was that at this point the Commerce Department altered the descriptions of the licensing records before they were provided to the House subcommittee: "Changes were made in 68 export licenses for Iraq . . . . Frank DeGeorge, Commerce Department inspector general, said . . . that the description of trucks on five license records—with a total value of about $1 billion—had been changed in Kloske's bureau 'to eliminate a reference to a design for military use.'"[77] These changes occurred at a time when both the White House and other departments subjected the Commerce Department to intense pressure to fend off congressional scrutiny in order to protect the White House. The Commerce Department's director of export licensing subsequently told investigators that "State [the State Department] said trucks classified as military vehicles should be re-classified as cargo trucks" and that "he thought Commerce had been set up, *as a conscious effort to distance Bush and Baker from Iraq beforehand.*"[78]

A year and a half later, when congressional investigators closed in on what the Commerce Department thus admitted to be "a conscious effort to distance Bush," Undersecretary of Commerce Dennis Kloske described the pressure he had received from on high to fend off oversight. He disclosed that during this period he was under "daily supervision" from aides to Commerce Secretary Robert A. Mosbacher.[79] Undersecretary Kloske said that he initially wanted to provide details of NSC Committee export license advice—a matter separate from, but related to, the records alterations—because "to do otherwise could be misleading and not fully responsive to Chairman Barnard's request for information." However, he was directed to do precisely what he considered misleading Congress: "I then asked the General Counsel to call the Counsel to the President, and we were informed that the White House would not approve the transmission of agency positions to Chairman Barnard. I was then instructed by the Commerce Department General Counsel to delete the interagency position from the first summary printout that went to Chairman Barnard's Subcommittee."[80] The attorney general's report, trying to minimize the matter, conceded blandly that the White House counsel had been involved on the ground that he had to decide if "executive privilege" applied.[81]

Chairman Barnard testified as follows, as the press summarized:

> Barnard said . . . he knows that members of the National Security Council staff—including Brent Scowcroft, assistant to the president for national security affairs—took a strong interest in the subcommittee's request for information.
>
> During fall 1990, when his panel was negotiating with Commerce for the records, Barnard said Kloske told the subcommittee: "Look, it's out of my hands; it's up to the White House."[82]

Scowcroft later claimed, on the eve of the 1992 election, "We have no reason to conceal any of [the Iraq policy] from Congress. The charge of a cover-up is outrageous and irresponsible." The attorney general later wrote, in defense of the White House counsel, that "[i]t is not a crime for officials in the Executive Branch to meet to consider claims of executive privilege. . . ."[83] Without actually invoking executive privilege—which would have led to a public confrontation with Congress—the White House counsel had implemented President Bush's strategy for keeping Congress in the dark about White House policy and errors.

Once the White House counsel's office had conveyed instructions to delete this kind of information, it was a short step for the Commerce Department to withhold other information by altering records. Commerce Department personnel took records to be provided to the Barnard Subcommittee, which would have reproduced the export applications' statements about "military use," and changed them to delete the mention of military use. They furnished these records to Congress without a hint about the changes. According to an inspector general interview of Undersecretary Kloske, "White House Counsel also reviewed the responses prior to transmittal." The interview noted that Kloske "concedes that the actions gave the appearance that [the Commerce Department] was stonewalling the committee."[84] As admitted by the Attorney General's Report, without disagreeing, even the Commerce Department inspector general, who took a highly self-protective line about the matter, termed the alterations "unjustified and misleading."[85]

Undersecretary Kloske's obedience to the White House counsel's instructions did not save him from White House scapegoating. In spring 1991, within forty-eight hours after Undersecretary Kloske testified to Congress about the White House origins of the lenient policy toward Iraq, aides to White House chief of staff John Sununu contacted the Commerce Department and "confirmed" that the undersecretary would retire "early." Ultimately, when the attorney general issued his report in August 1992 exonerating the NSC and the White House counsel, that report went out of its way to threaten that the Justice Department would "if appropriate, prosecut[e] Kloske or other non-covered officials for their actions."[86] It was a chilling demonstration of the White House's power to block congressional oversight, control agency officials, and escape accountability.

The April Glaspie Myth

In September 1990, Iraq released its transcript of the July 25 Glaspie meeting with Saddam Hussein.[87] As *Congressional Quarterly Almanac* put it, "Suspicions that the administration had appeased Iraq were crystallized by the case of April C. Glaspie," especially because "after the Iraqis released the transcript in September 1990, Secretary of State James A. Baker III appeared to distance himself from Glaspie, and repeated attempts by congressional committees to get Glaspie to testify were rebuffed."[88]

In 1991, when the end of the war freed Congress to conduct oversight, the administration employed its information-control powers to stage-manage the oversight of this critical incident. It let Ambassador Glaspie testify before Senate and House hearings in March 1991; the State Department withheld her cables regarding her instructions and what she had said at the meeting. Without cables to contradict her, she painted a glowing picture of how she had stood up to Saddam Hussein and denounced the transcript released by Iraq as "disinformation" and a "fabrication." Her presentation, not subject to cross-examination from her as-yet-undisclosed cables won over senators, who praised her personally. As the television coverage focused in typical fashion on personalities, the Glaspie hearing before the Senate committee generated the myth of the supposedly determined administration position.

Subsequently, on July 10, the administration did provide the cables to congressional committees. The contents of the cables, as reported by the media, reflected a far more conciliatory position toward Saddam Hussein, especially because one of the cables, dated July 28, 1991, on the virtual eve of the invasion, came in the name of President Bush himself. As the New York Times described the ensuing furious reaction, "Major Senators today accused the former United States Ambassador to Iraq of misleading Congress in March . . . ."[89] Chairman Pell of the Senate Foreign Relations Committee wrote, "The title 'Saddam's Message of Friendship to President Bush' is reflective of the tone of the cable."[90]

However, the administration refused to declassify the cables, even though Ambassador Glaspie already had testified publicly about the July 25, 1990, meeting and the media had already published purported texts of the cables. The administration gave the need for preserving diplomatic confidences as the reason, even though Saddam Hussein had already published a transcript. By that refusal, the administration prevented use of the cables in televised public hearings. The Senate Foreign Relations Committee held a second hearing for Ambassador Glaspie on November 21, 1991, but only behind closed doors. *Congressional Quarterly Almanac* reported: "Some senators reportedly expressed disbelief in her account. But the issue went no further because the hearings remained closed and the [key] cable remained classified."[91]

1992: DECLASSIFICATION AND INVESTIGATION

Declassification

The NSC's successes in stalling congressional oversight finally began giving ground in 1992. Iraq's $4 billion in illegal loans by the Banca Nazionale Del Lavoro came to light after a raid on August 4, 1989. The House Committee on Banking, Housing, and Urban Affairs, chaired by Representative Henry Gonzalez (D-Tex.), held its first hearings on the BNL in October 1990 and followed these up with subpoenas for documents in November 1990, a staff report in February 1991, and further hearings in April 1991 about the administration's pressuring of the Export-Import Bank to give loan guarantees to Iraq.[92] Also in April 1991, the committee voted to approve further subpoenas and spent the rest of the year obtaining and analyzing documents.

By February 1992, Chairman Gonzalez had accumulated an extensive body of documents and information about prewar administration policy toward Iraq. He unveiled them in a series of speeches on the floor of the House, on February 24 and March 2, 3, 9, 16, and 30. Chairman Gonzalez drew widespread attention to the NSC role, among other aspects of Iraq policy. The Washington Post reported the chairman's March 16 address in an article entitled "White House Curbed Release of Data on Prewar Support of Iraq, Hill Told," with specific reference to NSD-26: "Among the documents that the administration withheld on the basis of executive privilege, Gonzalez said, was an October 1989 National Security Directive signed by Bush—know as NSD-26—which ordered 'pursuit of improved economic and political ties with Iraq.'"[93]

The Banking Committee continued with hearings on May 21 and 29 that focused on the 1989–1990 approval by the NSC of aid for Iraq and the NSC's 1991 resistance of oversight. As the hearings unveiled, in 1991 the NSC counsel had convened seven meetings of his interagency group in 1991 to discuss the "coordination" of responses to congressional inquiries. When the Banking Committee requested the appearance at the hearings of White House Counsel C. Boyden Gray or the NSC counsel, the White House refused.[94] Its traditional position remained: There was no accountability in Congress for the NSC staff and the White House counsel.

Meanwhile, the Bush Administration began to give ground on declassifying Iraq-related documents. Another House subcommittee, chaired by Representative Sam Gejdenson (D-Conn.), called for extensive declassification and release of documents. Particularly in the face of Chairman Gonzalez's actions, the Gejdenson subcommittee won success in having about a hundred documents declassified and made public.[95]

Most notably, the administration finally declassified (in large part) NSD-26.[96] Thus, three years after NSD-26 had established the policy of befriending Saddam Hussein, the administration finally let the public see it.

Request for Independent Counsel

In June and July 1992, a push developed for appointment of an independent counsel. On June 2, the former manager of the BNL branch that had made the loans to Iraq, which observers now estimate at $5.5 billion, pleaded guilty to extensive fraud charges. The federal judge who received the plea expressed his indignation at the administration's handling of the case and expressed his sense that as a result, the BNL manager would not describe frankly the role of bank higher-ups and federal officials. "The case ought to have a special prosecutor because I'm not getting the information from Mr. [Christopher] Drogoul [the manager]," Judge Marvin H. Shoob said in a widely reported statement.[97]

The House Judiciary Committee held hearings on June 2 and 23 about whether to seek an independent counsel. These included testimony about meetings in October 1989, in the period immediately around NSD-26, that suggested that the administration knew, from its investigation of the BNL, that loans to Iraq "were used to procure nuclear-related equipment." An account of that information was supposedly furnished to Secretary of State Baker, but nevertheless the State Department, as previously described, wielded NSD-26 successfully in late 1989 to obtain approval of further loans to Iraq.[98]

On July 9, twenty House Judiciary Committee members made a formal request for appointment of an independent counsel. The letter included allegations about the original period of the courtship of Saddam Hussein. However, it focused on the later period of covering up: "activities . . . to attempt to conceal information about potential criminal activity from Congress through the making of false statements, the nonproduction, falsification or alteration of official records and other documents, and through otherwise misleading and obstructing Congress in its investigation of such matters." In this preelection period, the attorney general refused to follow his requirements, by the independent counsel law, to begin a preliminary investigation as a step toward an informed decision on whether to have an independent counsel appointed. Instead, he shut the whole matter down by rejecting the House letter, issuing a ninety-seven-page report that concluded "there is no basis to commence a preliminary investigation under the Statute."[99]

A number of points in that report have been noted previously. In particular, the attorney general refused to allow even a preliminary investigation of how the instructions from the White House counsel to Undersecretary Kloske to withhold export license advice might have influenced the records alteration. "White House and other high level officials" were involved in the withholding, but that was deemed such a "separate aspect of responding to the [Barnard subcommittee's] request"[100] from the records alteration that the attorney general would not allow a preliminary investigation.[101]

Rather, the report as a whole conveyed the Justice Department's decision to provide complete shielding for the NSC and the White House counsel. In so doing, it provided the skeleton of the Bush Administration's overall strategy. President Bush had found it agreeable to his personal style and his political situation to make foreign policy through the NSC rather than through accountable channels. With the election year upon him, his administration kept the public from scrutinizing the NSC's role by linking it to executive privilege. The Attorney General Report discussed the NSC staff's role in 1989 and 1990, showing that the ending of the Cold War had done nothing to diminish the White House's use of the NSC system to administer foreign policy: "The NSC is involved in export licensing policy in two capacities. General export licensing policy is set by an interagency committee that is chaired by the NSC. Additionally, the NSC will resolve disputes regarding particular export licenses within the interagency committee that is responsible for the actual licensing process."

This potent operational role thus gave the NSC staff the extraordinary tools to export militarily useful materials to Saddam Hussein on the basis of President Bush's personal views without having to consider those of the public, Congress, and the accountable departmental officers. However, as the report continued, the NSC could invoke the ultimate powers of the sovereign to block accountability: "At the NSC, Mr. Scowcroft's duties encompassed advising the President on matters involving possible claims of executive privilege concerning documents and testimony relating to national security matters." The report seemingly terminated further investigation by wrapping national security and executive privilege around all that had been done to govern without Congress.

There were two postscripts. First, the federal judge presiding over the BNL case in Atlanta became convinced that the matter did require an independent counsel and issued a sharp pronouncement to this effect. To head off this demand, the attorney general appointed as an in-house special counsel a retired judge, who commenced a preliminary inquiry in October 1992. Having an in-house sympathetic counsel start a preliminary inquiry so late succeeded in deferring the issue of a genuine independent counsel until after the election, much as the administration similarly deferred prior to the election the question of an independent counsel for the matter of political misuse of the passport office.

The Iraq-related special counsel did not complete his preliminary inquiry until December 1992. It revealed that in 1989 the Atlanta U.S. attorney's office, which conducted the investigation of the BNL, had warned about Iraq's use of credits for its weapons program but that the administration had followed NSD-26 and proceeded anyway with more credits. In 1990 that U.S. attorney's office had expressed only limited desires to defer oversight by congressional committees, but the attorney general had gone ahead anyway, with no basis except NSD-26, and cited "national security" reasons to block oversight. Predictably, the in-house special counsel saw no reason for an independent counsel on the Iraq matter.

The other postscript was that the Bush Administration faced intense criticism of its Iraq courtship during the 1992 campaign. In particular, Senator Gore released a lengthy, impressively footnoted address collecting the history of the matter. Governor Bill Clinton followed with shorter remarks. Enough had emerged, despite all efforts, to provide the principal foreign affairs criticism of the Bush Administration during the presidential campaign.

Still, the administration had avoided, delayed, or watered down oversight to a considerable extent by its sustained efforts over the years. The NSC staff both held the extraordinary vehicles of power and sought assiduously to protect itself from accountability. It had created NSD-26, it had run the NSC committee system, it had defeated Congress's efforts at sanctions, and it had stalled and deferred the efforts at oversight by vague hints at executive privilege. Then, when the most intense congressional inquiries uncovered this pattern, it deferred the resulting question of an independent counsel until after the 1992 election.

The Iraq matter epitomized, as nothing else could, the Bush Administration's general strategy on separation of powers. President Bush had conducted foreign policy toward Iraq as he liked, based on his personal hopes of a positive relationship with an unpopular foreign leader without regard to the contrary view of the public and Congress. He had done so not as his predecessor might have through appeals to the country to support his policy, but through the White House staff mechanism left over from the Cold War. Through this mechanism, he had succeeded in 1989 and 1990 at governing without Congress and in 1991 and 1992 at minimizing the electoral fallout from the revelation of his misjudgment in courting Saddam Hussein.

6

The Persian Gulf War Authorization

The Persian Gulf War of January and February 1991 capped one of the greatest controversies in U.S. history over a major subject of separation of powers: the great question of the war power. Congress has the constitutional power to declare war, and this should mean that the United States does not go to war unless Congress authorizes it as the nation's voice in democratic decisionmaking. War with a foreign power can be distinguished from other military steps that presidents have taken historically without congressional authorization, such as peaceful and defensive troop deployments or even landings to protect American citizens in danger. War is what took place by congressional advance authorization in 1812, 1846, 1898, 1917, and 1941 and by express ratification in 1861.

In the Cold War era, the nation temporarily accepted presidents who exceeded their powers and took the nation into war. President Truman took the nation into the Korean War without congressional authorization, and, arguably, the Vietnam War expanded without clear congressional authorization. Since the national reaction against the Vietnam War, other presidents have made statements about having the war power, but none before President Bush concretely threatened to take the country to war without congressional authorization.

In November and December 1990, President Bush clearly set out to go to war against Iraq and had indicated that he would do so, if he deemed necessary, without a vote on war by Congress. Presidential powers enthusiasts have even contended that in some sense he did go to war with Iraq without congressional authorization, notwithstanding the actual events of January 1991.[1] Thus, Iraq provided the ultimate test of postwar divided government after the Cold War: whether a president of one party would go to war without leaving the decision to a Congress with a majority of the other party. To put it in terms of the Bush Administration's general approach to the separation of powers, would the president commence a war on the basis of a sovereign's claimed prerogatives, that is, on his personal will without Congress?

The Constitution's express language and the Framers' intent give Congress the power to declare war. Yet the presidential exercise of war power during the Cold War, as in Korea, has focused much of contemporary analysis around how new situations fit with history. Accordingly, a discussion of presidential and congressional claims appropriately begins with a historical background up through the Reagan and early Bush administrations. Next comes the question of interpreting President Bush's offensive buildup of forces in Saudi Arabia in November and December 1990, which reflected his intention of deciding personally to go to war. Then can come a close examination of the circumstances and content of the public's confirmation that the decision is up to Congress, which occurred by January 1991. Finally, the significance of the taming of President Bush's claimed sovereign prerogative warrants further analysis.

THE HISTORICAL CONTEXT

From the time of the Framers through the beginning of the twentieth century, the proponents of Congress's unique role plainly held the upper hand. The Constitution had specified in the clearest terms, in Article I, section 8, clause 11, that "[t]he Congress shall have power . . . to declare War." Together with Congress's other powers, such as the power of the purse, this gave Congress the predominant role in decisions on initiating war.[2] American constitutional debate over the war power, particularly since the Vietnam War, divides between those adhering to the words of the Constitution and supporting Congress's predominance and those making a claim for presidential war power and relying largely on Cold War events.[3]

1789–1950: Congress Predominates

Nineteenth-century and early twentieth-century experience confirmed Congress's role. Later presidential proponents have attempted to promote "lists" of 56, 125, or 200 incidents supposedly reflecting unilateral presidential exercise of war power.[4] The examples range from bombardment of a Nicaraguan town in 1854 to the expedition against the Boxer Rebellion in China in 1900. These listed incidents show that presidents deployed forces in Third World contexts and that these forces even occasionally engaged in fighting, though rarely of significance on land. Most resemble President Reagan's Grenada intervention and President Bush's Panama intervention. The presidents justified these actions by the rationales of protecting American citizens abroad or of self-defense of the forces involved. Few of the incidents listed involve anything more than brief naval engagements, minor reprisals for piracy or banditry or the like, or landings of forces for occupations that were not effectively opposed though they were often disliked. None of the incidents would justify a war without congressional authorization.[5]

Wars before 1950 contrast sharply with such incidents. Congress authorized even the naval war with Republican France in 1798, the wars with the Barbary pirates in 1802 through 1812, and the landing in Veracruz in 1914.[6] War-hawk Congresses pushed reluctant presidents into the War of 1812 and the Spanish-American War.[7] Presidents did deploy forces in a manner that increased the likelihood of war, raising an analytical issue that recurred in President Bush's unilateral buildup in late 1990 in Saudi Arabia. President Polk sent the army into the disputed border of Texas and Mexico in 1845; President Lincoln ordered the Union forces to defend Fort Sumter in 1861 and then responded dramatically to the Confederate attack.

The 1846 action in particular raises a serious question about presidential ability if not directly to usurp Congress's power to declare war then indirectly to take provocative actions that end up forcing Congress's hand. However, in each of these cases the decision to declare war remained that of Congress. Even when presidents made provocative deployments that ripened into conflict, Congress still had the decision whether to commit to war or, by refusing a favorable vote (either of contemporaneous authorization or of subsequent retrospective ratification), to deny legitimacy to war. In 1846 and 1861, Congress ratified the president's actions and authorized war. On other occasions, Congress would not authorize the ultimate step and presidents had to retreat from bellicose military deployments, as President Grant had to back away from war with Haiti in 1872.[8] The nineteenth-century historical record involves many diverse instances and can often be complex, but it was not understood at the time to mean, and it does not support now the view, that the president decided on war without Congress.

In the twentieth century, Congress, not the president, declared that America would participate in World War I and World War II. Prior to, or absent, a congressional decision, presidents had limited power, although after declaration of war their power became very broad.[9] Before entering World War I in 1917, President Wilson awaited a congressional declaration of war, even though Germany had commenced unrestricted and brutal submarine warfare against American civilian ships. President Franklin D. Roosevelt pressed his powers in some respects in 1940 and 1941, but even then he held within limits rather than trespassing the ultimate war authority vested in Congress.[10] President Roosevelt illustrated a proper use of presidential power: not sovereign assertions that he would take the nation to war by personal will, but appeals to the nation and Congress to prepare for war.[11]

Upon review of this history, analysts have concluded appropriately that "with the sole exception of the protection of American citizens, no President ever claimed that congressional authorization [for war] could be assumed until President Truman did so in June 1950." Rather, "[s]uccessive Presidents, Congresses, and courts agreed that the scope of assumed authorization extended no further than the protection of American citizens in certain circumstances and the defense of the American state."[12]

Presidential Power During the Cold War

Just as the Cold War reflects a period of special presidential power in other areas of national security, so, too, it includes unilateral presidential action in the war power context. Congress simply did not authorize, or expressly ratify, the Korean War.[13] In 1964, President Johnson did obtain adoption by Congress of the Tonkin Gulf Resolution before his subsequent full-scale land intervention in Vietnam. However, what he obtained was not a clear authorization of the war that actually followed, but a symbolic expression provided in a virtually undebated context.[14] When the Vietnam War actually developed at full scale and cost in life, as the Nixon Administration openly enlarged it on the ground into Cambodia and Laos, the nation underwent a crisis over illegitimacy of the exercise of war power expressed through action in Congress.

Meanwhile, on other fronts of the Cold War, presidents had displaced Congress temporarily from its traditional role in the twilight zones of military or paramilitary measures short of war. Prior to 1950, Congress had given explicit authorization or ratification to a variety of such measures, from the 1798 undeclared limited naval war with France to President Wilson's occupation of Veracruz in 1914. With the start of the Cold War, presidents unilaterally directed proxy wars through the postwar "covert action" machinery, as in Cuba in 1961, or acted with meaningless symbolic resolutions from Congress, as with the Lebanon intervention in 1957.[15]

Yet even as the Vietnam War marked an enormous precedent for a type of imperfectly authorized presidential action, its course brought the most pronounced reaction in American history against presidential power claims and in favor of insisting on the originally intended constitutional role for Congress. The 1970s brought the end of the eclipse of the "declare war" clause of the Constitution, putting the responsibility and the authority on Congress. Enactment of the War Powers Resolution signified more than just the creation of procedures that later presidents might evade or dispute. It marked a major statement, even in the midst of the Cold War, that the country wished to insist on Congress's role to decide on future wars.[16] Ironically, the leadership of the armed forces, often incorrectly stigmatized as unconcerned about authorization, took the lesson of this period as much to heart as anyone else. From that time on, the military leadership and the civilian secretaries of defense insisted on not entering into war just on personal presidential will and demanded a display of national support—difficult to imagine except through Congress.[17]

Since the enactment of the War Powers Resolution, each U.S. action with war overtones has received intensive contemporaneous scrutiny, focusing on how it fits in the historic war power debate.[18] Presidential proponents have often tried to depict the president as not bound by the War Powers Resolution. Even the consistency of this claim warrants some scrutiny. Both the White House and the Justice Department, in soberer moments, have praised the War Powers Resolution and confirmed its constitutionality. As the Justice Department formally opined in 1980, "We believe that Congress may, as a general constitutional matter, place a 60-day limit on the use of our armed forces as required by the provision of [section 5(b)] of the [War Powers] Resolution." Even during the Reagan Administration, Secretary Weinberger in 1984 emphasized much the same necessity of congressional authorization for combat.[19]

More important, in terms of action rather than statements, the period from enactment of the War Powers Resolution in 1973 to the Iraq crisis of 1990 represented some measure of return to the sharing of authority with Congress as in the pre–Cold War era. During that period, presidents ordered many uses of the armed forces; these actions did not necessarily clash with the pre-1950 pattern, however. As noted earlier, even before the Cold War, presidents had engaged in unilateral actions justified as protection for American citizens or as reprisals not amounting to war. Many of the incidents from 1973 to 1991 resembled that prior history: the Indochina evacuations, the Mayaguez incident, the abortive 1980 Iran hostage rescue attempt, the Grenada landing, the Libyan air strike of 1986, and the Panama occupation in 1989. Other incidents involved deployments of disputed provocativeness but without actual directions to start combat: advisers in El Salvador, naval maneuvers off Libya, the reflagging of Kuwaiti vessels in 1987,[20] and, in a sense, the 1992 famine-control landing in Somalia. The validity of some of the actions may be questionable, particularly as to the lack of bona fide consultation with Congress. Still, these incidents did not radically surpass the pre-1950 pattern involving deployments below the level of initiation of land hostilities with a foreign power. The incidents may have strained the War Powers Resolution's procedures or expressed disdain for the spirit and duty of interbranch consultation, but they did not reach the level of outright usurpation of the Constitution's grant to Congress of the power to declare war.

On the contrary, Congress's enactment in 1983 of the Multinational Force in Lebanon Resolution represented a major marker of a return to the standard prior to Korea and Vietnam.[21] In many respects, the Lebanon troop commitment represented the most significant war power exercise of the period between Vietnam and Iraq. The implacability of the local forces in Lebanon made conflict with high American casualties more an immediate prospect than anything else during this interval. Tragically, the terrorist bombing of American headquarters facilities in Lebanon, which claimed 241 American lives, fulfilled the worst fears as to the cost of the commitment. In 1983, Senate Majority Leader Howard Baker played a historic role of go-between for the White House and Congress (particularly Speaker Thomas P. O'Neill, Jr.), helping President Reagan recognize the need for a congressional enactment explicitly in accord with the War Powers Resolution.

The Lebanon commitment constituted a key precedent and vindication of the War Powers Resolution: It confirmed that the exercise of the war power, and the concomitant expenditure in lives and treasure, should occur only with national consent through Congress. It might also be said that the tough congressional hearings and deliberations prior to adoption of that resolution, like those in late 1990, ventilated and clarified the issues surrounding the commitment. The false argument is often made that democratic debate undermines American resolve, either internally or in the world's eyes. In 1983, as in 1990 and at other times, the reality has been the opposite. Not merely the Congress but also the public and the military have more confidence in a considered decision than in one man's will.

Moreover, Congress also had buttressed its role regarding "covert action" proxy wars through another mechanism that stood the test of time. After the congressional investigations of the mid-1970s revealed the extensive postwar abuses of covert actions, Congress had enacted general legislative checks on the intelligence agencies. In particular contexts, the Clark Amendment had forbade a proxy war in Angola in the 1970s, and the Boland Amendments had limited the role of the U.S. government in a proxy war in Nicaragua in the 1980s. The Iran-contra congressional investigations revealed how far the Reagan NSC staff had gone to secretly violate the Boland Amendments, but that exposure hardly represented a vindication of the violations. Rather, the revelations occasioned a forceful denunciation of any similar future violations.[22]

Thus, as the Bush Administration began it received a legacy on war powers that made its actions subject to intense scrutiny and debate. Enactment of the War Powers Resolution and the limits on covert actions had made law out of the changed public view from the early Cold War period and had institutionalized the otherwise abstract constitutional issue. Congress had significantly restored the constitutional pattern of the pre-1950 history, attempting with some effectiveness to isolate and distinguish the Korea and Vietnam instances. The Bush Administration's major pre-Kuwait incident in Panama did not change this. Like so many other Latin American landings of the past two centuries, it received the justification in part of a need to protect American citizens from chaos. Also, it elicited no major congressional disputation and it did not involve a likelihood of land combat that would be costly in American lives. The Panama occupation represented another action that might be questioned for lack of bona fide consultation with Congress or on other grounds not discussed herein like the level of civilian casualties. Still, its critics compared it to pre-1950 excesses rather than contending it went far beyond them.

When the Cold War ended, it seemed entirely possible, for all the frequent rhetorical expressions of presidential war power, that Congress's effort over two previous decades to restore the pre–Korea and Vietnam pattern would be lasting. Kuwait clearly came as the unique test, without anything remotely comparable since Lebanon and without a true peer since Vietnam.

1990: TOWARD PRESIDENTIAL WAR

Following the Iraqi invasion of Kuwait on August 2, 1990, President Bush decided on a defensive buildup of American forces in Saudi Arabia. Then, having waited until after the 1990 midterm election, President Bush announced on November 8 a second-stage buildup that was clearly designed to provide an offensive option. That second stage, with its implication of a unilateral decision to go to war, occurred largely on his own power, not by congressional authorization. President Bush appeared poised to have the decision about war be his personal prerogative.

Before the 1990 Election: Defensive Buildup

President Bush made the initial decision for a buildup sufficient for defensive purposes during August 4 through 6, mainly in the context of discussion with Saudi King Fahd.[23] The president also employed diplomatic skill to swiftly assemble an international coalition. One might further note that the critics think that the president boxed in Saddam Hussein by the surprise of this reaction. To Iraq it must have come as a sudden jolt after President Bush's 1989–1990 courtship that President Bush refused to offer him a negotiated settlement on Kuwait that would allow him to save face. Saddam Hussein may have been morally wrong to expect an out, but it was a predictable expectation from what he had heard from the Bush Administration prior to the invasion.[24]

During the early period, in August and September 1990, the administration avoided serious challenge to Congress regarding war powers. It provided notice of the defense buildup in Saudi Arabia using the usual executive branch formula for evading the War Powers Resolution.[25] Congress responded by approving resolutions of support for that buildup, confirming the congressional position for authorizing noncombat deployments of such magnitude.[26] Prior to the announcement in November of an offensive buildup, the most bellicose statement on presidential unilateral prerogatives probably came in Secretary of State Baker's testimony before the Senate Foreign Relations Committee on October 17 and 18, 1990:

> We should not have a constitutional argument, it does not seem to me, about whether or not the President, as Commander in Chief, has the constitutional authority to commit forces. It has been done going all the way back, I think to World War II.
>
> You can look at Grenada, Panama, Libya, even at the unhappy experiences, too, such as Vietnam and so forth. . . .
>
> [I]t is important that we have the support of the American people. One way you get that is to have the support of the elected representatives. Therefore, we will consult.
>
> But, if were under an obligation to come back here and have hearings . . . that might drag out for a while while we debate, [']well, now wait a minute. If you are really talking about sending this force here and that one over there, is this the right thing to do and you really ought not to do that.[']
>
> I just want to make sure we all understand the position that would put the Commander in Chief in. So, we do have a constitutionally different view, I suppose, on the constitutional question of the authority to commit forces.[27]

The administration would sometimes get a bit more concrete in rejecting a member of Congress's request to acknowledge a need for congressional authorization:

> *Senator Kerry:* Therefore, I would reiterate whether or not, if what we are really talking about is going to war . . . would we not come to the Congress under those circumstances and ask for a declaration?
>
> *Secretary Baker:* . . . If we are saying, we want you to agree that nothing will happen while we are gone unless you get the approval of a majority of 535, that is something that we cannot agree to right now . . . .[28]

On October 29, President Bush reminded reporters of examples of action without congressional authority, including his Panama occupation. "'History is replete with examples where the President has had to take action. . . . I've done this in the past,' he said in apparent reference to Panama, 'and certainly would have no hesitancy [to do it again].'"[29]

After the 1990 Election: Going to War

President Bush's overall strategy applied precisely to the timing of his decision to prepare to go to war by personal prerogative. Rather than build public support or accept the public will, he used secrecy about the decision for an offensive buildup to take the war issue out of that election. As Congressional Quarterly noted: "[T]he November 1990 elections unfolded in a curious vacuum from the crisis brewing in the Persian Gulf. That was in part because President Bush waited until after Election Day to announce the deployment of 200,000 more troops to Saudi Arabia—and with them the greater capability for an offensive strike—that began to fragment congressional support."[30]

Keeping the issue out of the election fit with a general strategy of not engaging with Congress or the public. Externally, President Bush and Secretary Baker lined up support from other nations, particularly the Soviet Union, using President Bush's preferred personal style of leader-to-leader deals. He sought a United Nations Security Council Resolution indicating the use of force with a January 15 deadline for an Iraqi pullout. Internally, President Bush lined up military planning for the same action. He had positioned an enormous American military force that would have trouble engaging in war at all if it waited much longer than the January 15 deadline. In December, President Bush told foreign ambassadors that if he decided on war he would go ahead regardless of whether Congress and the American public agreed.[31]

Yet on this issue President Bush's effort to keep the decision an internal one in his own hands produced an escalating public reaction. Having not been engaged with, the public might well support Congress in challenging the president's subsequent attempts to act unilaterally by personal rule. Several times President Bush met with congressional leaders for what he called "consultations," though to them it may have seemed mere notifications. The key moment, on November 30, went thusly: "'If after January 15th you decide to go to war, you'll have to come to Congress,' Foley added. Senator Mitchell was emphatic on the same point: a vote was necessary and constitutionally required. As the Senate Majority Leader spoke, Bush stared coldly in the other direction."[32] The scene resembled the reproaches, from the leaders of Parliament in the seventeenth century to willful Stuart monarchs, that underlay the Constitution's clause that gave only to Congress the power to declare war.

The Senate Armed Services Committee, chaired by Senator Sam Nunn (D-Ga.), scheduled a series of hearings, held on November 27, 28, 29, and 30 and December 3. These historic hearings featured the views of two former chairmen of the Joint Chiefs of Staff and of a former secretary of defense, all skeptical about initiating hostilities instead of giving more time for sanctions. Chairman Nunn followed these hearings with skeptical questioning of Secretary of Defense Richard Cheney.[33] The hearings themselves, like the Fulbright hearings on the Vietnam War and the hearings on Lebanon in 1983, invoked one of Congress's strongest tools for insisting on its constitutional role of deciding on war.

On the war power issue, Secretary Cheney engaged in a widely publicized debate with Senator Edward Kennedy, marking the furthest extent of the administration's claim to unilateral power:

> *Senator Kennedy:* Now, barring an act of provocation, do you agree that the President must obtain the approval of Congress in advance before the United States attack Iraq?
>
> *Secretary Cheney:* Senator, I do not believe the President requires any additional authorization from the Congress before committing U.S. forces to achieve our objectives in the Gulf.
>
> [T]here have been some 200 times, more than 200 times, in our history when Presidents have committed U.S. forces, and on only five of those occasions was there a prior declaration of war. . . .
>
> *Senator Kennedy:* Well, Mr. Secretary, we are not talking about Libya, not about Grenada, not about Panama. We are talking about 440,000 American troops who are over there. . . . Do I understand from your response that you are prepared to tell the American people now that, barring provocation by Saddam Hussein, you believe he and he alone can bring this country to war?
>
> *Secretary Cheney:* [T]he President is within his authority at this point to carry out his responsibility.[34]

According to published reports, the president gave preliminary commands to the military by the end of December, reflecting his own conclusion in favor of hostilities. Bob Woodward's book, *The Commanders,* attributes the formal command to a National Security Directive drafted after an NSC Committee meeting,[35] which, if confirmed, would further reflect the awesome power invested in the NSC and its NSDs as instruments of secret decisions and law. One observer characterized the Defense Department's minimal role—despite its legal responsibility for military affairs—as one of "glorified messenger boys who must keep tuned to CNN to find out what decisions are evolving at the White House."[36]

As of December 1990, President Bush's sequence indicated that he asserted a "monarchical pretension" in the classic sense, namely, the personal power to decide on war. He had consulted with foreign leaders and with his military but had shrugged off the efforts at meaningful consultation by congressional leaders. It then became interesting to see how public opinion forced him, by early January 1991, to allow Congress to perform its constitutional role.

1991: CONGRESS VOTES THE WAR AUTHORIZATION

The Action Shifts to Congress

After the 1990 midterm congressional election, the announcement on November 8 of the offensive deployment led to Senator Nunn's hearings. In turn, at Senator Nunn's December 3 hearing, Secretary Cheney's dramatic testimony provided a trigger to a key step in the evolution of the congressional position: "Reacting to the statement, the House Democratic Caucus on Dec. 4 approved a resolution explicitly stating that the President should first seek such [congressional] authorization, unless American lives were in danger. The caucus voted 177-37 in favor of the non-binding policy statement."[37] This was the first legislative test vote. Congress had begun to discover, in the Nunn hearings and the December 3 Caucus vote, the strong national support for having Congress make the decision on war. In particular, it discovered that the support for this position exceeded the support either for or against war itself. Whereas a hard core on each side wanted the president to decide and favored war, or wanted the Congress to decide and opposed war, a middle position emerged that would accept war if, but only if, Congress voted for it.

The House Democratic Caucus statement had been drafted by Representative Richard Durbin and adumbrated a House Bennett-Durbin Resolution in January. Meanwhile, a federal judge, Harold Greene, on December 13 issued an opinion paralleling in many ways the sense of the Durbin Resolution. The opinion rejected the administration arguments for unilateral war making and supported the straightforward contention that the Constitution, in stating that Congress would have the power to declare war, gave that war-making power only to Congress.[38]

Congressional Quarterly Almanac stated the following conclusion about the year: "As 1990 ended . . . . Bush and Congress were also playing chicken, daring each other to make the first move to give lawmakers a decision-making role in the crisis."[39] In December, giving Congress a role would have required the extraordinary step of a special session of Congress—a "lame duck" session at that. With the end of 1990, both the president and the nation had the interregnum of the Christmas and New Year's holidays. Afterward, the dynamics changed for the January 3 convening of the new Congress. It now required no extraordinary step, as in December, for Congress to convene. Ordinarily, Congress might have adjourned after its initial convening, but this time congressional leaders kept it in session. Once the members assembled, they became a known quantity to themselves, to the president, and to the public and became a political force infinitely harder to ignore. Moreover, during the adjournment they had had a long period in which they could absorb the public mindset in their states and districts. The public mindset though not decisively favoring or opposing war, had crystallized, according to polls, around the view that Congress had to vote to make the war decision. Polls showed that although the public divided evenly on the use of force—46 percent for, 47 percent against—it supported a congressional vote almost two-to-one. The question "Do you think Congress should have to vote a declaration of war before American troops go into combat?" received a 60 percent "yes" and only 32 percent "no" response.[40]

Accordingly, on January 7, 1991, House Speaker Thomas S. Foley (D-Wash.) and Senate Majority Leader George Mitchell (D-Maine) both announced that their chambers would debate later in the week about authorizing the use of force against Iraq. [41]

President Bush Requests Congressional Action

On January 6 and 8, President Bush convened key meetings of his national security advisers. Secretary Cheney, true to his strong testimony at the Nunn hearings, opposed asking Congress for authority. "The administration, the coalition, the troops in the field could not afford a negative vote, Cheney said."[42] However, the next day President Bush apparently made his own tentative decision to ask Congress for authority. On January 7, "Bush began calling Senate and House Republicans that night to obtain a head count. He personally typed out the draft of a letter he could send to the Congress requesting that both houses endorse the 'all necessary means' language of the United Nations resolution."[43]

On January 8, President Bush convened a meeting of his legal and congressional liaison officers. He revealed his draft letter to Congress requesting authority. Secretary Cheney articulated again the case against making the request because a congressional "no" vote would be decisive and because the request would be seen as a precedent: "Cheney cautioned about sending the letter. The simple act of requesting the resolution would carry immense implications. No matter how the President's letter was phrased, it would be interpreted to mean that the President thought he needed a vote. . . . To go with the letter and lose [a vote] would be devastating."[44]

President Bush decided nonetheless to send the letter that day. As Secretary Cheney had predicted, the public recognized his request as a major shift. The New York Times summed up the general interpretation with a headline across the front page: "Bush Asks Congress to Back Use of Force If Iraq Defies Deadline on Kuwait Pullout." As the Times reported, "[T]he President's letter to Congressional leaders, end[ed] weeks of indecision by the White House over whether to seek support from Congress before sending American forces into combat. . . ."[45] An administration spokesman gave this insight into the request: "'We don't like the notion that the president is afraid to go to Congress because of fears he would lose. . . . We need to put that to rest.'"[46]

On the positive side for his own foreign policy strategy, President Bush, by making the request, increased the approval a war policy would obtain from Congress. "Democratic and Republican leaders said the direct Presidential request would be likely to win over some wavering lawmakers."[47] Moreover, he avoided a clash with what had solidified as the public's position on Congress's role.

Commentators urging an expansive view of presidential powers—and, as will shortly be described, the White House counsel—presented a rearguard argument on this point. They tried to suggest that the president had not changed his position by his request because his letter asked Congress for "support," not "authorization."[48] This nuance recalls the Tonkin Gulf Resolution and the predecessor resolutions of the 1950s and 1960s, which let presidents claim for themselves the power to authorize war and to allow for Congress a mere supportive role. Even to suggest this argument requires some strain, for although the letter did ask for "support" it avoided saying anything against receiving "authorization."

> I therefore request that the House of Representatives and the Senate adopt a Resolution stating that Congress supports the use of all necessary means to implement U.N. Security Council Resolution 678. Such actions would send the clearest possible message . . . .
> . . . I can think of no better way than for Congress to express its support for the President at this critical time.[49]

In fact, the argument that President Bush wanted support and did not want authorization rapidly breaks down in the light of the contemporary understanding. The resolution that shortly thereafter went to the Senate and House floor as the version desired by the administration provided not merely for support but for explicit authorization. The only reason the administration had not yet been explicit, as of January 8, as to the authorization it wanted was that the administration had not yet decided. On January 8, administration sources admitted this: "Facing the fluid situation in Congress, administration officials debated whether to ask for a clear endorsement of the U.N. resolution [i.e., a clear authorization of force] or a more vaguely worded request seeking support of Bush's gulf policies."[50] The White House had first worked on its draft NSD, then its draft letter to Congress, and only then on its draft congressional resolution.

In the two days following the letter, the administration made its decision to ask for authorization, reflected in the resolution it asked Congress to enact. By the time the White House came to draft that resolution on January 9, it had to work closely with congressional leaders who would shepherd the resolution through. Knowing the mindset of the public and Congress, the members of congress would never have allowed anything less than a clear request for authorization (as distinguished from mere support).

On January 9, a small working group came together to draft the administration's requested resolution. It included the two leading House cosponsors—Republican Leader Robert Michel (R-Ill.) and Democrat Steven Solarz (D-N.Y.)—among other senior members of Congress, along with Scowcroft, Sununu, and Gray.[51] In the Senate, Minority Leader Dole introduced the product on January 11 as the Dole-Warner Resolution,[52] the version that became the law. This resolution reflected the administration's decision at the crucial moment to seek explicit authorization rather than mere general support. It represented the abandonment of the initial presidential attempt to make the war decision a personal one, in the face of public and congressional insistence to the contrary.

Congress Adopts the Authorization

Starting on Thursday, January 10, and continuing until January 12, the House and Senate held the historic debates preceding their vote on the authorizing resolution. On January 11, Minority Leader Dole introduced the Dole-Warner Resolution,[53] the version the administration wanted. This version provided for explicit authorization rather than mere general support.

On January 12, the House adopted by the overwhelming vote of 302-131 the resolution of Representatives Durbin and Bennett. Representative Durbin had authored the December 3 Democratic Caucus resolution demanding congressional authorization prior to war, and this resolution insisted on the same: "The Congress finds that the Constitution of the United States vests all power to declare war in the Congress of the United States. Any offensive action taken against Iraq must be explicitly approved by the Congress of the United States before such action may be initiated."[54]

Virtually no one in the House spoke against the proposition cemented by the Bennett-Durbin Resolution. The minority manager on the resolution, Representative Henry Hyde (R-Ill.), was known as the ablest spokesman by far in the body for the presidential position on such questions regarding separation of powers.[55] Even Representative Hyde disclaimed any suggestion that the president was not seeking authority from Congress exactly as the Bennett-Durbin Resolution required. In asking for adoption of the Persian Gulf Resolution, Representative Hyde said, the president had made "an explicit request from this Congress for the authority that the Bennett resolution says the President must get."[56]

Similarly, the Senate debate reflected the overwhelming recognition that the president had asked for congressional authorization. Again, presidential supporters conceded this. As Senator Dan Coats (R-Ind.) said, "Now is not the time to enter into a bitter, partisan debate on the constitutional authority of the Commander in Chief. However one comes down on this issue, it is clear that the President is now requesting congressional authorization."[57]

The resolution put forth by the president's supporters represented a major choice in this regard. The administration finally chose a request with highly specific wording. As previously noted, the resolution that won a majority respectfully cited "the War Powers Resolution Requirements" and then stated: "SPECIFIC STATUTORY AUTHORIZATION—Consistent with section 8(a)(1) of the War Powers Resolution, the Congress declares that this section is intended to constitute specific statutory authorization within the meaning of section 8(a)(1) of the War Powers Resolution." That resolution spelled out that "[t]he President is authorized . . . to use the United States Armed Forces pursuant to United Nations Security Council Resolution 678 (1990)." This was a remarkable step for an administration that before January had tried to paint a picture of its being consistently opposed to the War Powers Resolution and of its being in this regard the same as its predecessor administrations in consistently opposing the War Powers Resolution.

The House adopted the resolution 250-183, the Senate by the closer vote of 52-47. This Senate vote itself constitutes powerful argument about the importance of Congress's authorization. Only fifty-two senators voted for war; forty-seven voted against. It was an extraordinarily strong statement that a hair short of half the Senate not only did not consider itself boxed in but would have given sanctions more time and actually avoided war. Moreover, in the entire debate no member of the House or Senate suggested that the president would or could go ahead if Congress voted no. Rather, the debate reflected the contemporary understanding that the decision on war belonged to Congress.

SIGNIFICANCE OF CONGRESSIONAL AUTHORIZATION

It seemed that if anything could stand as a clear precedent for Congress rather than the president in relation to going to war, the Persian Gulf Resolution does so. It was worded as law, not as a mere expression of symbolic support. It invoked specifically the provision of the War Powers Resolution that provides for war authorization, section 8(a)(1).

Most important, the Persian Gulf Resolution followed months of hearings and days of debate, in which at every step the gravity of the war decision had been discussed constantly. No one could say afterward that Congress had failed to face and to decide the hard issue of war itself. Nothing could contrast more dramatically either with the occasion when Congress had not spoken (Korea, 1950) or when it had adopted a resolution without awareness of the consequences (Vietnam, 1964) at the time of adoption of the Tonkin Gulf Resolution. President Bush's prior deployments and his diplomatic efforts shaped the situation, but this has been true of any number of historic situations in which deployment and even provocation occurred. Deployment decisions, even provocative ones, had not constituted a precedent for presidential power to make personal decisions on war itself. Some historians consider in retrospect that President Roosevelt's 1941 embargo on oil to Japan made war largely inevitable, as the Japanese military viewed it.[58] Few fail to distinguish foreign affairs steps, deployments, and even provocation from the deliberate initiation of war itself.

Those seeking to dispute the 1991 precedent thus urge, as they must, that in the period of the actual initiation of hostilities the president did not give up explicitly his claims about his having unilateral war power. His January 8 request letter, as noted, spoke of seeking "support" without mentioning, one way or the other, "authorization." On January 9, the president said publicly that he did not think he needed a congressional resolution. Later, after Congress had adopted the Persian Gulf Resolution, the president's counsel tried to confine the significance of the enactment. The president's signing statement for the resolution, which received virtually no attention at the time, made these assertions:

"As I made clear to congressional leaders at the outset, my request for congressional support did not, and my signing this resolution does not, constitute any change in the long-standing positions of the executive branch on either the President's constitutional authority to use the Armed Forces to defend vital U.S. interests or the constitutionality of the War Powers Resolution."[59] Those invoking this signing statement will cite the statements of President Bush and his secretaries of state and defense up to December 1990, quoted above, making vague claims of war powers.

This theory of presidential prerogative based on statements prior to, or after, the key debates on the Persian Gulf Resolution has no persuasive power when considered in the context of the actual enactment. As Secretary Cheney told President Bush on January 6 and 8, claims of unilateral presidential power would never be taken seriously after the president sent to Congress a request such as he did. No one has questioned in retrospect that the congressional enactment of the declaration of war in 1917 firmly established World War I as a precedent for congressional, not presidential, determination about war. It matters not a bit that President Wilson mentioned at the time that he felt he already had such authority "by the plain implication of my constitutional duties and powers" and that he had simply decided "in the present circumstances, not to act upon general implications."[60]

Moreover, the theory put forth in President Bush's signing statement simply ignored the president's change of position in making his request. What the president said to congressional leaders "at the outset," that is, in the period immediately after August 2, long predated the president's January 8 request. As the contemporaneous reporting captured vividly, months of presidential indecision about whether to ask Congress preceded the request letter, but that indecision ended with the sending of the letter.

The president had not made his request with any accompanying assertion of presidential prerogative, for that would have been wildly clashing and inconsistent, if not insulting, to the public and to Congress. Had any such assertion of presidential prerogative been expressed clearly enough to be taken seriously, it would have destroyed the two benefits President Bush reaped from his request: consonance with the strong public opinion in favor of having Congress vote to decide on war and added support within Congress from having made the request. President Bush had no intention of making such a foolish assertion at such a price, and he did not let any administration figures do so.

Such Bush White House signing statements often have offered false views of the preceding legislative history inconsistent with reality. A profile of C. Boyden Gray revealed that he was doing the same thing this time, for the true history was that he had sought, but failed, to impede the president's decision to ask Congress for the resolution: "Gray also argued that a congressional resolution in support of the Persian Gulf war would constitute an encroachment on presidential powers, but lost out to Bush's desire for political support."[61] For the president's counsel to suggest that the authorization the president got was not something he had asked for amounted to a naked attempt to rewrite history differently than it actually happened.

One other theory of presidential power warrants comment. The administration had pursued the strategy of having the Security Council adopt a resolution for use of force against Iraq. Executive power enthusiasts during this period had tried, and may well try again, to conflate international law on relations among nations with domestic law on relations among the branches of the American government. A Security Council resolution provided legal justification for use of force against another nation as a matter of international law, but it had nothing to do with American participation in war as a matter of domestic American constitutional law. Congress had not surrendered its power to decide on war to the United Nations any more than it had surrendered its powers to decide on taxes and appropriations. Security Council approval of force was an argument for Congress to consider, not a substitute for its action. A leading scholar, Professor Michael J. Glennon, commented, "It is laudable that the President succeeded in getting the approval of Ethiopia, Finland, Colombia and other members of the Security Council to use force, but . . . . [the fact that] the permanent representative of Ethiopia favors or opposes the introduction of the United States Armed Forces into hostilities is, constitutionally, a matter of the utmost inconsequence."[62]

In sum, President Bush initially tried to make of the Iraq war decision a supreme example of his Administration's general approach. He did succeed in delaying the issue until after the November 1990 midterm election, fulfilling his central desire to avoid having to make himself democratically accountable by appeals to the public. However, he failed in his effort commenced in November and December 1990 to govern without Congress by staking out a sovereign's prerogative to decide on war. Forces of public opinion and congressional determination in January 1991 proved too powerful for him. President Bush ultimately acknowledged that the president's place regarding the decision on war was to lead not by personal will, as at first he intended, but by persuading the country to grant him authority through the democratic process. Congress's efforts to confine the Cold War instances—Korea and Vietnam—to their particular period and to restore the pre-1950 constitutional division of authority regarding war reached fruition. The responsibility for the ultimate decision on war rested where it belongs: not in the rule of one man, but in the consent of the governed through their representatives in Congress.

7

Conclusion: Temporary Respite

On November 3, 1992, over 104 million voters went to the polls, making an extraordinary political statement both by the size and the results of their turnout. This level of participation broke not only past records but a historical trend of almost thirty years' duration. Voter participation had previously slid steadily downward, from lack of interest or alienation, to a low of 50.1 percent voter participation in 1988. The 1992 election excited potential voters to the highest turnout rate for any national election since 1968, a 55.2 percent level of participation. Bush, Clinton, and Ross Perot had fought down to the wire on issues high and low from economic policy to alleged lack of patriotism. The popular boom for Perot, who had dropped out of the race and then returned, added a major element of interest.

When the polls closed, President Bush had lost; candidate Clinton had won. That result captures two questions posed by the presidential strategy discussed in this book. The first chapter began by assessing how the 1988 Bush election, by bringing a president to office with no mandate, dealt the incoming administration its political hand. Subsequent chapters reviewed the play of that hand. The 1992 election allows its scoring. Thus, the first order of business in this final chapter is to examine whether the electorate's 1992 decision was a judgment about the Bush Administration's four-year strategy for a semi-sovereign presidency that tried to govern without Congress.

The question posed is, Did the 1992 electoral result put the semi-sovereign presidency to rest or only provide a temporary respite? Clinton's campaign and the early Clinton Administration indicated that a respite from sovereign claims would occur in presidential strategy. President Bush's strategy used White House staff and novel vehicles of power; the Clinton Administration strategy restored the primacy of public and congressional debate as the focus of policy decisions. President Bush had disengaged for reasons of personal style and political forces from policy appeals and compromises over legislation; candidate Clinton promised, and President Clinton acted, to push a major legislative program requiring active engagement both in public appeals and legislative compromises.

President Clinton's actions do not determine, however, whether the respite from the Bush Administration strategy will be permanent or temporary. This chapter analyzes the potential for the elements of the Bush Administration strategy to arise again, phoenixlike, at some time in the future. Tendencies toward personal rule and institutional abuses in the White House—the thrust toward attributes of sovereign rule—may be expected to recur. A last section, drawing on my experience with the judiciary in separation of powers cases, will suggest why the chief counterbalance to these recurring tendencies—the chief defense of the constitutional system of checks and balances—will remain not the judiciary but Congress.

THE 1992 ELECTION

Public opinion analysts found several appropriate measures of what the 1992 vote expressed. They started with the stunning dimensions of the public rejection of the Bush Presidency. In four years, the vote for George Bush declined from 53 percent in 1988 to 37 percent in 1992, a sixteen-point drop. Historians had few precedents for sitting presidents receiving under 40 percent of the popular vote in a quest for reelection or dropping in vote level by a margin as large as Bush's. As one analyst noted, "[e]xcept for Taft's 23.2 percent in the special party-bolt circumstances of 1912, this was the lowest ever recorded by an incumbent president seeking reelection."[1]

Professor Walter Dean Burnham explained that "Bush lost just under 30 percent of his 1988 voting base. Only Herbert Hoover in 1932, John Adams in 1800, and, of course, Taft in 1912 presided over worse coalitional collapses, and in the cases of Hoover and Adams they were not very much worse."[2] Considering that more voters came to the polls, President Bush suffered a huge drop in the absolute numbers, as well as the percentage, of his voter support. His 39.1 million votes in 1992 were nearly 10 million fewer than in 1988. To find a vote total for a Republican presidential candidate as low as Bush's 1992 figure required going back twenty-four years to a far smaller electorate.

Even Hoover, blamed for the nation's worst depression, had not fallen in percentage of voting support as low as Bush. As one analyst stated, in his article "Bush's Passive Presidency": "[v]oters dealt him a historic slap. Bush's 38 per cent share of the popular vote was the smallest received by any President in U.S. history other than William Howard Taft, who finished third with 23 per cent in 1912. Bush fared even worse (albeit in a three-way race) than Herbert Hoover did in drawing 39.6 per cent during the Depression in 1932."[3] It was, as Professor Burnham commented, "one of the great train wrecks of all time."[4]

Opinion poll analysts had no trouble finding the central theme of expression by the 1992 electorate. In contrast to 1988, when the country voted primarily for continuity, in 1992 it voted primarily for change. The public expressed an extraordinary depth of pessimism about the nation's economic and social situation coupled with cynicism about the federal government. One key indicator, the level of those agreeing that the nation was on the "wrong track," reached the peak of 80 percent. This figure had hit only 70 to 73 percent in pessimistic years such as 1974 (with the themes of Watergate and recession induced by the Organization of Petroleum Exporting Countries [OPEC]) and 1980 (with the themes of inflation and a brief rise in unemployment).[5] Voters on election day selected as the candidate quality mattering most that he "[w]ill bring about needed change." With 38 percent citing this quality as the most important, it far outranked experience, judgment in a crisis, honesty, caring, convictions, or party affiliation. It dominated the election.

President Bush had known the public mood of anger at government inaction earlier in the year. He tried to direct the anger at the Congress and failed. In early 1992, President Bush set a deadline for action on his own tax proposals. In March 1992 Congress responded by enacting an alternative package that raised taxes on very high incomes, and President Bush vetoed the bill. His accompanying speech condemned Congress, as *Congressional Quarterly* described:

> In a speech on March 20, Bush said Democrats "could not resist their natural impulse to raise taxes" and announced even before receiving the bill that he had signed his veto message. He used the occasion to launch a broad attack against the Democrat-controlled Congress, saying "it is no longer accountable to individual American citizens and voters, and this must change."
>
> The highly partisan speech capped a day of moves by the administration that signaled that Bush will try to salvage his slumping popularity with an election-year offensive against Congress.[7]

In August, President Bush's 1992 renomination acceptance speech likened him in fighting a Congress controlled by the opposition party to President Truman in 1948: "Join me in rolling away the roadblock at the other end of Pennsylvania Avenue. . . . [F]orty-four years ago, in another age of uncertainty, a different president embarked on a similar mission. His name was Harry S Truman."[8] By making that comparison, President Bush drew attention to the potential for lack of visible, accountable policymaking and ensuing public anger in the recurring postwar divided government. In 1948, President Truman had blamed gridlock—a term not yet invented, but a phenomenon well appreciated—on a Republican Congress. President Bush invoked Truman as a symbol of a president who succeeded in turning public anger at gridlock into feelings against Congress and a winning presidential reelection theme.

However, where Truman succeeded, Bush failed. Facing a divided government in 1947 and 1948, President Truman had put forth a major foreign and domestic agenda. In foreign affairs, he had reached a bipartisan agreement with the Republican Congress, notably the doctrine of containing the Soviet Union in Europe by the Marshall Plan for rebuilding Western Europe and the Truman Doctrine of propping up anticommunist forces in Greece and Turkey. In domestic affairs, Truman had not tried to govern through White House staff but had put his effort into public appeals for his specific legislative program and into publicly fighting with the "do-nothing" Congress for popular support.

In contrast, President Bush had declined Truman's course of conflict and compromise—of putting forth a major legislative agenda as the basis for public debate. Throughout his term, he had disengaged by not putting forth a program and instead resorted to the strategy of personal rule. In 1992, the public judged the ensuing gridlock as the president's fault, not, as in 1948, as a partisan fault of the Congress. Having selected change as the key quality, voters rejected President Bush as the antithesis of a change agent. He drew less than one in five, or 19 percent, of those outcome-determinative 1992 voters who considered the important quality in a president to be that he "[w]ill bring about needed change."

In polls on the question of whether "government would work better if all new people were elected this year," about the same number disagreed as agreed. Even as the vote for Bush plummeted from 1988, the partisan split in Congress changed little from the midterm congressional election of two years earlier. Republicans neither gained nor lost Senate seats and gained a mere ten House seats. Only twenty-four House incumbents were defeated on November 3, far fewer than earlier projections.[9] The nation did elect a large freshman House class, but for many reasons it did so without partisan or ideological shift. Many new freshmen resulted from the decennial redrawing of district boundaries after the 1990 census.[10] Together with reshuffling from redrawn boundaries, and issues that cut across party lines such as House bank overdrafts, extensive turnover from retirements and primary defeats replaced former members with new ones from the same party. These substitutions proved to have little partisan or ideological dimension. Apparently, the voters did not dislike the Congress's existing ideological views or its Democratic majorities in both chambers.

Voters did decide that they disliked divided government. Asked "which is better for the country," a "President and Congress of the same party," or "President of one party, Congress of other," 62 percent favored president and Congress of the same party and only 28 percent favored divided government.[11] By opposing divided government, and putting the blame on the president rather than the Democratic Congress, the popular vote and opinion constituted a major repudiation of the Bush Administration's strategy for dealing with divided government.

When polls asked the public which issues mattered most, 43 percent said the economy and jobs, 21 percent said the budget deficit, and 20 percent said health care.[12] Among the voters who thought foreign policy mattered most, President Bush obtained an overwhelming majority, but a meager 6 percent of voters included foreign policy among the issues that mattered most. The public's emphasis on the economic issues challenged the premises of the Bush Administration approach. Sununu's strategy in 1991 had contemplated running on "Kuwait, crime, and quotas." The Bush White House strategy for governance controlled two of those three issues, Iraq through national security channels and the 1991 Civil Rights Act through signing statements. Yet, in the 1992 election those issues subject to the White House strategy had the least impact with the public whereas the issues beyond the reach of the strategy mattered to the voters the most. President Bush's strategy for governing without Congress had not allowed him to do much about the economy, fiscal policy, or domestic sectors requiring legislative reform such as health care.

Of course, because voters cared most about the economy, it could be argued that President Bush simply fell victim to the recession, as other presidents before him had lost because of unpopular economic developments. Although the Bush Administration's economic activity or inactivity has not been the focus of this book, in some respects even the economy as an issue accords with the other themes of the Bush Administration. The public was concerned with the administration's style of disengaging from Congress instead of fighting or compromising, as well as the economy's performance. As observers pointed out in contrasting Franklin D. Roosevelt's success in 1936 with Herbert Hoover's failure in 1932, Roosevelt had failed to end the depression, just as Hoover had failed. However, President Roosevelt presented a style of vigorous activism and major legislative activity. He worked with Congress and showed results in the public arena. Notwithstanding the continuation of the depression, he won reelection in 1936 by a landslide. President Bush, who followed a strategy of disengagement, neither working with Congress nor fighting it, could not overcome the public's anger about economic problems and lack of visible governmental action.[13]

THE CLINTON ADMINISTRATION'S DIFFERENT STRATEGY

The Clinton Campaign

The election of 1992 put an end at least temporarily to the strategy of disengagement and the ideology of presidential "personal rule." Candidate

Clinton campaigned on a promise of policy change and won with a mandate for change, both sharply different from the campaign of candidate Bush in 1988. What the country expected after the 1992 campaign and outcome could not occur by White House fiat but required legislative action.

Candidate Clinton's campaign positions exhibited this quite clearly. Of course, he had used the word "change" and talked about change a great deal, but so had President Bush. The difference lay in the extent to which Clinton campaigned on specific positions that would require engaging with Congress and the public to produce legislative action. At the heart of his campaign lay promises of a new economic program and of health care legislation, issues that formed the main early themes in his administration. Also, candidate Clinton made additional promises to engage in a struggle for legislative action on many other issues.

The formal Clinton campaign book, *Putting People First: How We Can All Change America*, summed up the extent of proposals for legislative action. Clinton's plan started with bills passed by Congress that President Bush had vetoed and that Clinton would want to sign: bills on family leave, voter registration, and campaign finance. The plan went on to list a number of bills Clinton would want to get enacted: the Freedom of Choice Act regarding abortion, the Violence Against Women Act, the Brady Bill for gun control, a strengthened Community Reinvestment Act against redlining, and a bill to reform labor workplace organizing.[14]

Apart from these commitments to engage in an active process of legislating, Clinton made a number of commitments for change on issues that the Bush Administration had handled through its strategy of governing without Congress. Clinton's environmental policy pledges envisioned action against the positions established by President Bush through the Quayle Council and signing statements. These included Clinton pledges on wetlands, citizen environmental suits, and enforcement of the Clean Air Act. He challenged the Bush courtship of Saddam Hussein and the Bush signing statement on the 1991 Civil Rights Act.[15]

The point here is not that the positions taken by candidate Clinton were all clear or correct (or all unclear or incorrect) but that they committed him to an entirely different operating strategy than that of the Bush Administration. Clinton did not always disagree with President Bush's attempts to oppose Congress's constitutional powers: Candidate Clinton gave repeated and enthusiastic support to a demand for the line-item veto, just as President Bush had sought it.[16] Rather, the Clinton campaign's content of pledges for legislative action contrasted with the 1988 Bush campaign on symbols with its implicit promises of continuity and lack of substantive change. The 1989 Doonesbury cartoon caption for his predecessor's first day could not be rerun: "So far today, I've said the Pledge and I haven't joined the ACLU and I haven't furloughed any murderers. I've delivered on my entire mandate, and it isn't even lunch yet."

The Clinton Administration's Fiscal Program

Even an abbreviated view of the beginning of the Clinton term similarly reflects a sharp change from the disengaged Bush strategy and a redirection toward a quest for legislative action. Ironically, the closest parallel to Clinton's opening moves in 1993 lay in president Reagan's beginning in 1981, in his strategy of working through Congress even though the ideological thrust of the proposed program was completely opposite. President Reagan endorsed a massive tax cut for upper-bracket taxpayers in his 1980 campaign. President Clinton endorsed a tax increase for upper-bracket taxpayers in his 1992 campaign. Although going in diametrically opposite directions, they both promised major legislative action and they both came to Washington determined to obtain it.

Moreover, the subtle rules of congressional procedure even guaranteed that Presidents Reagan and Clinton would have to follow surprisingly similar initial sequences.[17] Under the congressional Budget Act, the chief tool for enactment of an overall program, Congress adopts a budget resolution each spring that serves as the general blueprint of its fiscal program for that year. Hence, both President Reagan in 1981 and President Clinton in 1993 had to engage first in the struggle to obtain enactment of a budget resolution with the broad outlines of their programs. For both, the budget resolution provided the necessary higher-level decisions about the scale of tax changes.[18]

Both differed in this regard sharply from President Bush in 1989. As *Congressional Quarterly Almanac* put it, on February 9, 1989, President Bush had made his budget speech for "laying out a fiscal agenda that had been virtually invisible during his campaign." With unusual acerbity, *Congressional Quarterly Almanac* described Bush's steps as making a "thinly detailed set of budget proposals for fiscal 1990" that amounted to a "nonbudget budget." A negotiated agreement with congressional leaders followed, which essentially avoided major legislation by optimistic economic assumptions; "the deal was based largely on the administration's premise that the nation's economy would not only continue to grow, but would do so at a healthier clip than most economists believed possible."[19]

In contrast to President Bush's 1989 strategy of ducking and avoiding the budget process as a means for legislating changes, Presidents Reagan in 1981 and Clinton in 1993 each embraced the process and girded themselves for a yearlong struggle to enact the desired changes. The Budget Act guaranteed each of them a double-header struggle. After the spring fight over the budget resolution, Clinton, like Reagan, would then face a second fight. Later in the year, Congress carried out the budget resolution by enacting the lengthy and detailed actual legislation that changes taxes and spending. This comes in the form of one or two bills that "reconcile" the current projected spending and revenue levels with the levels endorsed in the budget resolution. The effort to enact those "reconciliation" bills becomes the battlefield for a president—Reagan in 1981, Clinton in 1993—to fight for the detailed content of his program for fiscal change. The most significant procedural difference was in which chamber the fight would be hardest. For President Reagan, the nominal Democratic majority in the House ensured in 1981 the largest battle there. For President Clinton, the size and procedural rights of the Republican minority in the Senate, demonstrated by its successful April 1993 filibuster against his short-term stimulus package and by the June 1993 dropping of his proposed BTU energy tax, guaranteed the major battle there.

Clinton's struggle to obtain final passage of his deficit reduction bill in August 1993 created some strong contrasts with the Bush Administration. That administration had refused to attempt to move major legislation even when, after the Persian Gulf War, its favorable approval ratings soared to near 90 percent in spring 1991. In contrast, President Clinton fought for passage of his deficit reduction bill—the reconciliation bill attempting to reduce the deficit approximately $500 billion over five years—all the way to a razor-thin margin of victory in August 1993. The House passed the final conference version without a single representative to spare; the Senate passed it by a vote of fifty-fifty and the vice president's tie-breaking vote. President Clinton had demonstrated—as President Reagan had in 1981—determination to govern not by avoidance of Congress or unilateral fiat but by moving an entire fiscal program through hard-won success in the Congress. President Clinton demonstrated the same again in commencing in fall 1993 the massive effort to enact a system-wide program of health care reform.

The Clinton National Security Team

Clinton's campaign and early term gave a number of indications of some change in the realm of national security from the Bush Administration's strategy. The 1992 election was the first presidential election after the end of the Cold War. In the preceding four years the controversial international issue had been Iraq, not the communist bloc. In his campaign, Clinton endorsed a detailed position on Iraq put forth by vice-presidential candidate Al Gore on September 19, 1992, entitled "Bush-Quayle Iraq Policy: Profound Errors, Duplicity, Cover-Up." Gore gave a detailed and thoroughly documented address on the Bush Administration policy of courting Saddam Hussein.

Gore began by describing Bush's favorable views toward Saddam Hussein even after Congress turned against Iraq at the end of 1988. Then, Gore focused in on the National Security Directive on Iraq: "[I]n the midst of this flood of highly alarming information [about Iraq], on October 2, 1989, President Bush signed a document known as NSD-26, which established policy toward Iraq under his Administration. This document is the benchmark for judging George Bush's record for direction of American policy toward Iraq in the period that would ultimately lead to war. . . ." Gore found the fundamental errors of the Bush Administration policy toward Iraq inherent in NSD-26:

> NSD-26 mandated the pursuit of improved economic and political ties with Iraq on the assumption that Iraqi behavior could be modified by means of new favors to be granted. . . . The text of NSD-26 blindly ignores the evidence already at the Administration's disposal of Iraqi behavior in the past regarding human rights, terrorism, the use of chemical weapons, and the pursuit of advanced weapons of mass destruction.

Finally, Gore tied NSD-26 to the meeting on the brink of war between Glaspie and Saddam Hussein: "Much has been said about the record of our Ambassador to Iraq April Glaspie's famous interview of July 25th with Saddam Hussein. But the Ambassador's servile message was a clear expression of Bush's personal views. Her message was totally in line with US policy as laid down by President Bush in October 1989, and clung to until August 2, 1990, when Iraq invaded, conquered, and annexed Kuwait." Characteristically, Ross Perot, in the third presidential debate on October 20, 1992, challenged President Bush thusly: "Let's go back in terms of accepting responsibility for your actions. If you create Saddam Hussein, over a 10-year period, using billions of dollars of U.S. taxpayer money, step up to the plate and say it was a mistake."

The Clinton-Gore campaign had thus relied upon a critique of the Bush Administration's national security strategy, made possible by the Bush strategy of governing through the unaccountable tool of NSD-26.

Revelations about Iraqgate continued to emerge in 1993. One particularly official pronouncement came in an opinion by federal judge Marvin H. Shoob of Atlanta. In August 1993, he sentenced the lesser officials of the Banco Nazionale del Lavoro, whose Atlanta branch had illegally loaned about four billion dollars to Iraq. Judge Shoob's opinion outlined how information about BNL had flowed into the NSC system, which had nevertheless pressed forward with its program of supporting Iraq and opposing Congressional sanctions:

> In the fall of 1989, shortly after the raid on BNL-Atlanta . . . . [t]here were at least two telephone calls from a junior attorney in the White House counsel's

office to the chief prosecutor in this case; the calls sought information concerning the case in connection with the decision to approve loan guarantees. In the spring of 1990, the prosecutors and investigators were invited to Washington on at least one occasion to discuss the case with National Security Council staff members and other administration officials concerned about the approval of a second tranche of loan guarantees.[20]

With the start of the new administration, President Clinton indicated a change in strategy from that of Bush by his choice of the new national security team. His secretary of state, Warren Christopher, after his term as deputy secretary of state from 1977 to 1981, had authored one of the leading constructive approaches to relations between president and Congress in matters of foreign affairs.

Entitled "Ceasefire Between the Branches: A Compact in Foreign Affairs" and published in Foreign Affairs in 1982, Christopher's discussion began with an unusual acknowledgment of a former (and future) high executive branch official: "The ordeals of Vietnam and Watergate exposed grave perils to our constitutional structure—an accumulation of vast power in the President's hands, and room for enormous abuse."[21] The article admitted the correctness of much of the congressional critique of executive supremacy, blaming part of the war power disputes on "expansive constitutional premises originating in the Executive Branch" and recognizing that "neither absolute secrecy nor unfettered Executive supremacy is consistent with democratic ideals."

Christopher had thought about the same issues of constitutional separation of powers in foreign affairs that President Bush and his White House counsel had, but his conclusions contrasted sharply with Bush's 1991 Princeton Address. Where the Bush Princeton Address sought to justify secrecy against Congress as necessary for the president to conduct foreign policy on his own, Christopher embraced openness: "The obligation of comity holds especially for sharing information and for consultation, so that Congress can share in the broad design of policy and oversee its execution. There are cases, of course, where Executive privilege is appropriate, and where sensitive information must be closely guarded. But they should be understood as rare exceptions to the rule." He cited his own practice during the 1979–1980 Iranian Embassy hostage crisis as an example:

> In my own experience, I recall very few instances in which the added risk of a leak on Capitol Hill outweighed the potential damage that excessive secrecy would cause. During the 444 days the hostages were held, I provided periodic secret briefings on Iran and Afghanistan to the Senate and House leadership—sometimes daily, usually twice a week—and there was never a significant violation of the confidential relationship that was established.[22]

The Clinton Administration's choice of Christopher thus suggested the possibility of an era of informing and consulting with Congress, which would constitute a major shift not merely from the Bush Administration strategy but from most of the Cold War era.

President Clinton's choice of Anthony Lake as his national security adviser seemed to hold out a similar promise. Lake had spent most of his career as a foreign service officer or, during the Reagan-Bush years, as an academic. His formative experience in government appeared to have been his early work on the NSC staff in 1969 and 1970 as personal aide to Henry Kissinger. At the time when Kissinger built the position of national security adviser into an unrivaled instrument of unilateral presidential power, Lake had resigned in protest over the president's decision on the May 1970 invasion of Cambodia. This was a pivotal point in the development of congressional determination to curtail the extreme development of presidential sovereignty and was a crucial step in the evolution of the War Powers Resolution. Following Lake's resignation, the Nixon Administration wiretapped him as it had wiretapped a number of former Kissinger aides who also left in this period. It was an experience calculated to destroy Lake's or anyone else's illusions about the wisdom of having national security policymaking occur in a secretive and unaccountable NSC staff. As one observer concluded in 1993, "Lake and [his deputy Sandy] Berger, for the most part, are regarded as well-suited to the roles of honest brokers in the policy process and are not expected to try to dominate it the way Kissinger did when he ran the NSC for President Nixon."[23]

The new administration's team proved in practice far more willing than its predecessors to attend to public and congressional concerns with respect to overseas conflicts. In spring 1993, the House and Senate each adopted authorizations for the initial U.S.-led mission in Somalia. In September, Congress passed a resolution asking the administration to justify its operation. As the Somalian warlord inflicted casualties, Congress continued to react, and the president heeded congressional reaction. Even more pointedly, as proposals circulated for U.S. forces to participate in peacekeeping in Bosnia, President Clinton voluntarily embraced the kind of criteria that his predecessor had rejected until pressed by powerful national forces. President Clinton told a news conference that for U.S. forces to participate, "I would want a clear expression of support from the U.S. Congress."[24]

ONLY TEMPORARY RESPITE?

Likely Recurrence

Nevertheless, when a longer view is taken, a temporary cessation of the Bush "personal rule" approach to government provides little reason to expect the permanent demise of that approach, on either political or institutional grounds. A common political thread runs through the Watergate era in 1973 and 1974, the Iran-contra era in 1985 and 1986, and the Bush Administration. These peaks of attempts at presidential sovereignty all occurred during eras of divided government when the administration had just won a presidential election without a particularly clear mandate for legislative action. President Nixon in 1972 and President Reagan in 1984 won reelection without clear positive policy themes. They had done most of what they intended to do and could do in enacting legislation during their first terms.

Moreover, the 1972 and 1984 elections had both returned firm Democratic majorities to Congress, further denying the president a mandate for legislative action. The peculiarity of President Bush in 1988 lay in his arriving at that point—election without a theme and without support in Congress—when he had not even had a first-term program, denying him the initial periods of successful interaction in the public arena characterizing the first terms of Presidents Nixon and Reagan. The result was his reliance on White House staff much earlier in his tenure than his predecessors had in theirs.

Thus, this condition—first terms like President Bush's and second terms like President Nixon's and Reagan's—consists of presidents who win real election victories of their own but have no legislative program and face a Congress of the opposite party. Such presidents have White House staffs with the hubris of election victory but without the constraint of ties to a Congress of their own party. Lacking a program, those presidents and their staffs come to consider the system of checks and balances not as an opportunity for victory by successful legislative enactment but purely as an obstacle and an oversight burden that seems unfair in light of their presidential election victory. Moreover, there is no strong reason to think it matters unduly in such a situation which party in the divided government has the presidency. The one divided postwar government with a Democratic president—President Truman's after the 1946 election put Republican majorities into the House and Senate—did not manifest sovereign tendencies comparable to Watergate, Iran-contra, or the Bush Administration. However, it came at a time when divided government was still seen as the aberrant exception it had been in the first half of the twentieth century, and the president and his staff viewed their immediate condition as a temporary one, not, as it later came to be seen, a chronic one.

Moreover, President Truman did establish after his election the supreme postwar precedent of unilateral executive assumption of power, namely, the commitment of the nation to the Korean War in 1950 without Congress. Much later, looking back after Vietnam and Watergate, historians recognized that precedent as more than the Cold War oddity it seemed at the time but rather as a turning point toward unilateral presidential exercise of the war power. As Arthur Schlesinger put it, "By insisting that the presidential prerogative sufficed to meet the requirements of the Constitution [for war], Truman . . . . dramatically and dangerously enlarged the power of future Presidents to take the nation into major war."[25] Either party holding the presidency can play the sovereign's cards when it prefers not to work with the Congress.

Although the postwar decline of voter loyalty to party and the increase in ticket splitting increased greatly the frequency of divided government, that did not cause by itself the recurrent tendencies toward executive sovereignty. Sometimes even the president and Congress of a divided government conclude that the public elected them to achieve policy outcomes together. Depending in part on the president's own personal style, he may compromise or struggle with Congress in public and legitimate channels, as Presidents Truman and Eisenhower demonstrated in different ways. However, a president may be reelected, as in 1972 and 1984, or initially elected, as in 1988, both with a divided government, and with the further condition that his election does not seem to him to direct outcomes in the congressional and public arenas. Instead, the president may think himself justified in governing without Congress. Such circumstances nurture ideologies of unilateral executive governance in a president and his staff.

These combined conditions of divided government and perceived lack of need to engage with Congress have led in two directions. In one, selective pursuit of particular goals to the point of indifference to legality has led the White House staff to act without legal justification. Watergate and Iran-contra reflected this. In such circumstances, presidential staffs break the law, and faced with investigation they resort to perjury and obstruction. Alternatively, comprehensive pursuit of general disengagement from Congress allowed the Bush staff to take on new powers under a strategy calculated to use legal tools as cover. The first pattern is criminal; the second undermines the constitutional checks and balances. History suggests that in this postwar era of divided government, one or the other pattern may be seen as likely to occur following elections or reelections of presidents without legislative programs.

Preventive Arrangements

If political forces again create the simple conditions of divided government and electoral success without mandates, what will prevent recurrence of executive abuses? The chief question is whether institutional arrangements, including such matters as the War Powers Resolution or the system of intelligence oversight, can prevent or mitigate abuses. Believers in presidential prerogative posit an eternally power-greedy Congress capable of constantly expanding its control and paralyzing—"tethering" and "fettering"—the executive. Some reformers might imagine a Congress capable, in a good cause, of completely institutionalizing control.

The field of war powers suggests the more complex workings both of congressional interest and of institutional arrangements. Although members of Congress desire in general to take part in decisions on war, they only sometimes desire to do so enough to accept the responsibility of controversial record votes. In 1950 and 1964, the Korean and Vietnam wars occurred or expanded without clear congressional authorization not only because presidents did not seek such authorization when they should have but also because Congress did not seek responsibility when it could have. If President Truman would not ask for a vote on the Korean War, if President Johnson would ask only for a vague and undebated resolution of support (the Tonkin Gulf Resolution), then those in Congress also declined to insist upon more responsibility than they had been asked to assume. They did not insist on a meaningful authorizing vote, and by a guilty collaboration of the two political branches the war power slipped out of the hands intended by the Framers and expected by the public to hold it.

The same dynamics have occurred sometimes even after the War Powers Resolution, although the new institutional arrangements and soberer national mood have prevented anything as stark as 1950 and 1964. Perhaps the Persian Gulf tanker reflagging and convoy operation of 1987 provided the most serious example. Although the country could view it as a deployment of forces rather than a commencement of hostilities and ultimately it did not lead to war, it might well have done so. The United States sent major naval forces into the Persian Gulf war zone in a manner that could have led directly to war through either escalation of provocations or accident, when Iraq attacked the U.S. frigate *Stark* in May 1987 or when incidents occurred with Iranian forces in July and September 1987.

Both the House and Senate in 1987 gave serious consideration to fulfilling the spirit of the War Powers Resolution by voting on a measure to address the situation. Ultimately, however, the Senate passed a minimal resolution and the House passed nothing at all. This occurred, in part, from the lesson Congress had drawn from the adoption four years earlier of the Multinational Forces in Lebanon Resolution. Although the loss of American life in Lebanon in 1983 was tragic, at least the intervention had been debated and authorized by Congress. The precedent had confirmed the congressional role in war authorization. Hearings, debates, and votes gave Congress its proper role; they also focused national attention on the weak basis for the intervention, speeding the pullout that occurred after the terrorist attack on the Marine barracks.

Nonetheless, Lebanon apparently taught members of Congress the downside as well as the upside of the system of checks and balances, which led to shirking of responsibility over reflagging in 1987. As Barry M. Blechman concluded, in 1987 "[l]ike the Senate, the House feared the political consequences. . . . After the experience of Beirut, few members of Congress wished to share in the responsibility for future casualties."[26] Institutional arrangements such as the War Powers Resolution and precedents did not suffice to make Congress vote as its role in the separation of powers might suggest. Politics could drive Congress not into exercising its proper role but into evading it. The Cold War seems to have worked a change in public perceptions of the separation of powers that may outlast the Cold War itself.

This does not mean that protective legislation, institutional arrangements, and precedents are nullities. Just over three years later, regarding the Iraq war in January 1991, Congress again faced the question of whether to vote on an authorizing resolution. Institutional arrangements and precedents did help steel Congress's resolve. The public itself demanded a vote. In December 1990, the House Democratic Caucus took a crucial straw vote, which helped solidify the centrist moderate position that it was most important for a congressional decision to occur regardless of whether the result was for war or against war. The factors that brought about a legitimate congressional authorizing vote included public polls, the post-Vietnam military desire for concrete public authorization, the congressional straw votes, timing that allowed the new Congress to convene in time for a vote, and the fact that President Bush finally yielded to the advantages of seeking a vote.

In place of the conservative fantasy of a Congress always greedy for power—or, for that matter, the image often presented in the press of a Congress always cowardly shirking duties—these real examples suggest a more realistic model. Congress will sometimes take power and responsibility and sometimes avoid them. Much depends on institutions and precedents, on presidential attitudes, on the timing and particulars of the situation, and on the public's view. Constitutional understanding and institutional arrangements can help, but each situation is unique and requires an assessment of many factors.

A similar conclusion could come from other examples in this book. By 1986, Congress had tamed the Reagan Administration's regulatory review system. Despite the congressionally compelled reforms, the Quayle Council revived a much greater abuse of that system. It took from 1990 to 1992 for Congress to respond by investigation and appropriation provision, and even then, at the end of 1992, Congress had not enacted appropriation provisions, just as it had not enacted a reflagging resolution in 1987. Given the strong political base of business's dislike of regulation, Congress simply does not react reflexively against White House regulatory review. As with war powers, the response to executive assertions of prerogative depends on the mix of institutional arrangements and precedents, presidential actions, and the public's view.

The single biggest question regarding institutional arrangements in coming years will be whether the end of the Cold War will lead to a curbing of the NSC system. That system consists of an arrangement that is appropriate for wartime but has persisted in peacetime. It includes powerful White House staffs who come to expect to exercise authority; vehicles of secret law that propagate authority without public supervision; and doctrines of executive privilege that prevent accountability even to the responsible committees in Congress. Vague but ever-available doctrines of unilateral presidential supremacy in foreign affairs lie readily at hand to justify whatever grows out of the NSC system.

Past reforms have simply not dealt with the problem. The intelligence reforms of the 1970s curbed many abuses, but not those directly traceable to the NSC system. In particular, even the Hughes-Ryan provision requiring presidential findings to be reported to Congress did not prevent the NSC from covertly running a war in Nicaragua in 1985 and 1986. The scrutiny of Iran-contra curbed some abuses, notably the tendency of the NSC staff to take operational control of providing arms. Still, regarding the courtship of Saddam Hussein the NSC system evaded any prior checks, using its directives and committees to favor Iraq.

In the face of this record, the nation can expect only a temporary respite, not a permanent lesson, from presidential separation of powers strategies like those of the Bush Administration. Some of the post-Nixon efforts at buttressing the system of checks and balances may well occur. Just as impoundments became obsolete after the Nixon Administration, so, for some time in the near future, no president may make the kind of abuse of signing statements that characterized the Bush Administration. Moreover, abuse of regulatory review has a significant chance of being curbed for some time. Not only did the Clinton Administration abolish the Quayle Council, but in October 1993 it promulgated a new Executive Order 12866 on Regulatory Planning and Review. That order placed major responsibility in the Office of Information and Regulatory Affairs, a statutory office subject to oversight by Congress. It provided extensive assurances of a public record for outside communications and limited the role of the vice president and president to resolution of conflicts rather than conducting assignments at the behest of interested industries. The order appeared to provide numerous protections against the reappearance of a linkage of regulation-affected industries, campaign contributions, back-channel communications, and a White House staff with great power and no accountability.[27]

Yet the basic elements of presidential claims for personal power will remain. There is little reason to expect major institutional reform at the NSC. Sooner or later, an administration will want to use foreign policy powers without having to account to Congress or the public and without having to depend on the Departments of State and Defense. That administration will find the NSC staff, with its tools like directives and committees, still ready, willing, and able. Until the recurrence of some gross misjudgment on the scale of the courtship of Saddam Hussein, Congress and the public will find little to do about the revival of that approach.

As for signing statements, it is always possible, but far from certain, that the judiciary will develop legal doctrines to render them nonthreatening. The most likely judicial course would be simply to avoid the issue, citing signing statements when they accept something said in them and ignoring them otherwise, without ever making them a central focus. As a result, the signing statement would remain a tool for some future White House, particularly in those contexts, like foreign affairs and defense, which rarely lend themselves to adjudication in any case.

These post-Bush prospects suggest that in the postwar era some of the most fundamental aspects of the system of checks and balances have been altered in a lasting way. The American system of separated executive and legislative branches always contrasted with a parliamentary system that ensured same-party control of both branches. However, in the early twentieth century the political parties themselves maintained limited qualities of a parliamentary system. With divided government a rarity, same-party control tended to be the norm even without the requirements of parliamentary government. Voters could and did hold the elected branches responsible for unified action. Now, long-term divided government allows the executive branch to move recurrently into unilateral sovereign tendencies. Sharp congressional and public reactions—after Watergate, Iran-contra, and at the polls in 1992—are a much choppier and violent restorative of checks and balances than was necessary when it was supplemented by the unifying coordination of single-party government. The restoratives have worked each time from the 1970s to the 1990s, but not in a way to make an observer sanguine that they will always work well in the future.

CONGRESS, NOT THE JUDICIARY, PROVIDES THE BALANCE

Mention of the judiciary leads to one final discussion regarding the likelihood of recurrence after a temporary respite of the problem of presidential sovereignty. Those looking to the judiciary as a bulwark of the Constitution may express surprise that so little of this book concerns court cases. After all, the Constitution is law, and the general expectation is that the courts, which enforce the law, provide the main mechanism for enforcing the Constitution. If the White House sets up mechanisms for overstepping the system of checks and balances, then by this expectation resort to the judiciary should be expected to put the matter right.

Some might even point to examples during the Bush Administration to confirm the judicial role. Regarding the Iraq war, as briefly noted, Judge Harold Greene issued an opinion in 1990 indicating that war would require a congressional vote. This impressive opinion drew extensive publicity and just praise, had a serious impact, and will undoubtedly be cited for many years to come. In another matter, a federal judge in Atlanta gave a crucial opinion in late 1992 suggesting an administration cover-up in the BNL case.[28] At some future date, when the Supreme Court eventually interprets the Civil Rights Act of 1991, the Court's interpretation, on the points it covers, will either agree or disagree with President Bush's signing statement. Looking at these examples, some might even argue that this book has provided a distorted perspective by talking too much about the struggles between the administration and Congress rather than following what the courts did.

With all respect, the judiciary played a minimal role in responding to the strategy of the Bush Administration to escape the system of checks and balances. Judge Harold Greene's opinion on the Persian Gulf War, excellent as it was, actually supports this conclusion. It was a surprise that it occurred at all, given how the courts had brushed off war powers lawsuits throughout the Reagan Administration.[29] Furthermore, it was an opinion without the force of an order, and despite the eloquence of the opinion, that important difference was understood by the executive branch, which did not appeal the decision.

More important than any of these factors, the excellence of the opinion lay precisely in that the court did not purport to make the ultimate decision itself. It only said that the decision should come from Congress. Such a decision matters most when Congress helps itself, as it did, by public debate, meaningful hearings, and responsible votes. As counsel for the House of Representatives, I have participated in a number of cases concerning the system of checks and balances. These cases sometimes resolve important issues, particularly when strong jurists such as Harold Greene and Marvin H. Shoob perform their high function of courageously speaking truth to power. Still, my personal observation is that valuable as such decisions can be, Congress must depend on its actions of the kind from November 1990 to January 1991 regarding the Persian Gulf War—debate, hearings, and votes—which have benefit with or without such court decisions.

The essence of the system of checks and balances sometimes does not lie in what courts order or even in what they say without orders, vital as their wisdom may be in particular circumstances. The Framers established an important independent judiciary in Article III of the Constitution, but they gave little sign that they expected it to be the chief guardian of the system of checks and balances. Although the judiciary had performed a vital role throughout American history of protecting the liberty of the individual from the state, the political branches have performed the somewhat different vital role of protecting the system of checks and balances against personal rule threats. The ebbs and flows of president and Congress in the nineteenth century, with presidential peaks under Presidents Andrew Jackson and Lincoln and congressional peaks in the second half of the century, occurred largely without judicial involvement. The great war powers dramas of the twentieth century's first half—the actions of Presidents Wilson and Roosevelt to prepare for, but not to enter, World Wars I and II until Congress was ready—involved only the political branches, not the courts. Even the growth within the bounds of law of an enormous administrative state following the New Deal, for all the large role of judicially developed administrative law, also involved continuing congressional oversight and appropriations control and a vast interplay of the political branches quite apart from the courts.

The Iran-contra matter provides a recent example of this. Congress's extensive public investigation of Iran-contra in 1987 served at that time the great function of revealing the scandal to the public for its own judgment. For all the confusion of those public hearings, that investigation did set a public verdict against White House criminality. Subsequent indictments, guilty pleas, and trials of Iran-contra figures also served a purpose, but not the central one. To the extent that the shadow of Iran-contra forced the Bush Administration NSC, for all its desire to act without accountability, at least to avoid readily provable criminality, the shadow came in significant measure from the congressional investigation of Iran-contra.

There are some who blame Congress itself—in its grant of use immunity to witnesses at its hearings—for the limited impact of subsequent criminal prosecutions. The delays of the criminal justice system, the difficulty of applying that system to the unique world of national security, the impact of a judiciary filled by the appointments of the Reagan and Bush administrations, and other factors simply prevented criminal prosecution from accomplishments on the scale of congressional oversight. That there was an independent counsel at all owed to Congress's insistence, starting after Watergate, on enacting and renewing the independent counsel statute. Moreover, the ultimate availability in December 1992 of the Bush pardon, reminiscent of the 1974 pardon of Richard Nixon, was a reminder that the Constitution gave the presidency the power to block the cure of executive abuse by criminal prosecution. Only congressional investigations remain unstoppable by that barrier.

If the system of checks and balances depended solely on new institutional arrangements or judicial decisions, then the prospect of recurrent White House abuse would be daunting. American history records many problems addressed in the end, not by institutional arrangements or court cases but by the expectation of continuing congressional vigilance and responsiveness. The student of American history will recall many eras when Congress, not the judiciary, was the best hope for constitutional liberty.[30] During Reconstruction, the hope for the civil rights of the newly freed slaves lay with Congress, not the courts.[31] If Reconstruction did not permanently protect those civil rights, it was because that protection lay beyond what even the Congress of that era could accomplish, not for lack of giving the courts the task that for the following century they refused to carry out. During the period of the early labor movement, the hope for balance and peace between nascent unions and management again lay with Congress, not the courts. It was the enactment of labor legislation, in the face of judicial unwillingness to curb the labor injunction and the court-made doctrine of "liberty of contract," that ultimately resolved the issue.

The same has proven true in the contexts discussed in this book, such as war powers. Courts have played, and will continue to play, an important part.[32] However, the Supreme Court refused any role in adjudicating the legality of the various stages of the Indochina War of the 1960s and 1970s. The courts played little role in the doctrines that evolved into the War Powers Resolution or in the resolution's being followed in the Lebanon intervention of 1983. A host of doctrines by which the courts limit the occasions for decision—standing, political question, ripeness, mootness—keep them out of such controversies. Judge Greene's opinion in 1990, though significant, was only one thread in the fabric of the decision ultimately being made by Congress. Some day, the judiciary may assume an activist role in curbing executive war powers usurpation. For now, the judiciary is a distant hope rather than a realistic expectation.

However, with regard to war powers Congress is very much not a distant hope but a realistic expectation. Neither the War Powers Resolution nor any one single institutional arrangement will keep the decisions on war in their proper channel. What will do so is the simple dynamic of democracy: Absent the atmosphere of a Cold War, the public will expect a voice in the nation's decisions on war, and what it expects, it will obtain. It will speak its decisions through Congress, as it did before the Cold War, at the end of the Vietnam War, at the time of the Lebanon intervention in 1983, and at the decision point about Iraq in January 1991.

Tactics and institutions like signing statements and the Quayle Council can set back in the short term Congress's ability to make policy and to render executive offices accountable, but they will not disable Congress in the long term. Presidents can use such tools for some period of time to undermine new legislation and even to curb conditions on appropriations. However, presidents will never have legitimate ways to fund the government—including the operations conducted by their own White House staff—without coming back to Congress for appropriations. They may use laundered private or foreign funds as in Watergate and Iran-contra, or they may dispute appropriation conditions as in the Bush signing statements, but such schemes and disputes do not succeed in the long term. The hubris of those who believe themselves free to govern without the legislature, and the legislature's weapons of the investigation and the power of the purse, lead in the end to the kind of political showdown that only the side with public support can win. So long as the public ultimately decides, the system of checks and balances can have difficult times, but it will endure.

The progress of congressional intelligence oversight offers a model for what can take place over time in even the most difficult of fields for the normal operation of democracy. From the late 1940s to the 1960s, Congress significantly neglected such oversight.[33] Its initial efforts immediately after Watergate met strong resistance. Even after Congress created the institutional arrangement of the annual intelligence authorization process, with congressional oversight committees, hearings, reports, and an annual bill, Presidents Reagan and Bush still found ways to resist. Neither the courts, nor the instititutional arrangements, seemed willing or capable of curing the problem.

Yet in the end, Congress's determination to create an oversight system has brought a significant measure of accountability. Shortly after retirement, former CIA director Robert M. Gates spoke in praise of the system despite its having bruised him personally so much: "The United States has the most elaborate set of checks and balances on its covert activities of any country on earth . . . . These two [congressional intelligence] committees not only know the nature of the covert action that we are undertaking, but they also know exactly how the agency is doing it and they monitor every dime that is spent on it."[34]

Just as the professional military officers have viewed the requirement since Vietnam of congressional authorization for war as protecting them from the executive sending them into battle without a formal national debate and commitment, Gates declared that "Congressional oversight, in the eyes of the intelligence professional, is a protection against the misuse of the Agency by executive authority; and congressional review of our intelligence publications and analysis helps guard our objectivity." This veteran of the toughest battles between the legislative and executive branches of the past decade noted that "the process by which American intelligence agencies became accustomed to and positive about congressional oversight was a long and often difficult one." Yet now, "[c]ontrary to the image sometimes portrayed, most American intelligence officers *welcome* congressional oversight."

In short, future administrations may retrace the strategy of the Bush White House, and neither institutional arrangements nor the courts will deal, by themselves, with future abuse. A vigilant press may well be one of the nation's greatest resources, but it is still an unofficial one. One institution of government has the constitutional and political responsibility to serve as the voice of this nation's democratic system. For dealing with the recurring tendencies toward personal rule and institutional abuses in the White House, the institution that must and will respond is Congress.

Notes

PREFACE

1. Michael Duffy & Dan Goodgame, *Marching in Place: The Status Quo Presidency of George Bush* 11–12 (1992).

CHAPTER 1

1. John Jay used the famous phrase about "secrecy" and "dispatch" to describe the president's role solely in the phase of "the nego[t]iation of treaties" and not the making of foreign policy as a whole. Jay himself explained that he viewed the making of foreign policy as a power shared by the president and Congress (particularly the Senate). His phrase about secrecy and dispatch came immediately after a ringing reaffirmation of Congress's role in the making of policy through its unavoidable and proper role in treaty ratification and law enactment:

> There are few who will not admit that the affairs of trade and navigation should be regulated by a system cautiously formed and steadily pursued; and that both our treaties and our laws should correspond with, and be made to promote it. It is of much consequence that this correspondence and conformity be carefully maintained, and they who assent to the truth of this position, will see and confess that it is well provided for *by making the concurrence of the senate necessary both to treaties and to laws.* (*The Federalist No. 64* 434 [ed. Jacob E. Cooke 1961] [emphasis added]).

It would astound Jay to hear his explanation of the need for the Senate to pass on treaties and laws used to justify a system of directives with the effect of secret law that the Senate and Congress would not pass on or even see.

2. For more detail on these, see 1988 *Congressional Quarterly Almanac* at 10–19. "'It's probably the most productive Congress in a generation,' proclaimed House Majority Leader Thomas S. Foley," at the October 1988 adjournment. *Id.* at 10.

3. *Id.* 14-A (quote and House figures), 3-A (Senate figures); George C. Edwards III, "George Bush and the Public Presidency: The Politics of Inclusion," in *The Bush Presidency: First Appraisals* (eds. Colin Campbell & Bert A. Rockman 1991) (hereafter *First Appraisals*), at 130 (Bush running behind winning representatives). For discussion of Willie Horton, ACLU, and flag-pledging themes of the Bush campaign,

see Sidney Blumenthal, *Pledging Allegiance* 262–265 (1990); Marjorie Randon Hershey, "The Campaign and the Media," in *The Election of 1988* (ed. Gerald M. Pomper 1989), at 73, 86.

4. Charles O. Jones, "Meeting Low Expectations: Strategy and Prospects of the Bush Presidency," in *First Appraisals*, at 37, 51.

5. Barbara Sinclair, "Governing Unheroically (and Sometimes Unappetizingly): Bush and the 101st Congress," in *First Appraisals*, at 155, 160.

6. 1989 *Congressional Quarterly Almanac* 22-B. Bush's support level was 63 percent; the previous low in the first year of an elected president was for Nixon in 1969 of 74 percent.

7. Anthony King & Giles Alston, "Good Government and the Politics of High Exposure," in *First Appraisals* at 249, 275.

8. *Id.*, at 25.

9. *See, e.g.*, Bert A. Rockman, "The Leadership Style of George Bush," in *First Appraisals* 1, 32 ("elite deal-making").

10. Duffy & Goodgame, *supra*, at 214–215.

11. *Id.*, at 203.

12. Terry Eastland, *Energy in the Executive* 75 (1992).

13. Neil A. Lewis, *Turning Loyalty and Service to Bush into Power as Presidential Counsel*, New York Times, December 12, 1990, at B9.

14. Iran-contra details shed light on Bush Administration responses to reform bills in 1989. Accordingly, Chapter 3, in which I discuss those responses, provides further details.

On the eve of the November 1992 election, the press again focused on Vice President Bush's role. Among other matters, Howard Teicher, who had been Oliver North's superior at the NSC, released his own descriptions of how well briefed about the Iran initiative in 1986 Bush had been—how little he had been "out of the loop." Partly in response, Gray published an updated version of his defense of President Bush. C. Boyden Gray, *Iran-Contra: The President's Side*, Washington Post, October 4, 1992, at C7 (opinion editorial). Gray's piece relies three different times on the Tower Commission as a defense ("As the Tower Commission reported, the issues were never subjected to rigorous staff review or a full debate with all the NSC principals present. The then vice president criticized these failures in his interview with the Tower Commission . . . . [The latest charge] provides no new facts, . . . to demonstrate that George Bush played any greater role . . . than has been documented by the Tower Commission . . . .").

Teicher published his own rejoinder to Gray's piece. Teicher noted that news reports had reported "[c]urrent White House aides" as disagreeing with his account of Bush's depth of knowledge and involvement in the Iran initiative in 1986. Teicher summed up who he understood such aides to be by this quick background, after noting Gray's own role: "The president's special review board, the Tower Commission, was chaired by Gen. Brent Scowcroft, now the national security adviser . . . in addition to the late Sen. John Tower. Legal counsel for the review board was provided by Clark McFadden and Nicholas Rostow. Rostow is now responsible for legal matters at the NSC" (Howard R. Teicher, *In the Loop*, Washington Post, October 22, 1992, at A31 [opinion editorial]). Tower, Scowcroft, Rostow, and Gray had all received plum nominations or appointments in the Bush Administration's start. In sum, the analysis of an objective NSC insider—Teicher—was that Gray was relying on the Tower Commission; that Gray's reliance was understandable because of the way the Tower Commission meted out criticism only to the designated scapegoats (like Teicher himself) rather than Bush; and that the Tower Commission's approach could be understood best by seeing how Bush had rewarded the Tower Commission's members and staff.

15. Remarkably, the first conclusion of the Tower Report was that "[w]e recommend that no substantive change be made in the provisions of the National Security Act dealing with the structure and operation of the NSC system." Report of the President's Special Review Board, at V-5 (February 26, 1987).

16. Duffy & Goodgame, *supra*, at 123.

17. *Id.*, at 137.

18. Jim Hoagland, *The Value of Brent Scowcroft,* Washington Post, December 10, 1991, at A21.

19. "[I]n fall 1989, a strong secrecy motif emerged in evaluations of the administration. The way in which the Malta Summit between Bush and Mikhail Gorbachev and the Scowcroft/Eagleburger visit to China were arranged and sprung on Washington insiders and the nation alike aroused some fears . . . ." (Colin Campbell, "The White House and Presidency Under the 'Let's Deal' President," in *First Appraisals,* 185, 201). "[The press complained of] misleading statements from the White House designed to protect top-secret plans, such as meeting Gorbachev in Malta [and] the trips of high-level officials to China following the massacre in Tiananamen Square. . . ." (George C. Edwards III, "George Bush and the Public Presidency: The Politics of Inclusion," in *First Appraisals, supra,* 129, 149. Other details of these deceptions are in *Marching in Place, supra,* at 183–187.

20. 1989 *Congressional Quarterly Almanac* 403 (Tower), 639 (HUD).

21. Ironically, the administration started with one concession. In March 1989 it agreed with Congress to ask for terminal funding for the contras until the Nicaraguan election, subject to an informal legislative veto. The White House counsel, C. Boyden Gray, protested this as too great a concession to Congress about its control of appropriations. When this protest became public, President Bush "called Gray on the carpet on March 27" and publicly rebuked him. 1989 *Congressional Quarterly Almanac* 572.

22. *Id.*, at 130–131.

23. George C. Edwards III, in *First Appraisals,* at 131.

24. George Hager, *Bush's Success Rate Sinks to Near-Record Low,* 48 Congressional Quarterly Weekly Report 4183 (December 22, 1990).

25. 1990 *Congressional Quarterly Almanac* 901-02.

26. Carroll J. Doherty, *Uncertain Congress Confronts President's Gulf Strategy: Doubling of Forces Triggers New Demands for Role in Approving Military Action Against Iraq,* 48 Congressional Quarterly Weekly Report 3879 (November 17, 1990).

27. James A. Barnes, *Blown Off Course,* 24 National Journal 2472, 2473 (October 31, 1992).

28. Duffy & Goodgame, *supra*, at 81.

29. Bob Woodward, *The President's Key Men: Splintered Trio, Splintered Policy,* Washington Post, October 7, 1992, at A1 (part four of a four-part investigative series on behind-the-scenes economic decisionmaking).

30. 1991 *Congressional Quarterly Almanac* 252, 256.

31. 1991 *Congressional Quarterly Almanac* 261. For President Bush's signing statement of "authoritative interpretive guidance," *see Pub. Papers* 1702 (November 21, 1989).

32.

> [B]lack support for Clinton was accompanied by higher turnout. Dukakis garnered 6,351 votes in Macon County in 1988; Clinton drew 7,253 votes this year—an increase of 14 percent. Dukakis collected 159,407 votes in majority-black Washington; Clinton got 192,619—a 21 percent increase.
>
> The black support for Clinton on Nov. 3, says Ronald W. Walters, the chairman of the political science department at Howard University, "was more an anti-Bush than a pro-Clinton vote." (Rhodes Cook, *Republicans Suffer a Knockout that Leaves Clinton Standing,* 50 Congressional Quarterly Week Report 3810, 3812 [December 12, 1991]).

33. Barnes, *supra,* at 2474–2475.

34. Duffy & Goodgame, *supra,* at 93.

35. In particular, Gray demanded release, on the eve of the Michigan primary, of a regulatory decision sought by the automobile industry. Michael Weisskopf & Thomas W. Lippman, *From Fumes to Water, Bush Is Flexing Regulatory Rules,* Washington Post, March 7, 1992, at A1.

36. Eugene Robinson & Michael Weisskopf, *"No" Leaves U.S. Isolated at Summit,* Washington Post, June 6, 1992, at A1 ("The decision to reject Reilly's 11th-hour effort was made by White House domestic policy counselor Clayton Yeutter, after consulting with competitiveness council staffers and White House counsel C. Boyden Gray, according to administration sources in Washington.")

37. Paul Houston, *Bush May Launch Court Fight Over the Line-Item Veto,* Los Angeles Times, February 28, 1992, at A4. Barr's opposition is noted in Sharon LaFraniere, *Barr Takes Center Stage at Justice Department with New Script,* Washington Post, March 5, 1992, at A19.

38. Phillip A. Davis, *Politics, Drop in Senate Support Put Bush's Ratings in Cellar,* 50 Congressional Quarterly Weekly Report 3841 (December 19, 1992).

39. The independent counsel's postpardon report to Congress said regarding the Weinberger trial aborted by the pardon: "Administration officials called as defense witnesses, including particularly Meese and perhaps President Bush, would on public cross-examination have been subject to searching questions about the administration's conduct and their own in November 1986" (Lawrence E. Walsh, Independent Counsel for Iran/Contra Matters, *Fourth Interim Report to Congress* 72 [February 8, 1993]).

CHAPTER 2

1. Arthur M. Schlesinger, Jr., *The Imperial Presidency* 214 (1974)("monarchical"); Harold Hongju Koh, *The National Security Constitution: Sharing Power After the Iran-Contra Affair* 208 (1990) (Iran-contra "represented yet another challenge by the advocates of executive discretion to the constitutional principle of shared powers").

2. *INS v. Chadha*, 462 U.S. 919 (1983); *Bowsher v. Synar*, 478 U.S. 714 (1986).

3. Max Farrand, *The Records of the Federal Convention of 1787* (1966 ed.) at 65 (Pinkney) (fearing power grants that "would render the Executive a Monarchy, of the worst kind, to wit [sic] an elective one"); *id.* at 66 (Randolph) (fearing "the foetus of monarchy"); *id.* (Wilson) (agreeing "that he was not governed by the British Model"); *id.* at 83 (Franklin); *id.* (Butler) ("Gentlemen seemed to think that we had nothing to apprehend from an abuse of the Executive power. But why might not a Cataline or a Cromwell arise in this Country as well as in others"); *id.* at 101 (Mason) ("We are not indeed constituting a British Government, but a more dangerous monarchy, an elective one"); *id.* at 103 (Franklin) ("The Executive will always be increasing here, as elsewhere, till it ends in a monarchy"); *id.* at 113 (Mason). *See Youngstown Sheet & Tube Co. v. Sawyer*, 343 U.S. 579, 640–641 (1952) (Jackson, J., concurring); *Fleming v. Page*, 50 U.S. (9 How.) 603, 618 (1850).

4. Raoul Berger, *Executive Privilege: A Constitutional Myth* 29 (1974) (quoting speech by William Pitt, with the spelling and capitalization of the original).

5. The previously claimed monarchical power to "suspend" the laws had been rejected by the time-honored doctrine of "faithful execution" clause of the Constitution. Moreover, the Framers explicitly rejected the proposal of a power for the president to "suspend" the execution of laws. For this history, see Robert J. Reinstein, *An Early View of Executive Powers and Privileges: Trial of Smith and Ogden*, 2 Hastings Const. L. Q. 309, 321 (1975); *Ameron, Inc. v. U.S. Army Corps of Engineers*, 610 F. Supp. 750, 755 (D.N.J. 1985), *aff'd*, 809 F.2d 979 (3d Cir. 1976), *cert. dism'd*, 109 S. Ct. 297 (1988).

6. William D. Popkin, *Judicial Use of Presidential Legislative History: A Critique*, 66 Indiana L.J. 699, 702 (1991) (discussing signing statements about statutory intent). Use after World War II is discussed later.

7. The Framers mentioned the offices of the president's "heads of departments" in the Constitution but left their powers for creation by statute.

8. *Kendall v. United States ex. rel. Stokes*, 37 U.S. (12 Pet.) 524, 613 (1838).

9. Schlesinger, *supra*, at 216–217.

10. Article I, section 8 set forth that "[t]he Congress shall have Power . . . . [t]o regulate Commerce with foreign Nations. . . . [and] to declare War . . . ."

11.

> The provision [the appropriations clause of the Constitution] was framed against the backdrop of 150 years of struggle between the King and Parliament for control over the purse, often centering on military matters. In 1624, the House of Commons for the first time conditioned a grant of funds to the king. The Subsidy Act of that year prohibited the use of any military monies except for financing the navy, aiding the Dutch, and defending England and Ireland. Two years later Charles I attempted to wage war without popular support, but Parliament promptly denied him funds to conduct it. (*Congress and the Administration's Secrecy Pledges: Hearing Before the Subcommittee on Legislation and National Security of the House Committee on Government Operations*, 100th Cong., 2d Sess. 150 [1988] [Statement of Professor Glennon] [footnotes omitted.]

12. "No money shall be drawn from the Treasury, but in consequence of Appropriations made by law." U.S. Const., art. I, sec. 9, cl. 7. The appropriations power represents "the most complete and effectual weapon with which any constitution can arm the immediate representatives of the people, for obtaining a redress of every grievance, and for carrying into effect every just and salutary measure," *The Federalist*, No. 58 (J. Madison), and it was felt by the Framers to be particularly important in the areas of foreign policy and national security:

> Meeting in Philadelphia in 1787, the Framers were well aware of the tradition of parliamentary power over the purse and its use to check unwanted "national security" activities. . . . Madison considered it "particularly dangerous to give the keys of the treasury, and the command of the army, into the same hands." Accordingly, the Framers chose, in the words of Jefferson, to transfer the war power "from the executive to the legislative body, from those who are to spend to those who are to pay." (*1988* Hearings at 150–151 [Statement of Professor Glennon] [footnotes omitted].)

See Paul R. Q. Wolfson, *Is a Presidential Item Veto Constitutional?* 96 Yale L. J. 838, 841–844 (1987). Any notion that the president's powers override Congress's authority to withhold appropriations utterly defies the Framers' most basic doctrine of separation of powers: As George Mason stated it, "[t]he purse and the sword should not be in the same hands." Farrand, *supra,* at 144 (1966). This is the "most important single curb in the Constitution on presidential power." E. Corwin, *The Constitution and What It Means Today* 101 (1973 ed.).

13. Alexander Hamilton, usually the staunchest of defenders of presidential prerogative, admitted in the Federalist:

> The President is to be Commander in Chief. . . . In this respect his authority . . . [compared to] that of the King of Great-Britain . . . [is] in substance much inferior to it. It would amount to nothing more than the supreme command and direction of the military . . . while that of the British King extends to the *declaring* of war and to the *raising* and *regulating* of fleets and armies; all of which by the Constitution under consideration would appertain to the Legislature. *The Federalist No. 69* (Jacob E. Cooke ed. 1961) (emphasis in original)

See Schlesinger, *supra,* at 18; Berger, *supra* 56 (1974).

14. For critical scrutiny of the "lists" of incidents, see Francis D. Wormuth, "The Nixon Theory of the War Power," 60 Calif. L. Rev. 623, at 654–664 (1972); Francis D. Wormuth & Edwin B. Firmage, at 143–149 (1986); Koh *supra*, 81–88; Schlesinger, *supra,* 61–86.

15. For reviews of the pre–twentieth century record, both as to war powers and other aspects of national security, *see* Koh, *supra,* 74–88; Schlesinger, *supra,* 25–89.

16. The two quotes ("[s]uccessive Presidents . . . ." and "until President Truman") are from David S. Friedman, *Waging War Against Checks and Balances:*

The Claims of an Unlimited Presidential War Power, 57 St. John's L. Rev. 213, 226–227 (1983) (footnotes omitted).

17. President Truman could have obtained congressional authorization (or explicit ratification on the model of Congress's ratification of President Lincoln's steps after Fort Sumter). Even his congressional Republican critics said he would have received it, but he refused to ask for it. As a result, "[b]y insisting that the presidential prerogative sufficed to meet the requirements of the Constitution, Truman . . . . dramatically and dangerously enlarged the power of future Presidents to take the nation into major war." Schlesinger, *supra,* at 138. Still, it is worth noting, as I have discussed elsewhere, that Congress did enact for President Truman much legislation necessary for the extended conduct of the Korean War. Charles Tiefer, "The FAS Proposal: Valid Check or Unconstitutional Veto?" in *First Use of Nuclear Weapons: Under the Constitution, Who Decides?* 136, 156 (ed. Peter Raven-Hansen 1987).

18. John Hart Ely has argued eloquently, drawing on many materials released since the contemporaneous debate on the Indochina War, that the war was partly authorized and partly not authorized. He distinguishes the war in Vietnam, which he contends did receive a form of congressional authorization, from the other parts of the Indochina War, namely, the secret war in Laos from 1962 to 1969 and the secret bombing of Cambodia in 1969 and 1970 lacking such authorization. John Hart Ely, *The American War in Indochina, Part I: The (Troubled) Constitutionality of the War They Told Us About,* 42 Stan. L. Rev. 877 (1989); John Hart Ely, *The American War in Indochina, Part II: The Unconstitutionality of the War They Didn't Tell Us About,* 43 Stan. L. Rev. 1093 (1990). Ely's treatment is so exhaustive and balanced that it seems pointless to go over this ground.

Rather, the most relevant point for discussing the Bush Administration is to distinguish the sharply different natures of the Tonkin Gulf Resolution and the Persian Gulf Resolution. Congress intended the Tonkin Gulf Resolution of 1964 to be only a symbolic statement; it adopted the resolution in a virtually undebated context without intent to authorize the land war commitment the next year. That simply does not compare with the kinds of clear authorization given for pre-1950 wars. President Bush seemed initially to consider in 1990 going to war with Iraq based on a resolution like the Tonkin Gulf Resolution, but in January 1991 he ultimately asked for, and obtained, the full equivalent of a declaration of war.

19. For an introduction to the vast topic of covert action and war powers, *see* Jules Lobel, *Covert War and Congressional Authority: Hidden War and Forgotten Power,* 2134 U. Pa. L. Rev. 1035 (1986). For a discussion of the meaningless resolutions of this period, *see* Doyle W. Buckwalter, *The Congressional Concurrent Resolution: A Search for Foreign Policy Influence,* 14 Midwest J. Poli. Sci. 434 (1970).

20. For example, Congress delegated broad authority to the administration to devise multilateral restrictions on militarily useful trade with the communist bloc. It created classified budget systems to fund intelligence, including covert actions. During the Bush Administration, the wide-open presidential trade power became vital for the courtship of Saddam Hussein, and the attempts to curb the classified budget system met tough resistance through the White House counsel's signing statements.

21. "By 1947, the primary focus of American foreign policy was not on interna-tional trade, but on the perception of rising Soviet expansionism. . . . In 1947, America emerged from World War II only to find itself enmeshed in a cold war . . ." Koh, *supra,* 99, 101.

22. *See* Christopher C. Shoemaker, *The NSC Staff: Counseling the Council* 60 (1991) (Carter Administration); Harold C. Relyea, *The Coming of Secret Law,* 5 Gov't Info. Q. 97, 106–108 (1988); People for the American Way, *Government Secrecy: Deci-sions Without Democracy* 5 (1988); Robert Cutler, *The Development of the National Se-curity Council,* Foreign Affairs 441 (1956) (Truman and Eisenhower Administra-tions), reprinted in *Decision of the Highest Order: Perspectives on the National Security Council* 55, 60 (Karl F. Inderfurth & Loch K. Johnson eds., 1988).

23. The ground-breaking preliminary consideration of the issues came in the Senate Foreign Relations Committee's development of the National Commitments Resolution, S. Res. 85, 91st Cong., 1st Sess. (1969). For discussions of (and further sources on) the road to the War Powers Resolution, *see* Thomas M. Franck & Edward Weisband, *Foreign Policy by Congress* (1979) (also including a discussion of the contemporaneous congressional cutoffs that ended the Indochina War); Mi-chael J. Glennon, *Constitutional Diplomacy* 88–93 (1990). For a sample of the exten-sive literature on the War Powers Resolution, *see, e.g.,* Jacob K. Javits, *War Powers Reconsidered,* 64 Foreign Affairs 130 (Fall 1985) (review written by key author of original resolution); Note, *A Defense of the War Powers Resolution,* 93 Yale L.J. 1330 (1984); Michael J. Glennon, *The War Powers Resolution Ten Years Later: More Politics Than Law,* 78 Am. J. Int'l. Law 571 (1984); Stephen L. Carter, *The Constitutionality of the War Powers Resolution,* 70 Va. L. Rev. 101 (1984).

24. James L. Sundquist, *The Decline and Resurgence of Congress* (1981). For exam-ple, where there had once been an open-ended delegation of authority regarding arms-type exports, now Congress reemployed its constitutional role regarding "foreign commerce" to enact the Arms Export Control Act and the Nuclear Non-Proliferation Act. Where there had once been open-ended appropriations for the intelligence community, now Congress enacted annual intelligence authorizations, with "classified annexes" describing the amounts and details and conditions that could not be publicly disclosed.

25. For one of the fullest treatments, *see* Glennon, 71–122, and sources cited.

26. As noted earlier, even from 1789 to 1945 presidents had engaged in unilat-eral deployments, including fighting, justified as protection for American citizens, or reprisals. Incidents of similar rescues and reprisals from 1973 to 1991 resembled that prior history: Indochina evacuations, the Mayaguez incident, the abortive 1980 Iran hostage rescue attempt, the Grenada landing, and the Libyan air strike of 1986. The Grenada landing, in particular, involved debatable issues over the stated rationale of a landing to protect Americans but not the issue presented in 1990 re-garding the suggestion of an Iraq war without congressional authorization. The is-sue here is not to debate all the war powers questions together, but to isolate out what history says about when a full congressionally enacted authorization—not just consultation, not just appropriations, but a declaration of war or the equiva-lent—is necessary.

Other incidents not for rescue or reprisal involved deployments without en-gagement in actual combat, such as advisers in El Salvador, naval maneuvers off

Libya, and the Persian Gulf tanker reflagging of 1987. Like the pre-1950 experience, these involved provocative deployments, not war. They involved important and debatable issues about presidents exceeding their proper powers but not the issue starkly presented in 1990 regarding the suggestion of an Iraq war without congressional authorization.

This subject receives more detailed discussion in the chapter below regarding the 1991 Persian Gulf Resolution. For documentation and discussion of the post-1973 incidents, see Subcomm. on Arms Control, International Security and Science of the House Comm. on Foreign Affairs, 100th Cong., 2d Sess., *The War Powers Resolution: Relevant Documents, Correspondence, Reports* (May 1988 ed.) (periodically updated series).

27. "We believe that Congress may, as a general constitutional matter, place a 60-day limit on the use of our armed forces as required by the provisions of [section 5(b)] of the Resolution." (4A Op. Office of Legal Counsel, Department of Justice 185, 196 [1980] [seminal opinion on the War Powers Resolution during the Carter Administration]). President Carter endorsed the War Powers Resolution as a "constructive safeguar[d]." *President's Message to the Congress on Legislative Vetoes, Pub. Papers* 1146, 1149 (1978).

28. Gary W. Cox & Samuel Kernell, "Introduction: Governing a Divided Era," in *The Politics of Divided Government* 2 (eds. Gary W. Cox & Samuel Kernell 1991) (hereafter *Divided Government*). The divided governments occurred from 1911 to 1913, 1919 to 1921, and 1931 to 1933.

29. Cox & Kernell, *supra*, at 1.

30. See Cox & Kernell, *supra*, for studies of these; Samuel Kernell, *Going Public: New Strategies of Presidential Leadership* (2d ed. 1993), on the particular subject of public appeals; and *The Bush Presidency: First Appraisals* (eds. Colin Campbell & Bert A. Rockman 1991) for particular studies of why the Bush Presidency used veto bargaining but few public appeals.

31. 343 U.S. 579 (1952).

32. Regarding President Nixon's "administrative presidency," *see* Richard P. Nathan, *The Administrative Presidency* (1983).

Legislative vetoes were statutory provisions that authorized future rejection, by resolution of one or both Houses, of an executive action after enactment, such as administrative rulemaking or implementation of an energy plan. Under a legislative veto provision, Congress would later adopt a resolution of rejection of the executive action. Congress would not submit that resolution to the president for signature or veto.

Presidents mindful that they had no legitimate role in lawmaking other than veto, but that they did have that veto role, thus had to devise a vehicle to respond when Congress enacted a bill with a provision—a legislative veto—denying them their future veto on a future congressional enactment. When presidents responded to legislative vetoes with signing statements, they were not devising a general power to declare provisions void. Rather, such presidents were employing a poor substitute for the veto they would be denied on the subsequent congressional resolutions that would take effect pursuant to the legislative veto provision. The problem was ultimately resolved when the Supreme Court declared the legislative veto unconstitutional.

Such statements let presidents "go on record," as the Supreme Court put it in *Chadha*, at the time of signing of the legislative veto provision.

33. The quote, and a discussion of the pre-Reagan regulatory review systems, is in Morton Rosenberg, *Regulatory Oversight and OMB*, in *Office of Management and Budget: Evolving Rose and Future Issues*, Sen. Comm. on Governmental Affairs, 99th Cong., 2d Sess. 185, 200 (1986) (committee print prepared by the Congressional Research Service); see also Morton Rosenberg, *Beyond the Limits of Executive Power: Presidential Control of Agency Rulemaking Under Executive Order 12,291*, 90 Mich. L. Rev. 193 (1981). What the Nixon Administration had done was change what had been the Bureau of the Budget in the Treasury Department to the Office of Management and Budget (OMB) in the White House, thereby initially seeming to shield it from congressional oversight. Yet, even the maneuvers surrounding the OMB had almost wholly to do with other issues, such as impoundment, rather than regulatory review.

34. I gave an account of this sequence and its significance in my testimony in *Constitutionality of GAO's Bid Protest Function: Hearings Before a Subcomm. of the House Comm. on Government Operations*, 99th Cong., 1st Sess. 279 (1985). For an excellent description of the prior history, see Louis Fisher, *Presidential Spending Power* (1975). The enactment of the Regulatory Flexibility Act of 1980 created, within the OMB, the statutory Office of Information and Regulatory Affairs (OIRA) with a Senate-confirmed head. At that point, Congress appeared well on the way to bringing regulatory review within the well-established system of authorization by enacted law and accountability.

35. President's Committee on Administrative Management, [Reorganization of the Executive Departments, Sen. Doc. No. 8, 75th Cong., 1st Sess. (1937)], 5, quoted in Peter M. Shane & Harold H. Bruff, *The Law of Presidential Power: Cases and Materials* 22 (1988). The role in the 1981 to 1988 regulatory review system of Vice President Bush's task force was trivial compared to the one that the Quayle Council came to play.

36. Cox & Kernell, "Conclusion," in *Divided Government* at 242 (citation omitted).

37. Even enthusiasts for Attorney General Meese's positions marked the loss of authority. "'Meese's own clout, as a result of his troubles, is, if possible, even lower than the rest of the Administration,' wrote *National Review* in June 1988." Terry Eastland, *Energy in the Executive* 210 (1992).

38. Barry M. Blechman, *The Politics of National Security: Congress and U.S. Defense Policy* 200 (1990) (citing, among other matters, the 1980s Congress intelligence oversight, enactment of restrictive defense authorization and appropriations, 1986 Goldwater-Nichols reorganization of the armed forces, and sweeping role in arms control).

39. Walter J. Oleszek, "The Context of Congressional Policy Making," in *Divided Democracy: Cooperation and Conflict Between the President and Congress* 95 (ed. James A. Thurber 1992).

40. For a description of some of the post-Watergate statutory oversight framework, see Tiefer, *The Constitutionality of Independent Officers as Checks on Abuses of Executive Power*, 63 B.U.L. Rev. 59 (1983). The defense of the constitutionality of the

independent counsel statute in that article was vindicated when the statute was upheld in *Morrison v. Olson*, 487 U.S. 654 (1987).

41. Among the most prominent examples would be President Lincoln's suspension of habeas corpus and President Wilson's post–World War I intervention in the Russian Revolution.

CHAPTER 3

1. The few exceptions were like the few pre-Nixon impoundments—special circumstances or expressions of unique or minor points—not a full-fledged pretension to a lawmaking role after signing. That not one single scholarly commentary was ever written before the Reagan Administration about signing statements reflects the lack of any presidential claim to their being a major mechanism of power.

2. Neil A. Lewis, *Turning Loyalty and Service to Bush Into Power as Presidential Counsel*, New York Times, December 12, 1990, at B9.

3. For descriptions of the OMB Unconstitutionality Bulletin and the entire CICA sequence, see *Ameron v. United States Army Corps of Engineers*, 909 F.2d 979 (3d Cir. 1986) (*affirming* 610 F. Supp. 750 [D.N.J. 1985]), *cert. dismissed*, 109 S. Ct. 297 (1988); *Constitutionality of GAO's Bid Protest Function: Hearings Before a Subcomm. of the House Comm. on Government Operations*, 99th Cong., 1st Sess. (1985); *The President's Suspension of the Competition in Contracting Act Is Unconstitutional*: H.R. Rep. No. 138, 99th Cong., 1st Sess. (1985); *Department of Justice Authorizations Act Fiscal Year 1986*: H.R. Rep. No. 113, 99th Cong., 1st Sess. (1985).

4. Marc N. Garber & Kurt A. Wimmer, *Presidential Signing Statements as Interpretations of Legislative Intent: An Executive Aggrandizement of Power*, 34 Harv. J. Legis. 369 (1987). The issue concerned the provision for noncitizens who were unfairly denied jobs to sue employers for discrimination. The president said that they could win lawsuits only if they could prove that the employer acted with discriminatory intent. However, the bill's draftsmen had actually required victims only to prove that the employer's acts had a discriminatory effect. Congressional and academic commentators criticized the president for claiming the power to modify the law's meaning after its passage. *See* 1986 *Congressional Quarterly Almanac* 67.

5. William D. Popkin, *Judicial Use of Presidential Legislative History: A Critique*, 66 Indiana L.J. 704–705 (1991).

6. See the source cited in the prior footnote and *Lear Siegler, Inc. v. Lehman*, 942 F.2d 1102, 1121 (9th Cir. 1988) (subsequently vacated en banc in part on a separate issue regarding attorneys' fees).

7. Garber & Wimmer, *supra*, at 363. William D. Popkin, *Judicial Use of Presidential Legislative History: A Critique*, 66 Ind. L. J. 699 (1991); Brad Waites, *Let Me Tell You What You Mean: An Analysis of Presidential Signing Statements*, 21 Georgia L. Rev. 755 (1987). One defense was in Frank B. Cross, *The Constitutional Legitimacy and Significance of Presidential "Signing Statements,"* 40 Admin. L. Rev. 209 (1988).

8. As a conservative supporter of the Reagan Administration said, "[t]he time to have made that argument [about the Boland Amendments not applying to the NSC] (and others) was at the moment of presentment in a veto message or at least in a signing statement." Terry Eastland, *Energy in the Executive* 99 (1992). President Reagan could either have declared the Boland Amendments invalid overall for in-

fringing presidential prerogatives or construed them into uselessness, for example, as not forbidding foreign solicitation or not applying to the NSC staff. He did none of those things; his NSC staff told Congress it was obeying "the letter and the spirit" of the laws, and his Cabinet officials conceded the laws barred solicitation.

It may be argued that the Reagan Administration's not using signing statements against the Boland Amendments reflected a political calculation. The White House may have preferred not to stir up the trouble with Congress and the public that would have resulted from using a constitutionally dubious and controversial technique in such a context.

9. For example, Congress used the annual intelligence authorization as a vehicle for an immediate response to the Iran-contra scandal by tightening up both the Boland Amendment and the CIA inspector general's reporting duties. 1988 *Congressional Quarterly Almanac* 521–525. Congress used the annual defense authorization bill to nail down obedience to the ABM Treaty, among other points. President Reagan vetoed a first version of the bill, but after negotiation of a compromise he signed a later one rather than claiming power to affect the bill's interpretation by signing statements. *Id.* at 399–400; *see* also Barry M. Blechman, *The Politics of National Security: Congress and U.S. Defense Policy* 109–110 (1990).

10. The staff search that turned up Gray is described in Owen Ullmann, *Soul Brothers*, Washingtonian, May 1992, 145. See Charlotte Allen, *Bush's Right-hand Eminence*, Washington Times, August 12, 1991, at 34 (regarding Gray's law firm work as business lobbyist). The Alibi Club memberships are in Sarah Booth Conroy, *A Peek at Privilege: Inside the Alibi Club*, Washington Post, June 22, 1992, at B1.

11. Bush's roles in Iran-contra included two matters having to do with quid pro quos, as discussed later—the Bush trip to Honduras in 1985 and McFarlane's having informed him in 1985 of the solicited Saudi contributions to the contras. Bush's roles in Iran-contra also included his support for the Iran arms-for-hostages initiative at the key White House meetings in August 1985 and January 1986; the visits with him by his agent in Oliver North's contra resupply operation, Felix Rodriguez; and his meeting with Amiram Nir, the Israeli enthusiast for continued arms-for-hostages efforts, prior to renewal of those efforts in summer 1986. Bush also had difficulty explaining about his national security adviser, Donald Gregg, who denied knowledge after the October 1986 shoot-down by a resupply plane even though the press quickly tied him to the resupply operation through Felix Rodriguez. Gregg adhered to increasingly strained recountings for years after of the vice president's supposedly not having been briefed by Rodriguez. These issues recurred in Gregg's 1989 Senate hearings when Bush nominated him as ambassador to South Korea.

12. For the late defense, see C. Boyden Gray, *Iran-Contra: The President's Side*, Washington Post, October 4, 1992. The Tower Commission, appointed by President Reagan, was made to order for sympathy with Bush. Of its three members, one was Senator Tower, a fellow Texas Republican who Bush nominated later for secretary of defense; another was Brent Scowcroft, who had worked with Bush in the Ford Administration (Scowcroft as national security adviser, Bush as CIA director) and who Bush picked later for national security adviser. Bush never submitted to interviewing or questioning by the congressional Iran-contra committees. He did have a 1988 interview by the independent counsel.

13. George Lardner, Jr. & Walter Pincus, *Diary Shows Bush "Trying to Weather the Storm" on Iran-Contra,* Washington Post, January 17, 1993, A26.

14. For a description of the office's normal functioning, see Bradley H. Patterson, Jr., *The Ring of Power: The White House Staff and Its Expanding Role in Government* 141–150 (1988). When Oliver North needed a written opinion from a lawyer that the pertinent laws did not apply to him, he turned not to the White House counsel's office, which he did not trust, but to the counsel to the Intelligence Oversight Board. *Testimony of Elliott Abrams, Albert Hakim, David M. Lewis, Bretton G. Sciaroni, and Fawn Hall: Jt. Hearings Before the Sen. Sel. Comm. on Secret Military Assistance to Iran and the Nicaragian Opposition and the House Sel. Comm. to Investigate Covert Arms Transactions with Iran,* 100th Cong., 1st Sess. (June 8, 1987) (Bretton G. Sciaroni), at 406–411. Legal drafting for the Iran deal was performed by a hand-picked CIA lawyer.

15. Ullman, *supra,* at 78.

16. *Id.* at 78.

17. Lewis, *supra,* at B9 (quoting John Buckley). Gray's stock may have been particularly high because Bush inherited from the Reagan Administration his attorney general, Richard Thornburgh, in whom he would not invest such trust.

18. Michael Wines, *A Spotlight on Counsel with Clout,* New York Times, November 25, 1991, at A16.

19. W. John Moore, *The True Believers,* National Journal, August 17, 1991, at 2021.

20. *See, e.g., Congress Investigates 1792–1974* (eds. Arthur M. Schlesinger, Jr. & Roger Bruns 1975). That tradition went back to preconstitutional days and to the earliest major congressional investigation of an executive branch "national security" fiasco in 1792, with ensuing statutory reforms. Congress followed the Panic of 1907 by creating the Federal Reserve System; it followed the economic collapse of the 1930s with statutory alteration of the Federal Reserve System and creation of numerous new systems of financial regulation; it followed Watergate with campaign finance reform and with the Ethics in Government Act of 1978, notably including a statutory system for special prosecutors; it followed the revealed intelligence abuses of the 1970s with the Hughes-Ryan controls for covert action and the system of annual intelligence authorizations. In fact, later presidents, like Harry Truman and Lyndon Johnson, had built part of their congressional reputations on the cycle of abuse, investigation, and reform—Truman during World War II, Johnson in the aftermath of Sputnik.

21. "McFarlane also testified he informed selected members of the executive branch of the funding. 'Within a day or so,' he told Vice President George Bush . . . ." *Report of the Congressional Committee Investigating the Iran-Contra Affair,* S. Rept. No. 216 & H. Rept. No. 433, 100th Cong., 1st Sess. (1987), at 39.

22. Paragraphs 52 and 58, Stipulated Facts, *United States of America v. Oliver L. North,* Crim. No. 88-0080-02-GAG.

23. 1989 *Congressional Quarterly Almanac* 541.

24. For example, a key Senate debate and test vote on the CIA statutory inspector general provision, with the administration lobbying intensively to defeat the provision, nevertheless upheld the provision by 64-34. For analysis of the debate and vote, *see* 1989 *Congressional Quarterly Almanac* 549–550. Obviously, that was

not a veto-proof majority, but there were limits to President Bush's eagerness, and that of his Senate supporters, for a veto fight to protect Iran-contra abuses.

25. *See Nomination of Robert M. Gates to be Director of Central Intelligence,* Exec. Rept. No. 19, 102d Cong., 1st Sess. (1991). The report summarizes the review of Gates' role in Iran-contra on pages 6–41. In the context of that scrutiny, it would have been impossible for the nominee to sustain a position antagonistic to Iran-Contra reforms.

26. Samuel Kernell, "Facing an Opposition Congress: The President's Strategic Circumstance," in *The Politics of Divided Government* 101–108 (eds. Gary W. Cox & Samuel Kernell 1992).

27. Pub. Papers 1573 (Nov. 21, 1989) (emphasis added).

28. The report of the Iran-contra congressional committees noted:

> It is a mistake for the United States to engage in what Assistant Secretary of State Elliott Abrams called "tin cup" diplomacy. It is unseemly for a global superpower to ask other nations to finance its foreign policy. Moreover, allowing foreign policy to be conducted with funds supplied by . . . foreign governments is likely to create the expectation by the donor nations that they can expect something in return for their largesse. . . .
>
> But by seeking . . . third-country aid for the Contras without Congressional notification—much less approval—the Administration did more than engage in an unfortunate fundraising effort that opened the door to expectations of secret return favors. This clandestine financing operation undermined the powers of Congress as a coequal branch and subverted the Constitution. (*Report of the Congressional Committees Investigating the Iran-Contra Affair,* H. Rept. No. 433 & S. Rept. No. 216, 100th Cong., 1st Sess. 391 [1987].

Even the most explicit quid pro quos could rarely be proven in the absence of congressional ability to examine foreign personnel and records or administration cooperation in the proof.

29. When the Senate had the Obey Amendment before it, and the supposedly explanatory colloquy took place, Senator Kasten offered his own differently worded amendment. The Kasten Amendment—in contrast with the amendment for which it would have substituted, the Obey Amendment—did use the words "express condition." Senator Kasten had said, "I understand that this provision is intended only to cover an actual quid pro quo," and Senator Rudman had said, "the words 'in exchange for' in the amendment must be understood to require an agreement . . . [with] an express condition." 135 Cong. Rec. S 16362-63 (daily ed. Nov. 20, 1989). The amendment in question was Kasten's, not Obey's.

30. Senator Kasten defended his own Kasten Amendment by saying, "It is essential, therefore, to adopt substitute language which makes clear that providing assistance is only prohibited when it is done . . . as an express condition . . . ." The Kasten Amendment is at *id.* 16361; the quoted statement, at *id.* S 16362. Although Senator Kasten offered his "explicit condition" amendment and explained why it

was "essential" to adopt its language substituting for the Obey Amendment, he followed up not by having the Kasten Amendment adopted but by having it withdrawn. "I will not press this amendment which, if adopted, would force this bill to go back to the House of Representatives and to an uncertain fate, based on the readings that we are getting from the leadership there." *Id.* at S 16362.

31. 135 Cong. Rec. H 9088-89 (daily ed. Nov. 20, 1989) (emphasis added).

32.

> I support both the amendment of the Senator from Wisconsin [Senator Kasten], and his decision to withdraw the amendment, for the reasons he has cited.
>
> I want to affirm what he has already said—that the White House is very concerned about the so-called leveraging language as some have interpreted it. Senior White House officials have told me that they would advise the President to veto the bill unless this matter is satisfactorily clarified. (135 Cong. Rec. S 16363 [daily ed. Nov. 20, 1989] [Senator Dole])

33. As to the trade of arms for hostages with Iran, the CIA came in as a result of the January 1986 NSC meeting attended by Bush. That agency provided the support for the May 1986 arms-for-hostages mission to Teheran, regarding which the NSC staff briefed Bush. He and Gray kept contending that he was "out of the loop" on this, but his own concealed diary notes from November 1986 showed otherwise.

As to the contra resupply, Felix Rodriguez, who had a key role in the resupply operation, had been reporting to Gregg and had met with Bush himself. In October 1986, when Nicaraguans shot down a resupply plane and captured the crew member Eugene Hasenfus, Gregg and Bush became trapped in denials that they had learned anything from Rodriguez, even though Rodriguez called the vice president's office the very day of the shoot-down to alert it of the connection to the North operation about which Gregg knew already anyway. *See* 1989 *Congressional Quarterly Almanac* 538–540 (describing the 1989 Gregg nomination controversy). From similar denials of knowledge in October 1986, one CIA official, Alan Fiers, pled guilty for lying to Congress, and another, Clair George, was convicted of lying to Congress. President Bush pardoned both in December 1992.

34. Report, at 425.

35. Former CIA station chief Joseph Fernandez, who had helped the contra resupply operation, was charged with making false statements to the CIA inspector general. President Bush's attorney general, Richard Thornburgh, caused dismissal of the charges against Fernandez by refusing to allow the use of documents at trial on classification grounds. 1989 *Congressional Quarterly Almanac* 555, 564.

As the Senate Intelligence Committee noted in its 1989 report of a bill for an inspector general, "the existing [nonstatutory] Inspector General is a member of the CIA management team," depending on staff rotated to and from other CIA assignments. "It is difficult to expect thoroughness and objectivity with these inherent institutional constraints." A previous discussion of the constitutionality of statutory inspectors general is in Charles Tiefer, *Independent Offices as Checks on Executive Abuse*, 63 B.U.L. Rev. 59 (1983).

36. Congress had initially included in the intelligence authorization bill a title regarding notice of covert actions within forty-eight hours. After extensive bargaining over a veto threat, Congress had detached the issue of covert action notice from the bill. President Bush's signing statement acknowledged and even expressed gratitude for the arrangement. For a description of the enactment process, see 1989 *Congressional Quarterly Almanac* 543–550.

37. Quotations are from the message at *Pub. Papers* 1609–1611 (November 30, 1989).

38. "Moreover, the Office of Inspector General should be staffed by individuals knowledgeable and experienced in intelligence operations." Presidential Statement at 1609. The Senate Intelligence Committee had noted that "performance of the office has been affected by an over-reliance upon CIA employees who are rotated into the office as inspectors and investigators who have no previous training or experience in such work, and who must return to positions in other parts of the Agency once their tour with the Inspector General is completed."

39. This quote is from the independent counsel's postpardon report to Congress, which explains "Vice President Bush . . . was present for a national security briefing in 1985 at which McFarlane explained the Hawk shipment." The report adverts to the (unpublished) December 12, 1987, FBI interview of Vice President Bush, in which "Bush then went on, however, to describe a landing rights problem that arose with respect to the *November* 1985 shipment. Thus, although Bush confused the dates, it appears that he was recalling a national security briefing on the HAWK missile shipment either before or immediately after the November 1985 Geneva summit. Such briefings ordinarily included the President, Vice President, and chief of staff." Lawrence E. Walsh, Independent Counsel for Iran/Contra Matters, *Fourth Interim Report To Congress* (February 8, 1993), at 67 and n.142. The "landing rights problem" described by Bush was precisely what led Dewey Clarridge into the perjury charges that Bush pardoned in 1992.

40. *United States of America v. Caspar W. Weinberger*, Cr. No. 92-0416 (Indictment filed October 30, 1992), paras. 27, 28, and 32. Technically, prior to President Bush's pardon of Secretary Weinberger, this part of the indictment had been dismissed and instead other parts of the indictment were pending. However, there is little reason to doubt that, absent the pardon, the trial would have covered this subject. Weinberger discussed these meetings in his notes. While the meetings would not come into the trial in connection with dismissed counts (about Weinberger's withholding the notes), they would come into the trial in connection with the remaining counts (about Weinberger's denying he had notes).

41. Report at 418 (stating committee conclusion and citing Weinberger views).

42. Walter Pincus, *Shultz Memoirs Say Bush Misstated Arms-for-Hostages Role*, Washington Post, January 31, 1993, at A1 and A16.

43. When the congressional Iran-contra committees described the NSC meeting on January 7, 1987, concerning whether to go ahead with the deals, at which "Secretary Weinberger and Shultz continued to object strenuously," the committee had to admit that "[t]here is no record that the Vice President expressed any views." Iran-Contra Report, *supra*, at 203. When Weinberger's diary entry became available, it read: "George Shultz & I opposed—Bill Casey, Ed Meese & VP favored—as

did Poindexter." *United States of America v. Caspar W. Weinberger,* Cr. No. 92-0416 (indictment filed October 30, 1992), para. 22.

44. 1989 *Congressional Quarterly Almanac* 542.

45. *Pub. Papers* at 1693 (December 12, 1989).

46. *Ameron,* 610 F. Supp. at 755 (quotation omitted, in which the court quoted my congressional testimony.)

47.

James II was forced into exile in the Glorious Revolution of 1689, and the English Bill of Rights was enacted. The first article of that historic charter of freedom declared "That *the pretended power of Suspending of Laws,* or the *Execution of Laws by Regal Authority,* without Consent of Parliament *is Illegal."* Scholars have concluded that the "'faithful execution' clause of our Constitution is a mirror of the English Bill of Rights' abolition of the suspending power," that is, the abolition of what the English Bill of Rights had called the "pretended (Royal) power of Suspending". . . . *(Id.)*

48. *Lear Siegler,* 842 F.2d at 1124 (quotations omitted).

49. *Ameron* at 756.

50. *Lear Siegler,* 842 F.2d at 1124 (quotations omitted).

51. Blechman, *supra,* 90–111.

52. *Pub. Papers* 1767, 1766–1767 (1990).

53. Pat Towell, *Democrats Continue March Toward Big Defense Cuts,* Cong. Q. Week. Rep. 2930, 3931 (1990) (quoting House Armed Services Committee Chairman Les Aspin, who opposed the burden-sharing amendment).

54. *Id.* at 2931.

55. The president invoked similar claims of power regarding funding for an air base in Italy (later cancelled as Congress suggested) and regarding use of the Army and Navy Reserves. These were provisions he chose to construe away rather than explicitly say he was striking them down.

56. *Pub. Papers* 1767 (1990).

57. This section of the law read: "(b) Research, Development, Test, and Evaluation Objectives.— . . . . (2) LIMITED PROTECTION SYSTEMS—The Limited Protection Systems program element shall include . . . systems and components which, if deployed as a limited defense, *would not be in violation of the 1972 ABM Treaty"* (104 Stat. 1512 [emphasis added]).

58. For a description, see Michael J. Glennon, *Constitutional Diplomacy* 134–145 (1990); Blechman, *supra,* at 109–110; 1988 *Congressional Quarterly Almanac* 425–428.

59. In much the same spirit, the president "raise[d] constitutional difficulties" about a requirement concerning military antidrug efforts in Peru and Bolivia, where Congress merely asked for legislative proposals to square that military aid with American policy.

60. Section 1702 provided in pertinent part:

(k) NEGOTIATIONS WITH OTHER COUNTRIES.—

(1) . . . The Secretary of State, in consultation with the Secretary [of Commerce], [and] the Secretary of Defense [and others], shall be responsible for

conducting negotiations with those countries participating in . . . the Missile Technology Control Regime . . . regarding their cooperation in restricting the export of goods and technology in order to carry out—. . . .
(B) United States policy opposing the proliferation of chemical, biological, nuclear, and other weapons and their delivery systems . . . .
(2) OTHER COUNTRIES—The Secretary of State . . . shall be responsible for conducting negotiations with countries and groups of countries not referred to in paragraph (1) . . . . In cases where such negotiations produce agreements . . . the Secretary may treat exports . . . to countries party to such agreements in the same manner as exports are treated to countries that are MTCR adherents.

61. *Pub. Papers* 1766–1767 (1990). Commentators have noted the new understandings needed between president and Congress as American foreign policy increasingly shifts from bilateral arrangements to multilateral arrangements. When the old bilateral arrangements—one-on-one treaties and agreements—had received reservations in the course of congressional ratification, bilateral renegotiation had been comparatively simple. By contrast, if multilateral arrangements receive congressional ratification with reservations, that might require renegotiation on a multilateral basis—a very complicated matter. Because Congress cannot easily impose reservations afterward, as it had during traditional ratification of bilateral agreements, it must give its conditional "advice and consent" in advance for these new multilateral deals. Hence, in an era of multilateral agreements there is an obvious need for arrangements such as section 1702 for advance structuring of authority and responsibility.

62. A 1988 staff report for the House Armed Services Committee Investigations Subcommittee had stated:

The Congress and the media have expressed a growing interest in what are often called "black programs" (i.e. highly classified programs in the Department of Defense [DOD]) . . . . The official terms for highly classified programs is Special Access Programs or SAPs. . . .

The recent past growth in SAP funding and likely prospects of further growth in the future raise fundamental questions about DOD's oversight . . . . In fact, SAPs have sometimes been created and continued without adequate justification. (Housed Armed Services Committee Investigations Subcommittee, "Staff Inquiry into Department of Defense Special Access Programs" [February 1988], at 1, 5)

Subsequently, there appeared a work based on a Pulitzer Prize–winning news series, T. Weiner, *Blank-Check: The Pentagon's Black Budget* (1990).

63. It provided that "[t]he Classified Annex prepared by the Committee of Conference to accompany the conference report on the bill H.R. 4739 of the One Hundred First Congress and transmitted to the President shall have the force and effect of law as if enacted into law." 104 Stat. 1681 (1990).

64. *Pub. Papers* 1767 (1990).

65. 1990 *Congressional Quarterly Almanac* 812.

66. 1990 *Congressional Quarterly Almanac* 464.

67. Jefferson Morley, *Bush and the Blacks: An Unknown Story,* New York Review of Books, January 16, 1992, at 19, 20.

68. 484 U.S. 49 (1987).

69. Gwaltney argued that its past discharges were nonrecurring past violations and these did not show the company still, at that time of the lawsuit, "to be in violation." The suggested barrier against suit, that past discharges would not support litigation, meant that courts would routinely close their doors to citizen groups that observe environmental violations and sue; defendant polluters need only claim those violations were only past and nonrecurring.

70.

[I]f Congress were to grant private citizens enforcement powers coextensive with those of the government, serious constitutional questions would arise.[34]

[34]Article III of the Constitution requires that a plaintiff, at a minimum, show that he personally has suffered some actual or threatened injury . . . .
. . . . However, a citizen who brings suit simply to obtain a judicial assessment of civil penalties for nonrecurring past violations would fail to meet Article III's requirements . . . . Indeed, if Congress were to give private citizens untrammeled authority to seek penalties for wholly past violations . . .—it would intrude upon the Executive's responsibility to "take Care that the Laws be faithfully executed" (U.S. Const. Art. II, §3) and the prosecutorial discretion inherent therein. (Brief for the United States at 21–22 and n.34 [quotations omitted])

71. 484 U.S. at 57.

72. Section 707 of Pub. L. No. 101-549, 104 Stat. 2683 (1990).

73. Moore, *supra,* 2018, at 2022; *The Fettered Presidency* 214–216 (eds. L. Gordon Crovitz & Jeremy A. Rabkin 1989). Gray did have enthusiasm for particular clean air causes like alternative fuels and market mechanisms. Richard E. Cohen, *Washington at Work: Back Rooms and Clean Air* 52, 58–60 (1992).

74. *Pub. Papers* 1825 (November 15, 1990). In practical terms, a citizen group may see some facility illegally polluting on a few occasions and want to bring suit. *Gwaltney* said Congress could draft a law to allow the group to sue, and Congress had. Now, the president's statement said that this would not suffice for suing a polluter who asserted that these were "purely past" violations.

75. So thoroughly has the Justice Department lost every effort to create such barriers that it declined to join with industry attacks on statutes using such theses. The *qui tam* statutes, regarding which the Justice Department declined to join in constitutional challenges, are the clearest case in point.

The argument has not even won out in the context where it has more of a chance—a limitation on suits, not against polluters, but against the government to make it act. In *Lujan v. Defenders of Wildlife,* 112 S. Ct. 2130 (1992), the court denied environmental organizations the standing to require federal agencies aiding projects overseas to heed the Endangered Species Act. Justice Antonin Scalia tried, in his opinion for the court, to import a discussion of "faithful execution." 112 S. Ct. at 2145. However, of the five other justices who subscribed to his opinion, two wrote separately and talked only of the "injury-in-fact" requirements for cases. 112 S. Ct. at 2146-47 (Kennedy and Souter, JJ., concurring in part and concurring in the judgment). They did not talk of "faithful execution." At this time, the "faithful execution" theory remains a theory that might still go somewhere—in the direction of preventing Congress from letting citizens protect the environment when the executive branch will not—but the theory has not yet gotten the necessary acceptance from the moderate justices.

76. Terry Eastland, *George Bush into the Breach*, National Review, November 4, 1991, 41, 42.

77. The minority participation provision sets aside

> at least 10 per centum of Federal funding for the development, construction, and operation of the Superconducting Super Collider [to] be made available to business concerns or other organizations owned or controlled by socially and economically disadvantaged individuals . . . including historically black colleges and universities and colleges and universities having a student body in which more than 20 percent of the students are Hispanic Americans or Native Americans. (Section 304 of the Energy and Water Development Appropriations Act, Fiscal Year 1992, 105 Stat. 510, 532 [1991])

78. *Pub. Papers* 1143 (August 17, 1991).

79. Both the broadcasting provision, and the Supercollider ones, were appropriations provisions. The broadcasting provision had been just about as specific as the Supercollider one. It was the conservative dissent in the broadcasting case, not the majority, that kept insisting that the courts should sustain such remedies only when "Congress had identified discrimination" in the particular industry and the conservative dissent had complained that a congressional report "identifies no discrimination in the broadcasting industry." *Metro Broadcasting, Inc. v. FCC,* dissent at 6, 11.

80. Representative Louis Stokes (D-Ohio) authored the provision. Representative Stokes has a reputation for precision and caution in factual assertions, developed as he has chaired the House Assassinations Committee, the House Intelligence Committee, and the House Ethics Committee. Representative Stokes based this provision on a "recent report by the congressional established task force on women, minorities and the handicapped in science and technology." He reviewed the past "de facto exclusion of qualified contractors from such projects," particularly "minority-owned businesses, historically black colleges and universities, and other minority educations institutions." He justified the provision in order "to enhance and guarantee minority involvement in the scientific and technological industries . . . ." 136 Cong. Rec. H 1981 (daily ed. May 2, 1990).

81. Moore, *supra,* at 2018. Gray's views against civil rights drew unwanted attention in other instances, such as when "he backed an Education Department proposal to eliminate minority scholarships because the federal government should be 'colorblind.' The proposal was quickly dropped after it caused a political fu-

ror." (Owen Ullman, *Soul Brothers*, Washingtonian, May 1992, 76, 148). For a discussion of the controversy, *see* 1991 *Congressional Quarterly Almanac* 376.

82. 401 U.S. 424 (1971).

83. *Wards Cove Packing Co. v. Atonio*, 109 S. Ct. 2115 (1989).

84. To be more specific, these were burden of proof (complainants, rather than employers, had to offer proof on central points); the "business necessity" standard (making it easier for employers to claim that their employment practices weeded out minorities only for necessary reasons); and "cumulation" or "particularity" (complainants had to prove discrimination on a practice-by-practice basis instead of showing the overall or cumulative result of the overall employment approach).

85. Michael Duffy & Dan Goodgame, *Marching in Place: The Status Quo Presidency of George Bush* 116 (1992).

86. 1990 *Congressional Quarterly Almanac* 472–473 (Bush veto message; Senate attempted override vote).

87. Sharon LaFraniere, *Businesses Reject Talks on Rights Bill, Citing Bush Stance,* Washington Post, May 3, 1991, at A1.

88. Ann Devroy, *Bush Saw Gains in Deal, Officials Say,* Washington Post, October 26, 1991, at A1 (the quote of "strongly expressed" is from White House officials); 1991 *Congressional Quarterly Almanac* 256 (naming two Republican senators who would no longer oppose an override).

89. Joan Biskupic, *Overturning Precedents,* 49 Cong. Q. Week. Rep. 3125 (October 26, 1991).

90. 137 Cong. Rec. S 15276 (daily ed. October 25, 1991).

91. Washington Post, November 14, 1991, at A23 (emphasis supplied).

92. The provision was adopted at 137 Cong. Rec. S 15362 (daily ed. October 29, 1991). It appears in the bill as finally passed by the Senate at 137 Cong. Reg. S 15504 (daily ed. October 30, 1991). For more details, see Joan Biskupic, *Skirmish Over Spin,* 49 Cong. Q. Week. Rep. 3204 (November 2, 1991).

93.

> The following Monday [Oct. 28], the administration proposed an innovative statutory provision[] specifically designed to enforce the Thursday night [Oct. 24] agreement. This provision directed the courts to ignore any legislative history (such as the description of the agreement given by Kennedy on Friday) apart from the two sentences originally agreed to. Sens. Kennedy and Danforth objected to this proposal, while administration negotiators felt they had to insist. Tense meetings ensued, and it seemed at points that there might be no civil rights bill after all.
>
> On Tuesday [Oct. 29], Sens. Dole and Orrin Hatch engaged in heroic efforts to hold Sen. Kennedy and his allies to the agreement. Republican Leader Dole's arguments were particularly effective—that night, without any debate or a recorded vote, the Senate accepted a slightly modified version of the administration proposal enforcing the deal. (Gray, *supra*, at A23).

94. Ann Devroy & Sharon LaFraniere, *U.S. Moves to End Hiring Preferences,* Washington Post, November 21, 1991, at A1.

95. For the interesting story of how President Reagan and Attorney General Meese had backed away from the proposal to roll back the executive order on affirmative action, see Gary L. McDowell, *Affirmative Inaction: The Brock-Meese Stand-off on Federal Racial Quotas*, Policy Review, Spring 1989, at 32.

96. See Joan Biskupic, *Bush Signs Anti-Job Bias Bill Amid Furor Over Preferences*, 49 Cong. Q. Week. Rep. 3463 (daily ed. November 23, 1991); Devroy & LaFraniere, *supra*. The draft terminated existing federal guidelines on employment discrimination and it ordered the termination of set-asides and preferences throughout the government.

97. Augustus J. Jones, Jr., "Kinder, Gentler? George Bush and Civil Rights," in *Leadership and the Bush Presidency: Prudence or Drift in an Era of Change?* (eds. Ryan J. Barilleaux & Mary E. Stuckey 1992), 176, 184.

98. *Pub. Papers* 1702 (November 21, 1991).

99. Washington Post, November 14, 1991, at A23.

100. Devroy & LaFraniere, *supra*.

101. Beth Donovan, *Partisanship, Purse Strings Hobbled the 102nd*, 50 Cong. Q. Week. Rep. 3451 ("tax restructuring . . . ."), 3452 (Davidson quote).

CHAPTER 4

1. Woodward & Broder, *Quayle's Quest: Curb Rules, Leave 'No Fingerprints,'"* Washington Post, January 9, 1992, at A1 (hereafter *No Fingerprints*). The article is reprinted in 138 Cong. Rec. S 13210 (daily ed. September 10, 1992).

2. *No Fingerprints* at A17.

3. *Id.*

4. Michael Duffy, *Need Friends in High Places? For Industries Trying to Skirt the Law, Dan Quayle's Council on Competitiveness Is a Good Place to Start*, Time, November 4, 1991, at 25.

5. Daniel Isaac, *They Can't Compete*, Legal Times, September 7, 1992, reprinted in 138 Cong. Rec. S 13208, 13209 (daily ed. September 10, 1992) (referring to study by Public Citizen's Congress Watch).

6. His wife was Quayle's chief fund-raiser in his 1980 Senate campaign. He managed former Delaware governor Pierre S. du Pont IV's 1988 presidential campaign, was Bush's deputy convention manager in 1988, and was vice chair of Dan Coats's Senate campaign for the seat left vacant by Quayle. Christine Triano & Nancy Watzman, *All the Vice President's Men: How the Quayle Council on Competitiveness Secretly Undermines Health, Safety, and Environmental Programs*, Public Citizen's Congress Watch (September 1991), at 35; *No Fingerprints* at A16; Kirk Victor, *Quayle's Quiet Coup*, National Journal, July 6, 1991 1676, at 1677.

7. This is not to minimize the several in-depth treatments given to the Quayle Council. Besides the Washington Post account previously cited, there is Christine Triano & Gary D. Bass, *The New Game in Town: Regulation, Secrecy, and the Quayle Council on Competitiveness*, 9 Gov't Info. Q. 107 (1992); Triano & Watzman, *supra*. As to legal theory, there is Thomas O. Sargentich, *Normative Tensions in the Theory of Presidential Oversight of Agency Rulemaking*, in American Law J. (forthcoming 1993).

8. The hearings are discussed in Morton Rosenberg, *Regulatory Management at OMB*, in Sen. Comm. on Governmental Affairs, 99th Cong., 2d Sess., *Office of Man-*

agement and Budget: Evolving Roles and Future Issues, S. Prt. No. 134, at 185 (1986); see also Erik D. Olson, *The Quiet Shift of Power: Office of Management and Budget Supervision of Environmental Protection Agency Rulemaking Under Executive Order 12,291,* 4 Va. J. Nat. Res. Law 1 (1984).

9. The legislative action and Gramm procedures are described in Christopher H. Foreman, Jr., "Legislators, Regulators, and the OMB: The Congressional Challenge to Presidential Regulatory Relief," in *Divided Democracy: Cooperation and Conflict Between the President and Congress* (ed. James A. Thurber 1991), 123, 135–138. The Gramm procedures themselves are in a June 13, 1986, memorandum, reprinted in *Regulatory Program of the United States Government for April 1, 1991–March 31, 1992* 683–685 (1991).

10. OMB Watch, April 12, 1991, at 7, gave this retrospective view of Gray's role on the Reagan-era Task Force:

> Gray has been deeply involved in regulatory review initiatives. He was Executive Director of Reagan's 1981 Task Force on Regulatory Relief while then–Vice President Bush was chair. During that time, he developed a "hit list" of regulations that were to be reviewed by the Task Force and OIRA. His deregulatory campaign ginned up the OIRA machine and resulted in what has become commonly known as the OMB "Black hole," where regulations are known to have been sent, only to disappear from public reach for indefinite periods of time.

The Bush Administration fought hard and successfully to block public review through the Freedom of Information Act of records relating to the Bush-chaired task force. *Meyer v. Bush,* 981 F.2d 1288 (D.C. Cir. 1993).

11. Letter of John L. Howard, Counsel to the Vice President, July 25, 1991, to Paul R. Q. Wolfson of Public Citizen, responding to the latter's Freedom of Information Act request for Quayle Council documents.

12. Most sources attribute the executive order authority to the June 1990 grant discussed later. Even the April 12, 1989, "Fact Sheet" of the vice president's office stated the jurisdiction of the council in the modest terms quoted from the April 4 press briefing, namely, "The Council will review regulatory issues, and such other issues as may be referred by the President, bearing on competitiveness." However, that "Fact Sheet" then added in a paragraph on "Structure of the Council" that "In order to accomplish these purposes, the President has established a Council on Competitiveness, with the same authorities over the matters it reviews that were given to the Presidential Task Force on Regulatory Relief over regulatory issues in Executive Order No. 12291 (February 17, 1981) and No. 12498 (January 4, 1985)."

If that "Fact Sheet" were correct that the Quayle Council had the executive order authorities in April 1989, it would be hard to understand the fuss made when those authorities were conferred over a year later in June 1990. The more likely explanation is that the vice president's office simply boasted and overreached in its April 1989 claims. The murk is typical of authority conferred without congressional oversight or judicial review.

13. Victor, *supra,* at 1677.

14. *No Fingerprints,* at A16.

15. Duffy, *supra,* at 25.

16. 138 Cong. Rec. S 13222 (daily ed. Sept. 10, 1992).

17. *No Fingerprints,* at A17. After its June 28 meeting, the Quayle Council held meetings and issued press releases in 1990 on September 27 and December 19 concerning a variety of new laws and regulations, such as the regulations for the Clinical Laboratories Improvement Amendments of 1988, regulations concerning pension plans and working at home, and the president's pocket veto of the orphan drug law.

18. For a full discussion of the development of the recycling rule, *see Quayle Council Expected to Kill EPA Proposal to Require Recycling,* BNA Rep. on Regulation, Economics and Law, December 19, 1990, at A-6. Even the administration's antiregulation bible, its annual regulatory program published by OMB, noted in connection with this rule that "nearly half of the 6,000 landfills currently in use [will] be filled or closed down within 5 years. This impending shortage is creating more interest by local officials in recycling . . . ." Office of Management and Budget, *Regulatory Program of the U.S. Government: April 1, 1991–March 31, 1992* 530 (1991).

19. *Quayle Council Expected to Kill EPA Proposal to Require Recycling, supra,* at A-6.

20. Rosewicz, *Panel Led by Quayle Helped Kill Plan to Require Certain Waste Recycling,* Wall Street Journal, December 20, 1990, at A4.

21. Accordingly, "in light of the views of his colleagues on the Council, Administrator William Reilly stated his intention to remove the source separation requirement from the final Municipal Waste Combustor Rule." President's Council on Competitiveness Fact Sheet, December 19, 1990, at 1–2.

22. Fact Sheet of December 19, 1990, at 1 (public document issued by vice president's office) (quoted about executive order); Rosewicz, *supra,* at A4 (environmentalists called it "silly").

23. *South Carolina v. Baker,* 485 U.S. 505 (1988); *Garcia v. San Antonio Metropolitan Transit Authority,* 469 U.S. 528 (1985).

24. Victor, *supra,* at 1680 (quoting Paley).

25. 1990 *Congressional Quarterly Almanac* 278.

26. At 1825.

27. Fact Sheet of September 27, 1990, at 2.

28. Letter from Allen B. Hubbard to Chairman John Glenn, October 22, 1991, at 9.

29. Letter of October 22, 1991, from Hubbard to Chairman John Dingell of the House Energy and Commerce Committee.

30. At 1825.

31. The changes were at page 361 (and an unnumbered page of "Insert A" and "Insert B" following that page) of the McIntosh memorandum. These provisions for changes in permits violated a number of sections of the Clean Air Act, including section 502(b) (6) (governing permit changes).

32. The changes were at 361–362 of the McIntosh memorandum. These violated the "operational flexibility" provision in the act, section 502(b) (10).

33. The changes were at page 357 of the McIntosh memorandum. These violated the restrictions in the allowance trading provision in the act, section 503(f).

34. Fact Sheet of May 7, 1991, at 3.

35. See, regarding ITT, Raoul Berger, *Executive Privilege: A Constitutional Myth* 255 (1975); regarding Kissinger, Stephen W. Stathis, *Executive Cooperation: Presidential Recognition of the Investigative Authority of Congress and the Courts*, 3 J. Law & Politics 183, 258, 264–265 (1986); and regarding Watergate, Philip B. Kurland, "The Watergate Inquiry, 1973" in *Congress Investigates: 1792–1974* 467 (eds. Arthur M. Schlesinger, Jr., & Roger Bruns 1975).

36. McFarlane pled guilty but was pardoned by President Bush in December 1992. Poindexter had been convicted in a jury trial, but the conviction was reversed on appeal, so he needed no pardon.

37. Besides the hearing, see Triano & Watzman, *supra*, at 16.

38. The Waxman subcommittee released a May 8, 1991, memorandum from Richard Scmalensee of the Council of Economic Advisers to William Rosenberg of the EPA. The memorandum stated: "I had been led to believe that EPA would use the Administration's legislative proposal as the basis for crafting its WEPCO rule," meaning, "the Administration position as spelled out in my letter to Senator Ford on July 23, 1990." In other words, the CEA took it that the *rejected* administration position would be the basis for regulatory action.

39. The subcommittee hearing on July 22, 1991, included a staff report tracing the sequence. *See* also Triano & Watzman, *supra*, at 12.

40. 1990 *Congressional Quarterly Almanac* 413.

41. John H. Cushman, *Federal Regulation Growing Despite Quayle Panel's Role*, New York Times, December 24, 1991, at A1, A14. ("[C]onservatives [say] that [the] office on regulatory affairs is far less effective now than it was in the Reagan Administration. It has no politically appointed administrator and relatively little influence, they say."). Conservative commentators viewed Quayle's actions as reinvigorating OIRA. Warren Brookes, *Quayle's Sharper Edge*, Washington Times, May 15, 1991, at G1 ("As vice president, Mr. Quayle has singlehandedly revived the Office of Information and Regulatory Affairs . . . after Dick Darman had neutered it.")

42. *No Fingerprints* at A17.

43. Triano & Watzman, *supra*, at 9 n.1.

44. Fact Sheet of May 6, 1991, at 3.

45. *No Fingerprints* at A17. The deal had been that the proposed wetlands definition would require fifteen consecutive days of saturation, but public comments would be elicited on a ten- to twenty-day saturation period. Triano & Watzman, *supra*, at 11.

46. *No Fingerprints* at A17.

47. Triano & Watzman, *supra*, at 11 n.5 (citing Washington Post, August 8, 1991).

48. *Id.*

49. Sidney Blumenthal, *All the President's Wars*, New Yorker, 62, 68–70 (December 28, 1992).

50. James P. Pfiffner, *The President's Chief of Staff: Lessons Learned*, Working Paper No. 92:19, October 1992, at 22.

51. For a sample, see *Wetlands Conservation: Hearings Before the Subcomm. on Fisheries and Wildlife Conservation and the Environment of the House Comm. on Merchant Marine and Fisheries,* 101st Cong., 1st Sess. (October 16 and November 21, 1991).

52. Philip J. Hilts, *U.S. Aides Retreat on Wetlands Rule,* New York Times, November 23, 1992, at 1, 10.

53. Jim Sibbison, *Dan Quayle, Business's Backdoor Boy,* Nation, July 29, 1991, at 141; Victor, *supra,* at 1676; Jeffrey H. Birnbaum, *White House Competitiveness Council Provokes Sharp Anger Among Democrats in Congress,* Wall Street Journal, July 8, 1991, at A8.

54. The October letter listed the following as the Quayle Council meeting dates in 1990: June 8, September 27, and December 19. In 1991, the meetings took place on February 11, May 6 and 14, June 27, and July 22 and 29. The working groups were entitled biotechnology, civil litigation reform, deregulation, the drug approval process, product liability reform, and commercialization of government research. A letter of response in April had simply forwarded public record documents with a few paragraphs of pleasantries.

55. November 18, 1991.

56. Holly Idelson, *Glenn Trying to Shed Light on Rule-Making Process,* 49 Cong. Q. Week. Rep. 3449 (November 23, 1991). The bill was numbered S. 1941.

57. Michael Weisskopf, *White House Defends Competitiveness Chief: No Conflict of Interest Found, Aide Reports,* Washington Post, December 10, 1991, at A19. Later he put his holdings in a blind trust. Weisskopf, *Amid Conflict Questions, White House Official to Put Holdings in Blind Trust,* Washington Post, December 11, 1991, at A23.

58. 138 Cong. Rec. H5736 (daily ed. July 1, 1992).

59. Dana Priest, *Competitiveness Council Under Scrutiny: Critics Charge Panel Lets Industry Exert Back-Door Influence on Implementing Laws,* Washington Post, November 26, 1991, at A19; *see* Philip J. Hilts, *Questions on Role of Quayle Council: Panel's Influence in Writing Rules Draws Criticism and Subpoena in Congress,* New York Times, November 19, 1991, at B12 (regarding issuance of subpoena).

60. *Council on Competitiveness and FDA Plans to Alter the Drug Approval Process at FDA: Hearing Before the Human Resources and Intergovernmental Relations Subcomm. of the House Comm. on Government Operations,* 102d Cong., 2d Sess. (1992). See these hearings at 176–177 (1990 documentation activating the Quayle Council) and 164–175 (Subcommittee subpoena).

61. Kirk Victor, *Tale of the Red Tape,* National Journal, March 21, 1992, 684, at 685.

62. Both the president's remarks and his memorandum are in *Pub. Papers* 727, 729 (1992).

63. Eugene Robinson & Michael Weisskopf, *"No" Leaves U.S. Isolated at Summit: Leak of Memo Urging Treaty Approval Said to Upset EPA Chief,* Washington Post, June 6, 1992, at A1 (emphasis added).

64. Nancy Watzman & Christine Triano, *Defund Quayle's Autocratic Competitiveness Council,* Los Angeles Times, June 24, 1992, Metro Section, 7 (opinion editorial).

65. Jessica Mathews, *Unfriendly Skies,* Washington Post, February 9, 1992, at B7 (columnist).

66. Dana Priest & Helen Dewar, *Critics of New Pollution Rules Threaten Lawsuits, Legislation,* Washington Post, June 27, 1992, at A6.

67. *Treasury, Postal Service, and General Government Appropriations for Fiscal Year 1993: Hearings Before a Subcomm. of the House Comm. on Appropriations,* 102nd Cong., 2d Sess. 239 (March 17, 1992) (submission for the record by White House).

68. H.R. Rep. No. 618, 102nd Cong., 2d Sess. 35 (June 25, 1992).

69. 138 Cong. Rec. H 5736-37 (daily ed. July 1, 1992). The Committee on Appropriations had approved Representative Skaggs's provision to defund the Quayle Council before the bill came to the floor. On the floor, Representative Joseph McDade (R-Penn.) offered an amendment to restore the defunded amount, which the House defeated. *Id.* at H 5733.

70. Eric Pianin & Bill McAllister, *Administrative Spending Freeze Voted*, Washington Post, July 29, 1992, at A21.

71. 138 Cong. Rec. S 13225 (daily ed. Sept. 10, 1992) (statement of Senator Dennis DeConcini [D-Ariz.]). In conference, the Senate's position in favor of funding prevailed, H.R. Rep. No. 919, 102d Cong., 2d Sess. 48 (Sept. 28, 1992) (Senate prevails on Amendment No. 58), as part of the general congressional approach of not offering up veto bait to the president but letting the issues be resolved by the election.

72. Michael Weisskopf & Thomas W. Lippman, *From Fumes to Water, Bush Is Flexing Regulatory Rules*, Washington Post, March 7, 1991, at A1.

73. Of the 25 percent of the petitioners that got to meet personally with the Quayle Council staff, "[w]ith the exception of three companies, the winners were major corporations or associations representing major corporations, and all were big donors to the Bush Quayle campaign, the Republican National Committee or events—such as the President's Dinner—sponsored by the RNC" (Dan Isaac, *They Can't Compete*, Legal Times, September 7, 1992 [reprinted in 138 Cong. Rec. S13208 (daily ed. September 10, 1992)]).

74. Bob Davis & Jill Abramson, *Many of Competitiveness Council's Beneficiaries Are Firms That Make Big Donations to the GOP*, Wall Street Journal, October 13, 1992, at A22. One particular issue received study: how major oil companies used the Quayle Council to weaken a regulation of the burning of used motor oil, which contains high toxic levels: "The used-oil controversy shows how big contributors try to influence the course of regulation. In this battle, big contributors worked together to secretly persuade the council to release a weak Environmental Protection Agency proposal they favored . . . ."

75. James A. Barnes, *Cash Crunch Slows GOP Ground War*, National Journal, October 31, 1992, at 2505. The article details how the president scheduled forty fundraising events from the end of September to the end of October. The Wall Street Journal article showed the value of the Quayle Council in obtaining attendance at those events.

76. William Schneider, *A Loud Vote For Change*, National Journal, November 7, 1992, 2541, at 2544 (table of exit polls). Eight percent of voters had listed choice of vice president as one of the candidate qualities that mattered most; 6 percent of voters had listed the environment as one of the issues that mattered most.

CHAPTER 5

1. R. Jeffrey Smith & John Goshko, *Ill-Fated Iraq Policy Originated Shortly After Bush Took Office*, Washington Post, June 27, 1992, at A7.

2. Some NSC directives would be classified, but that is not why they are withheld from Congress. Through its intelligence committees, Congress routinely re-

views matters of much higher and more sensitive classification than NSC directives, namely, the operations of, and intelligence gathered by, intelligence agencies.
NSC directives that are either unclassified or are at a much lower classification
level are withheld to shield the White House.

3. *Presidential Directives and Records Accountability Act: Hearing Before a Subcomm.
of the House Comm. on Government Operations*, 100th Cong., 2d Sess. 92 (1988) (hereafter *Presidential Directives Hearings*). GAO made its estimate by looking at the last
(highest) number of declassified directives. (The directives are consecutively numbered.) For the Carter Administration that number was 54. For the Reagan Administration, at that time (half a year before the administration's end), the number was
298.

4. Christopher C. Shoemaker, *The NSC Staff* 61 (1991).

5. Constantine C. Menges, *Inside the National Security Council: The True Story of
the Making and Unmaking of Reagan's Foreign Policy*, 14 (1988); see *id.* at 94.

6. Menges, *supra*, at 154.

7. In 1983, a congressional hearing focused on an NSDD that greatly expanded
secrecy requirements for federal employees, muzzling whistleblowers and former
officials. *Hearing Before a Subcomm. of the House Comm. on Government Operations*,
98th Cong., 1st Sess. (1983). The NSDD expanded the signing of nondisclosure
agreements—forced pledges that would block whistleblowing on defense procurement scandals—to 2.5 million government and 1.5 million contractor employees.

The directive also expanded greatly the portion of these employees required to
sign lifelong agreements to submit their writings forever to prepublication review.
This lifelong submission to censorship allowed the administration to muzzle any
timely news commentary by experts who had left the government, thus effectively
precluding criticism to the news media regarding missteps or botched policies of a
current administration. The directive's commands of law also greatly expanded
the use of polygraphs in investigations of leaks of classified information, putting
the fear of technological inquisitions into all those being forced to sign these documents as a condition of employment.

8. During the Reagan Administration, congressional hearings on NSDDs had
the simple facts about the system. For example, the 1983 hearing on NSDD 84 contained the full text of that directive, and extensive testimony occurred on the
NSDD. Even an archapostle of government secrecy, former assistant attorney general Richard Willard, considered it entirely appropriate as it was to publish details
behind that NSDD in a defense of the directive. Richard K. Willard, *Law and the National Security Decision-Making Process in the Reagan Administration*, 11 Houston J. of
Int'l Law 129 (198). Similarly, a 1987 congressional hearing on National Security
Decision Directive 145, a directive further intensifying Defense Department information control, contained full open discussion of the directive. *Computer Security
Act of 1987: Hearings Before a Subcomm. of the House Comm. on Government Operations*, 100th Cong., 1st Sess. (1987).

During the Bush Administration, in contrast, the chairman of the House Committee on Government Operations, Representative John Conyers (D-Mich.), when
introducing a bill in 1991 to regulate the directives, described the blocking of the
most basic oversight effort: "During the past year, as chairman of the Government

Operations Committee, I have been engaged in an ongoing dialogue, with General Scowcroft, the President's National Security Adviser. The White House has refused to provide even a list of NSD's issued by the Bush administration. I did not seek the actual NSD's themselves, just a numbered list with the titles and a brief summary of each" (137 Cong. Rec. E2022 [daily ed. June 4, 1991]).

9. These diary entries, respectively from November 10, November 18, and December 20, 1986, were published in *Was Vice President Bush in the Loop? You Make the Call*, Washington Post, January 31, 1993, at C6.

10. *Presidential Directives Hearings, supra.*

11. *Id.* at 29.

12. *Id.*

13. The conviction was overturned on the grounds of his immunization during the congressional hearings. For a discussion of the immunization issue, *see* George Van Cleve & Charles Tiefer, *Navigating the Shoals of "Use" Immunity and Secret International Enterprises in Major Congressional Investigations: Lessons of the Iran-Contra Affair*, 55 Mo. L. Rev. 43 (1990).

14. Staff Report to the Senate Committee on Foreign Relations, 100th Cong., 2d Sess., S. Prt. 148, at viii (1988).

15. The fullest study of that development is Kenneth R. Timmerman, *The Death Lobby: How the West Armed Iraq* (1991) (hereafter *Death Lobby*).

16. As a New York Times reporter described this turning point in her book on the Kuwait crisis, "To continue its war with Iran, Iraq had relied on roughly $40 billion in interest-free 'loans' and grants from the rich Gulf states—which it expected to be forgiven. Iraq also owed as much as $35 billion to Europe, Japan, and the United States that it would now have to pay back in increasingly scarce hard currency, and about $7 billion to $8 billion to the Soviet bloc" (Elaine Sciolino, *The Outlaw State: Saddam Hussein's Quest for Power and the Gulf Crisis* 187 [1991]).

17. *Id.* at 188.

18. *Chemical and Biological Weapons Threat: The Urgent Need for Remedies, Hearings of the Sen. Comm. on Foreign Relations*, 101st Cong., 1st Sess. (January 24, 1989).

19. *Id.* at 3.

20.

Iraq modified a Soviet-produced SCUD—extending its range to some 325 nm—and used it with devastating effect against Iran's cities. . . .

Many states noted Iraq's effective use of chemical weapons against both its own Kurdish population and Iranian forces. The tacit acceptance of this development could encourage other states to obtain or improve their CW capability. . . .

NUCLEAR CAPABILITIES . . . . Those actively pursuing a capability include Libya, Iraq, and Iran. (*H.R. 2461 Department of Defense Authorization for Appropriations for Fiscal Year 1990: Hearings Before the Subcomm. on Seapower and Strategic and Critical Materials Subcomm. of the House Armed Services Comm.*, 101st Cong., 1st Sess. 38-49 [February 22, 1989] ([declassified version of testimony by Rear Admiral Thomas Brooks, director of U.S. naval intelligence])

21. *Death Lobby* at 327.

22. The suppressed Department of Energy warnings are detailed in a hearing chaired by Representative John Dingell (D-Mich.) in 1991, regarding which the Congress could not obtain declassification until spring 1992. *Nuclear Nonproliferation: Hearing Before the Subcomm. on Oversight and Investigations of the House Comm. on Energy and Commerce Concerning Failed Efforts to Curtail Iraq's Nuclear Weapons Program*, 102nd Cong., 1st Sess. (April 24, 1991). For the discussion when the information became public, see R. Jeffrey Smith, *DOE Official Discounted '89 Warning on Iraq's Nuclear Program*, Washington Post, April 21, 1992, at A15.

23. See 139 Cong. Rec. H 7872-76 (1992) (June 1989 knowledge of Defense Intelligence Agency).

24. The hearings were *Global Spread of Chemical and Biological Weapons: Hearings Before the Sen. Comm. on Governmental Affairs and its Permanent Subcomm. on Investigations,* 101st Cong., 1st Sess. (1989). The Pell-Helms bill was S. 195, 101st Cong., 1st Sess., reported by S. Rep. No. 166, 101st Cong., 1st Sess. (1989). The companion House bill was H.R. 3033, 101st Cong., 1st Sess., reported by H. Rep. No. 334, Parts I and II, 101st Cong., 1st Sess. (1989). For discussions of these, *see* 1989 *Congressional Quarterly Almanac* 501–503.

25. S. Rep. No. 131, 101st Cong., 1st Sess. 171 (September 14, 1989), contains the provision, though without explaining that its obscure language was directed at Iraq. That was made clear during Senate enactment. 135 Cong. Rec. S 11491 (daily ed. September 20, 1989). *See* 1989 *Congressional Quarterly Almanac* 784.

26. In June 1984, Vice President Bush apparently called the chairman of the Export-Import Bank to extend financing for an Iraqi pipeline project. After the call, the chairman agreed. This "marked the point at which George Bush had begun to take an active role in the covert policy to tilt toward Iraq." Murray Waas & Craig Unger, *In the Loop: Bush's Secret Mission*, New Yorker, November 2, 1992, at 64, 71. In spring 1987, Vice President Bush apparently again talked to the chairman (a new chairman) of the Export-Import Bank to extend short-term financing to Iraq. After the talk, the chairman agreed. The vice president could then tell this to the Iraqi ambassador at a meeting on March 2, 1987. *Id.* at 81. The related documentation, primarily the talking points for the vice president in these discussions, has been published in the Congressional Record. 138 Cong. Rec. H. 519-20 (1992).

27. *Id.* at 78–79.

28. Paul A. Gigot, *A Great American Screw-Up: The U.S. and Iraq, 1980–1990*, The National Interest, Winter 1990/91, 3, at 6–7. For further discussions of Fairbanks, see *Death Lobby* at 222-23.

29. John M. Goshko, *Before the Gulf War, Iraq was a 'Sixth-Floor Problems,'"* Washington Post, July 7, 1992, at A17.

30. Smith and Goshko, *supra*, at A7.

31. *Id.*

32. Don Oberdorfer, *Missed Signals in the Middle East: Why Was the Administration Blindsided by Iraq's Invasion of Kuwait?* Washington Post Magazine, March 17, 1991, 19, at 21. Another lengthy press account of this can be found in Sciolino, *supra*, at 173. One also appears in 1990 *Congressional Quarterly Almanac* 723.

33. Elaine Sciolino, *'89 Bush Order Says Ply Iraq with Aid*, New York Times, May 29, 1992.

34. 138 Cong. Rec. H 865 (daily ed. March 2, 1992).

35. *Id.*

36. Department of Justice, *Report to the House Committee on the Judiciary Concerning July 9, 1992 Request to Seek the Appointment of an Independent Counsel* 14 (August 10, 1992).

37. Report at 15. Secretary Baker had approved a memorandum recommending that he make the call, dated October 26, 1989, which explained, "Earlier this month, the President signed NSD-26, mandating pursuit of improved economic and political ties with Iraq." The memorandum is reprinted in *Need for an Independent Counsel to Investigate U.S. Government Assistance to Iraq: Hearings Before the House Comm. on the Judiciary,* 102nd Cong., 2d Sess. 438 (1992) (hereafter *Independent Counsel Hearings*).

38. 135 Cong. Rec. H 867 (daily ed. March 2, 1992). The talking points are also in *Independent Counsel Hearings* at 442.

39. 138 Cong. Rec. H 520 (daily ed. February 24, 1992).

40. Sciolino, *The Outlaw State,* at 173.

41. 138 Cong. Rec. H520-21 (daily ed. February 24, 1992).

42. 135 Cong. Rec. S 11491 (daily ed. September 20, 1989). Senator Kasten (R-Wisc.) offered the amendment for Senator Heinz and made the comment.

43. 55 Fed. Reg. 4826 (February 9, 1990).

44. *Developments in the Middle East: Hearings of the Subcomm. on Europe and the Middle East of the House Comm. on Foreign Affairs,* 101st Cong., 2d Sess. 60–61, 97–100 (1990).

45. *The Middle East in the 1990s: Hearing Before the Subcomm. on Europe and the Middle East of the House Comm. on Foreign Affairs,* 101st Cong., 2d Sess. 41 (1990).

46. *United States-Iraqi Relations: Hearing Before the Subcomm. on Europe and the Middle East of the House Comm. on Foreign Affairs,* 101st Cong., 2d Sess. 4 (1990).

47. *Id.* at 3, 21.

48. House Republican Research Committee, "Task Force on Terrorism and Unconventional Warfare, *Chemical Weapons in the Third World,* section 2 ("Iraq's Expanding Chemical Arsenal"), at 12 (1990). The report's seventy-three footnotes provide a cogent map to the literature in the United States and abroad on the Iraqi weaponry of mass destruction.

49. 1990 *Congressional Quarterly Almanac* 200 (describing the Pell-Helms bill, S. 195).

50. H.R. 4918, 101st Cong., 2d Sess. (introduced May 24, 1990, by Rep. Dan Burton (R-Ind.) et al.).

51. S. 2779, 100th Cong., 2d Sess., introduced by Senator Inouye June 22, 1990, provided for sanctions for Iraq.

52. The column was reprinted by Representative Lantos in the Congressional Record, 136 Cong. Rec. E2523 (daily ed. July 27, 1990).

53. 136 Cong. Rec. S10904 (daily ed. July 27, 1990).

54. The two quotes are from 136 Cong. Rec. H 5743 and 5752, and the vote is at 5755 (daily ed. July 27, 1990).

55. 136 Cong. Rec. S11047 (daily ed. July 30, 1990).

56. Around then, according to a Washington Post report, the administration also received, but ignored, planning papers from the State Department warning

that its Iraq policy was fundamentally wrong. The following report in Oberdorfer, *supra*, at 19 and 22, concerns the early weeks of 1990:

> About the same time, Rick Herrmann and Steve Grummon, two junior aides on the Policy Planning Staff at State, were writing internal papers arguing that the policy was not just flawed in its execution but fundamentally wrong. One of their papers, "Containing Iraq," went to Policy Planning director Dennis Ross, one of the handful of close Baker aides in a position to get an immediate and serious hearing from the secretary. The paper asserted that Iraq had emerged from the war much stronger than Iran and argued—in contrast to the prevailing administration view that Tehran was the focal point of danger—that Saddam Hussein's regime was the main threat to stability in the area and should be contained.

57. *Death Lobby* at 371. The meeting is also described in Oberdorfer, *supra*, at 20, 22 ("the thrust of the Iraqi leader's remarks to Kelly had suggested a desire for better relations with Washington rather than more distant or even unfriendly ones").

58. 136 Cong. Rec. H 1111 (daily ed. March 9, 1992) (reprinting of NSC memorandum of May 18, 1990, which was produced in response to the April 16 meeting).

59. The participants are reflected in the May 18 memorandum cited in note 58 and in *United States Exports of Sensitive Technology to Iraq: Hearings Before the Subcomm. on International Economic Policy and Trade of the House Comm. on Foreign Affairs* (hereafter *Iraq Technology Hearings*) 102nd Cong., 1st Sess. 50 (April 8, 1991).

60. *Iraq Technology Hearings* at 50.

61. *Id.* at 51.

62. *Id.* at 92.

63. The paper's format stated "pro" and "con" positions on options, apparently avoiding commitments to positions in case the document was leaked but signaling implicitly its antipathy for congressional sanctions legislation. Regarding congressional sanctions on chemical warfare, the paper stuck to what had been, and continued to be, the administration's ground for opposing the Pell-Helms proposal and ultimately vetoing what Congress passed. This ground was that no law should be passed because even without a law the administration would take care of export controls and licensing by proposals of its "non-proliferation PCC [Policy Coordination Committee]"—another NSC committee. Memorandum of May 16, 1990, reprinted in 136 Cong. Rec. H1111 (daily ed. March 9, 1992).

64. Oberdorfer, *supra*, at 36.

65. A Wall Street Journal reporter wrote:

> The April remarks finally got [Dennis Ross's (head of the State Department's Policy Planning office)] attention. Ross and John Kelly, the assistant secretary for Near Eastern affairs, have told reporters they went to Secretary of State James Baker and urged a new policy of limited sanctions against Iraq. Baker is said to have agreed.

But the policy died aborning. Baker turned the effort over to Robert Kimmitt, State's undersecretary for political affairs, who made a case to the interagency [NSC] "deputies committee," a set of officials just below the Cabinet level. Accounts differ on what happened next. By State's account, its initiative died after it met resistance from the Commerce Department and the NSC staff, including NSC adviser Brent Scowcroft.

Other sources, the majority by far, insist that State never really made much of an effort. (Gigot, *supra,* at 7)

66. Reportedly, Ambassador Glaspie was told to reiterate to the Iraqi government the standard administration position that the United States had "no position" on Arab border disputes (the United States merely opposed use of force). Jean Edward Smith, *George Bush's War* 56n. (1992). (On July 23, 1991, the Washington Post printed what it reported as the texts of the cables.)

67. *Id.* at 56 (emphasis deleted). The transcript was published in the New York Times on September 23, 1990.

68. Smith and Goshko, *supra,* at A7.

69. The House Foreign Affairs Committee actually marked up the bill on August 1, one day before the invasion. For the description of the bill's passage, see 1990 *Congressional Quarterly Almanac* 725.

70. For a description of the veto, see *id.* at 198.

71. Report of Frederick B. Lacey on the Preliminary Investigation, December 8, 1992, at 105 (NSD, "overstated") and 96 (quoting letter with "national security," conceded to be "unfortunate").

72. Memorandum to the Secretary of Agriculture of April 17, 1991, in 138 Cong. Rec. H 1279 (daily ed. March 16, 1992).

73. NSC Memorandum of April 8, 1991, in 138 Cong. Rec. H 1279 (daily ed. March 16, 1992).

74. Memorandum to the Secretary of Agriculture, *supra,* at H 1280.

75. *U.S. Government Controls on Sales to Iraq: Hearing Before the Commerce, Consumer, and Monetary Affairs Subcomm. of the House Comm. on Government Operations,* 101st Cong., 2d Sess. (1990).

76. The letters and subpoena vote are described in *Strengthening the Export Licensing System:* H.R. Rep. No. 137, 102d Cong., 1st Sess. 42 (July 2, 1991).

77. *Id.* at 1896.

78. *Id.* (quoting March 1991 interview by Commerce Department auditors; emphasis added).

79. Carroll J. Doherty, *State Department Official Tells of Warning About Saddam,* 50 Cong. Q. Week. Rep. 1895, 1896 (June 27, 1992); *Independent Counsel Hearings* at 501 (Representative Chuck Schumer [D-N.Y.] explaining what Undersecretary Kloske had told in interviews).

80. *Independent Counsel Hearings* at 781 (written statement of former Undersecretary Kloske); R. Jeffrey Smith, *Decision to Withhold Some Iraq Export Data Laid to White House,* Washington Post, June 26, 1992, at A10.

81. "White House and other high level officials were involved in a separate aspect of responding to the [Barnard] Subcommittee's request: the decision whether

to release or assert privilege with respect to the positions that other agencies had taken on whether to approve the export licenses . . . . [T]here were several discussions between lawyers and other officials at various agencies and departments about whether executive privilege protected the interagency positions." Attorney General Report at 30.

82. Carroll J. Doherty, *Of Documents and Doctoring*, 50 Cong. Q. Week. Rep. 1616 (June 6, 1992) (describing statements at June 2 House Judiciary Committee hearing). For the full testimony, see *Independent Counsel Hearings* at 158.

83. Scowcroft calls the "cover-up" charge "irresponsible" in Brent Scowcroft, *We Didn't "Coddle" Saddam*, Washington Post, October 10, 1992, at A27 (opinion editorial). The report quote is in Attorney General Report at 96.

84. *Independent Counsel Hearings* at 528.

85. Attorney General Report at 30.

86. *Id.* at 31.

87. The Iraqi transcript of the meeting was published in the New York Times on September 23, 1990.

88. 1991 *Congressional Quarterly Almanac* 455 ("suspicions"); 1991 *Congressional Quarterly Almanac* 436 ("attempts rebuffed").

89. Elaine Sciolino, *Envoy's Testimony on Iraq is Assailed*, New York Times, July 13, 1991, at 1.

90. 1991 *Congressional Quarterly Almanac* 456 (quoting Pell letter which, in turn, purports to quote cable title).

91. *Id.*

92. *Banca Nazionale del Lavoro Affair and Regulation and Supervision of U.S. Branches and Agencies of Foreign Banks: Hearing Before the House Comm. on Banking, Finance and Urban Affairs*, 101st Cong., 2d Sess. (1990); Staff Report of the House Comm. on Banking, Finance and Urban Affairs, 102d Cong., 1st Sess., *The Role of Banca Nazionale Del Lavoro in Financing Iraq, the Failure of the Federal Reserve Under the Federal "Umbrella" Bank Regulatory Structure and Interference by the State of Illinois* (1991); *Iraqi and Banca Nazionale Del Lavoro Participation in Export-Import Programs: Hearing Before the House Comm. on Banking, Finance and Urban Affairs*, 102d Cong., 1st Sess. (1991).

93. George Lardner, Jr., *White House Curbed Release of Data on Prewar Support of Iraq, Hill Told*, Washington Post, March 17, 1992. The administration responded with criticism of Chairman Gonzalez for disclosing documents bearing executive branch classification markings and threats from Attorney General Barr that the administration would withhold documents thereafter. Timothy J. Burger & Glenn R. Simpson, *Bush Administration Charges Gonzalez Bares "Classified" Documents in "Record,"* Roll Call, April 13, 1992, at 11; Carroll J. Doherty, *Democrats Aim to Reignite Iraqi Aid Controversy*, 50 Cong. Q. Week. Rep. 1457 (May 23, 1992) (describing Barr letter of May 15). Representative Larry Combest (R-Texas) offered a privileged resolution to have Chairman Gonzalez investigated by the House Ethics Committee, but the House voted to table the resolution. 138 Cong. Rec. H 8739 (daily ed. September 18, 1992).

94. George Lardner, Jr., *GAO Investigators Decry Delays on Iraq Inquiry*, Washington Post, May 30, 1992, at A15.

95. Carroll J. Doherty, *Democrats Aim to Reignite Iraqi Aid Controversy, supra,* at 1459; R. Jeffrey Smith, *Democrats Widen Iraq Policy Debate to Include Issue of a Coverup,* Washington Post, July 13, 1992, at A6.

96. Sciolino, *'89 Bush Order, supra.*

97. Carroll J. Doherty, *Panel Democrats Poised to Ask for Probe of Help to Saddam,* 50 Cong. Q. Week. Rep. 1615 (June 6, 1992). The manager subsequently withdrew his plea.

98. Doherty, *State Department Official, supra,* 1895–1896.

99. Attorney General Report at 97. The mechanism for the House Judiciary Committee members' letter and the attorney general's response is described in the law regarding independent counsels, 28 U.S.C. § 592 (g).

100. Attorney General Report at 30.

101. "We are aware of suggestions that there may have been White House involvement in the decision to change the description of the trucks [as "military use"]. We have uncovered no evidence that supports the suggestion that anyone in a higher position of authority than Kloske directed or authorized changing the description of the trucks" (Attorney General Report at 30). Of course, the White House counsel and NSC counsel had declined to testify before Congress on the matter.

CHAPTER 6

1. For examples of presidential supremacists on this subject, *see* J. Gregory Sidak, *To Declare War,* 41 Duke L.J. 27, 33, 120 (1991) (congressional enactment of the Persian Gulf Resolution was "a legal nullity, a merely precatory or hortatory gesture," and "legally insignificant"); Terry Eastland, *Energy in the Executive* 126 (1992) ("the President's very powerful exercise of executive power" in the period leading up to the congressional enactment of the Persian Gulf Resolution was "a rebuke to the unconstitutional assumption of the War Powers Resolution that the entire domain of foreign policy may be managed by the legislative branch").

2. Early Supreme Court cases, early examples, and early commentaries reflected this original vision of congressional preeminence. David Gray Adler, *The Constitution and Presidential Warmaking: The Enduring Debate,* 103 Poli. Sci. Q. 1 (1988); Charles A. Lofgren, *War-Making Under the Constitution: The Original Understanding,* 81 Yale L.J. 672 (1972); Abraham Sofaer, *War, Foreign Affairs and Constitutional Power* (1976); Francis D. Wormuth, *The Nixon Theory of the War Power: A Critique,* 60 Calif. L. Rev. 623 (1972); Raoul Berger, *War-Making by the President,* 121 U. Penn. L. Rev. 29 (1972).

3. For some of the major books in the debate, particularly those not cited as to particular contexts, *see, e.g.,* Thomas Eagleton, *War and Presidential Power: A Chronicle of Congressional Surrender* (1974); W. Taylor Reveley III, *War Powers of the President and Congress: Who Holds the Arrows and Olive Branches?* (1981); Marc E. Smyrl, *Conflict or Codetermination? Congress, the President, and the Power to Make War* (1988) John Lehman, *Making War* (1992); Francis D. Wormuth & Edwin B. Firmage, *To Chain the Dog of War* (2d ed. 1989).

4. Unofficial "lists" and treatment by presidential proponents started with J. Reuben Clark, *Right to Protect Citizens in Foreign Countries by Landing Forces* (3d ed.

1924); M. Offutt, *The Protection of Citizens Abroad by the Armed Forces of the United States* (1928); and James Grafton Rogers, *World Policing and the Constitution* (1945). The lists emerged into the heart of modern debate when cited officially by the State Department as justifications for the Korean and Vietnam wars. U.S. Department of State, *Authority of the President to Repel the Attack in Korea*, 23 Dep't State Bull. 173, 177–178 (1950); U.S. Department of State, *Armed Actions Taken by the United States Without a Declaration of War, 1798–1967*, Research Project No. 806A (August 1967). More detail on the history of "list" theory is in Wormuth & Firmage, *supra*, at 142 – 145.

5. For critical scrutiny of the "lists" of incidents, see Wormuth, *supra*, at 654–664; Wormuth & Firmage, *supra*, at 143–149; Harold Hongju Koh, *The National Security Constitution: Sharing Power After the Iran-Contra Affair* 81–88 (1990); Arthur M. Schlesinger, Jr., *The Imperial Presidency*, 61–86 (1974).

6. Wormuth & Firmage, *supra*, at 42 and n. (Veracruz), 60 (France 1798), and 63–64 (Barbary pirates).

7. For reviews of the pre–twentieth century record, both as to war powers and other aspects of national security, *see* Koh, *supra*, 74–88; Schlesinger, *supra*, 25–89.

8. For example, President Grant ordered the Navy to protect Santo Domingo from Haiti as part of a project to annex part of the island. Yet when Congress would not agree, he canceled the project and thereafter deferred to Congress as the acknowledged "war-making power of the country." Schlesinger, *supra*, 86 (quoting Grant).

9. After the Spanish-American War, the president had American troops put down the Philippine Insurrection; after World War I, the Wilson Administration had American troops intervene against the Russian Revolution. *See, e.g.,* Koh, *supra,* and sources cited, at 88–90. The particular war powers question thereby raised concerns when conflict, once authorized, continues after the original enemy is no longer in the field and the new enemy was not the one originally contemplated by Congress. Presidential power once war has been authorized is so magnified that even precedents of that nature, involving such altered conflicts, simply do not bear on the Persian Gulf War question in 1990 of what a president could do prior to, or absent, any congressional authorization at all.

10. For discussions of the contrast between Roosevelt's actions—the destroyer deal, the naval war with German submarines, and the deployments to Greenland and Iceland—and his holding back from committing troops to battle on foreign soil, *see* Berger, *supra*, at 66, and sources cited.

11. Congress's unwillingness to break the bonds of isolationism during the period of Nazi and Japanese expansion proved, in retrospect, so unadmirable as to constantly be invoked in the postwar era to support unilateral presidential claims. Only much later, from the 1970s on, could observers look back at the 1940–1941 period in the only positive way. When the nation is as divided about war as it was in 1940 and 1941, the only way in which war could come with its tremendous sacrifice, however necessary and just the war, was by events decisive enough to persuade Congress.

12. The preceding quote and this are from David S. Friedman, *Waging War Against Checks and Balances: The Claims of an Unlimited Presidential War Power*, 57 St. John's L. Rev. 213, 226–227 (1983) (footnotes omitted).

13. President Truman could have obtained congressional authorization (or explicit ratification at an early point after the defensive Korean War began, on the model of Congress's explicit ratification of President Lincoln's steps at an early point after the firing upon Fort Sumter). Even his congressional Republican critics said he would have received it, but he refused to ask for it. I have previously noted that Congress did enact much legislation necessary for the extended conduct of the Korean War. Charles Tiefer, "The FAS Proposal: Valid Check or Unconstitutional Veto?" in *First Use of Nuclear Weapons: Under the Constitution, Who Decides?* 136, 156 (ed. Peter Raven-Hansen 1987). Simple enactment by Congress of necessary measures does not amount to explicit ratification, although because Congress acted supportively the precedent thereby created is not one for sole presidential power.

14. John Hart Ely has drawn brilliantly on newly released documents and memoirs to reconstruct the legal context of the Indochina War. He has argued that the war in Vietnam did receive sufficient congressional authorization whereas the other parts of the Indochina war, namely the secret war in Laos from 1962 to 1969 and the secret bombing of Cambodia in 1969 and 1970, lacked such authorization. John Hart Ely, *The American War in Indochina, Part I: The (Troubled) Constitutionality of the War They Told Us About,* 42 Stan. L. Rev. 877 (1989); John Hart Ely, *The American War in Indochina, Part II: The Unconstitutionality of the War They Didn't Tell Us About* (1990). His treatment is so exhaustive and balanced that it seems pointless to do anything other than simply to refer the reader to his pieces as models of analysis of war powers in the context of a particular war. The questionable point in his approach is his arguments from Congress regarding voting appropriations for the Vietnam War, which fell far short of authorization. In any event, in drawing the contrast with the Persian Gulf War, what matters is not so much the question as to whether what the war in Vietnam received should be considered congressional authorization. Rather, the most relevant point is to distinguish the sharply different natures of the merely symbolic Tonkin Gulf Resolution enacted after an empty debate and the decisive Persian Gulf Resolution enacted after knowing debate upon the basis discussed in the following section.

15. For an introduction to the vast topic of covert action and war powers, *see* Jules Lobel, *Covert War and Congressional Authority: Hidden War and Forgotten Power,* 2134 U. Pa. L. Rev. 1035 (1986). For a discussion of the meaningless resolutions of this period, see Doyle W. Buckwalter, *The Congressional Concurrent Resolution: A Search for Foreign Policy Influence,* 14 Midwest J. Poli. Sci. 434 (1970).

16. The ground-breaking preliminary consideration of the issues came in the Senate Foreign Relations Committee's development of the National Commitments Resolution, S. Res. 85, 91st Cong., 1st Sess. (1969). For discussions of (and further sources on) the road to the War Powers Resolution *see* Thomas M. Franck & Edward Weisband, *Foreign Policy By Congress* (1979) (also including a discussion of the contemporaneous congressional cutoffs that ended the Indochina War); Michael J. Glennon, *Constitutional Diplomacy* 88–93 (1990). For a sample of the extensive literature on the War Powers Resolution, *see, e.g.,* Jacob K. Javits, *War Powers Reconsidered,* 64 Foreign Affairs 130 (Fall 1985) (review written by key author of original resolution); Note, *A Defense of the War Powers Resolution,* 93 Yale L.J. 1330 (1984); Michael J. Glennon, *The War Powers Resolution Ten Years Later: More Politics Than*

Law, 78 Am. J. Int'l Law 571 (1984); Stephen L. Carter, *The Constitutionality of the War Powers Resolution,* 70 Va. L. Rev. 101 (1984).

17. The point is made numerous times in Bob Woodward, *The Commanders* (1991), about the military's insistence with respect to the prospect of war with Iraq in 1990 on much clearer national authorization than presidential power enthusiasts consider necessary. In 1990 the military used every mechanism to privately and to publicly express this insistence, from reluctance in planning for offense to leaks of White House proposals to supportiveness for testimony by their proxy spokesmen such as former military chiefs of staff. Also of note is Secretary Weinberger's classic 1984 statement, cited in the following section.

18. For some of the fullest treatments, see Glennon, *Constitutional Diplomacy* 71–122, and sources cited; Smyrl, *supra,* 63–140.

19. 4A Op. Office of Legal Counsel, Department of Justice 185, 196 (1980) (seminal opinion on the War Powers Resolution during the Carter Administration). President Carter endorsed the War Powers Resolution as a "constructive safeguar[d]." *President's Message to the Congress on Legislative Vetoes, Pub. Papers* 1146, 1149 (1978).

Secretary of Defense Caspar W. Weinberger laid down, as a classic test for committing American forces to combat overseas, that the commitment should "have the support of the American people and their elected representatives in Congress," Barry M. Blechman, *The Politics of National Security* 189–190 (1990) (quoting Weinberger address from New York Times, November 29, 1984); Louis Fisher & Neal Devins, *Political Dynamics of Constitutional Law* 185 (text of 1984 Weinberger address) (1992). Secretary Weinberger's position contrasts thoughtfully with the book by his secretary of the navy, John Lehman, *Making War* (1992).

20. For documentation and discussion of the post-1973 incidents, see Subcomm. on Arms Control, International Security and Science of the House Comm. on Foreign Affairs, 100th Cong., 1st Sess., *The War Powers Resolution: Relevant Documents, Correspondence, Reports* (May 1988 ed.) (periodically updated series); Barry M. Blechman, *The Politics of National Security: Congress and U.S. Defense Policy* 171–186 (1990) (especially on reflagging); Smyrl, *supra,* 128–134 (reflagging).

21. Absent those 1983 hearings, and the guarantee of more to come, President Reagan might not have so readily understood the need to quickly extricate the marines from the Lebanon quagmire. For discussions of the Lebanon commitment, see Note, *The Future of the War Powers Resolution,* 36 Stan. L. Rev. 1407, 1423–1427 (1984); Note, *The War Powers Resolution: A Tool for Balancing Power Through Negotiation,* 70 Va. L. Rev. 1037 (1984); Blechman, *supra,* at 180–184; Smyrl, *supra,* at 96–117.

22. For a general review of Congress's role on intelligence matters, see Frank J. Smist, *Congress Oversees the United States Intelligence Community 1947–1989* (1990); Gregory F. Treverton, "Intelligence: Welcome to the American Government," in *A Question of Balance: The President, The Congress and Foreign Policy* (ed. Thomas E. Mann. 1990); Blechman, supra, at 137–166.

23. For accounts of the decision during August 4 through 6, 1992, to make the buildup, *see* Woodward, *supra,* 228–256; Jean Edward Smith, *George Bush's War* 80–95 (1992); Roger Hilsman, *George Bush vs. Saddam Hussein: Military Success! Political Failure?* 1, 45–47 (1992).

24. This is the extensively developed analysis of Smith, *supra*, particularly focused on how unexpected to Saddam Hussein must have been President Bush's immediate efforts in the days after August 2 to head off any renewals of the type of talks and reciprocal gestures so freely offered to Iraq until then. *Id.* at 76–77, 89–90, 94–99, and 126–127.

25. President Bush took the following position, in his letter to Congress of August 9, 1990, regarding the deployment of forces: "I do not believe involvement in hostilities is imminent; to the contrary, it is my belief that this deployment will facilitate a peaceful resolution of the crisis. If necessary, however, the Forces are fully prepared to defend themselves." The president never changed his position that the deployment of forces had not made hostilities imminent and, in fact, that neither the deployment nor the blockade of Iraq and the other sanctions provoked combat. It required the later American decision, not some provoked Iraqi initiation, to start combat.

26. The House adopted House Joint Resolution 658 on October 1; the Senate adopted Senate Concurrent Resolution 147 on October 3.

In that regard, it is noteworthy that the president had sought, and Congress had provided, significant legislative authorization for the buildup. Besides the standing armed forces, President Bush used two major tools for the buildup: American reserves and foreign funds. He called up the reserves in a deployment that required them for long-term duty. Following Vietnam, the military force structure necessitated such a call-up of reserves, with the ensuing guarantee that a president would have trouble going to war, at least by some routes, without the national debate and, presumably, the national support inherent in such a call-up. By pre-1990 law, such a call-up could last only six months (without presidential assertion of special authorities). In 1990, Congress enacted a provision in the annual defense appropriation bill allowing the call-up to last longer, sanctioning the Desert Shield call-up.

Similarly, when President Bush received massive financial support from his coalition partners, particularly Arab nations, Japan, and European nations, he required affirmative legislation to expend these funds. Congress enacted the provisions for receiving and expending those funds, without which their use would have been either illegal or at least highly dubious.

27. *U.S. Policy in the Persian Gulf: Hearings Before the Sen. Comm. on Foreign Relations*, 101st Cong., 2d Sess. (October 17, 1990).

28. *Id.* at 108–109.

29. Smith, *supra*, at 198 (quoting Washington Post, October 30, 1990).

30. Holly Idelson, *National Opinion Ambivalent as Winds of War Stir Gulf*, 49 Cong. Q. Week. Rep. 14 (January 5, 1991).

31. Hilsman, *supra*, at 91 (citing Anthony Lewis, *On his Word Alone*, New York Times, January 12, 1992). That may have been December 21. Woodward, *supra*, at 338.

32. Woodward, *supra*, at 325. The picture of President Bush rejecting or disputing the congressional position recurs in many accounts of that period: "Senate Majority Leader George J. Mitchell of Maine and House Speaker Thomas S. Foley of Washington have tirelessly argued that only Congress has the constitutional authority to decide whether the country goes to war. Although Bush disputes that as-

sertion, it is a widely shared view on Capitol Hill." (Caroll J. Doherty, *Congress Faces Grave Choices as Clock Ticks Toward War*, 49 Cong. Q. Week. Rep. 7, 9 [January 5, 1991]). For pertinent examples for Parliament's clashes with the Stuarts, *see* Raoul Berger, *Executive Privilege: A Constitutional Myth* 124–125 (1974).

33. *Crisis in the Persian Gulf Region: U.S. Policy Options and Implications: Hearings Before the Senate Comm. on Armed Services*, 101st Cong., 2d Sess. (1990).

34. *Id.* at 701–702.

35. Woodward, *supra*, at 341–342.

36. Clay Blair, Washington Post National Weekly Edition, at 35 (May 13–19, 1991) (quoted in Hilsman, *supra*, at 250).

37. 1990 *Congressional Quarterly Almanac* 742.

38. *Dellums v. Bush*, 752 F. Supp. 1141 (D.D.C. 1990). For the administration's rejected arguments, *see* Fisher & Devins, *supra*, at 183–184.

39. 1990 *Congressional Quarterly Almanac* 746.

40. *Id.*

41. Also, the Senate Judiciary Committee held an interesting set of hearings on January 8, but the administration did not testify. *The Constitutional Roles of Congress and the President in Declaring and Waging War: Hearings Before the Sen. Comm. on the Judiciary*, 102 Cong., 1st Sess. (January 8, 1991).

42. Woodward, *supra*, at 343.

43. *Id.* at 344.

44. *Id.* at 346.

45. Adam Clymer, *Bush Asks Congress to Back Use of Force if Iraq Defies Deadline on Kuwait Pullout*, New York Times, January 9, 1991, at A1.

46. Dan Balz, *Bush Asks Congress to Back Force Against Iraq*, Washington Post, January 9, 1991, A1, at A16.

47. Clymer, *supra*, A1, at A6.

48. Sidak, *supra*, at 31. "President Bush formally requested that Congress pass a resolution *supporting* (not authorizing) 'the use of all necessary means.'" Eastland, *supra*, at 119 ("the measure Bush sought would have only *supported*, not authorized, the use of force"). (Both italics are in the originals.)

49. The letter is reprinted in 1990 *Congressional Quarterly Almanac* 747.

50. Balz, *supra*, A1, at A16.

51. The drafting meeting occurred on January 9, after the meeting of Secretary of State James Baker and Iraqi foreign minister Tariq Aziz in Geneva ended with Aziz's globally publicized intransigence, which destroyed the last chance to avoid a decision on war. Lawrence Freedman & Efraim Korsh, *The Gulf Conflict 1990–1991* 292 and n.29 (1993).

52. 137 Cong. Rec. S231 (daily ed. January 11, 1991).

53. *Id.*

54. H. Con. Res. 32, 102d Cong., 1st Sess., 137 Cong. Rec. H390 (January 12, 1991).

55. Among other occasions, Representative Hyde sat on the House Iran-Contra Committee, and during its hearings he made countless effective presentations in defense of executive prerogatives.

The only speaker (besides Representative Hyde) against the Bennett-Durbin resolution, Representative Campbell, did not really take issue with its meaning in this context. In fact, he said: "The Bennett-Durbin resolution before us correctly states that only the Congress can declare war. This is a view I have long applied to the Persian Gulf crisis." Rather, he drew the distinction that the president might, on his own authority, take a limited action such as a retaliation against the individual Abu Abbas, the terrorist then in Baghdad responsible for murder of an American. 137 Cong. Rec. H 403 (daily ed. January 12, 1991). Not one representative rose to express the view that the president could initiate full-scale war against Iraq without congressional authorization.

56. 137 Cong. Rec. H391 (daily ed. January 12, 1991).

57. 137 Cong. Rec. S364 (daily ed. January 12, 1991) (Senator Coats).

58. See Sidak, *supra*, at 76–77.

59. *Pub. Papers* 14 (January 14, 1991).

60. The quotation from Wilson's statements, and a discussion of the context, are in Schlesinger, *supra*, at 99.

61. Owen Ullmann, *Soul Brothers,* Washingtonian, May 1992, 76, at 147.

62. Michael J. Glennon, *The Constitution and Chapter VII of the United Nations Charter,* 85 Am. J. Int'l Law 74, 86 (1991). For similar past distinctions between United Nations views as international law support for force and the necessities under the Constitution for a congressional decision to warrant American participation in war, *see* Schlesinger, *supra*, 137; *Constitutional Diplomacy* 192–222 (addressing mechanisms of both the United Nations and treaties such as NATO).

CHAPTER 7

1. Walter Dean Burnham, "The Legacy of George Bush: Travails of an Understudy," in *The Election of 1992: Reports and Interpretations* 1, 31 (ed. Gerald M. Pomper 1993).

2. *Id.* at 31.

3. Burt Solomon, *Bush's Passive Presidency,* 24 National Journal 2628 (November 14, 1992).

4. Rhodes Cook, *Clinton Climbs to Power on Broad, Shaky Base,* 51 Cong. Q. Week Rep. 188 (January 23, 1992) (quoting Burnham) (statistical analyses at 191).

5. James A. Barnes & Burt Solomon, *Bill Clinton's Clear/Fuzzy Mandate,* 24 National Journal 2680 (November 21, 1992).

6. Solomon, *supra*, at 2544.

7. David S. Cloud, *Final Push Clears Tax Bill; Bush Announces Veto,* 50 Cong. Q. Week. Rep. 712 (March 21, 1992).

8. *Bush Takes Off the Gloves, Comes Out Fighting,* 50 Cong. Q. Week. Rep. 2556, 2559 (1992) (reprinting text of August 20 nomination acceptance speech).

9. Dave Kaplan & Charles Mahtesian, *The House: Election's Wave of Diversity Spares Many Incumbents: Record Number of Women, Minorities Sweeps into the Chamber, but Partisan Alignment Shifts Only Slightly,* 50 Cong. Q. Week. Rep. (1992).

10. The Bush Administration had supported nationwide litigation efforts to use the Voting Rights Act to produce minority-oriented districts. As a result, district lines changed much more than necessary simply to accommodate population change. For example, Georgia gained only one district. However, it redrew its district lines to create two new black-majority districts. Creating such districts, which

drained off so many of the local Democratic votes, had the effect of also creating new Republican districts. Hence, the new Georgia House delegation had two new freshman black Democrats and three new freshmen Republicans. A swollen freshman class could thus come from such redistricting, aside from voter decisions to change the House.

11. Solomon, *supra*, at 2544.

12. *Id.*

13. *Id.* at 2629 (tracing analysis by William E. Gienapp, a Harvard historian).

14. The Family and Medical Leave Act alone received eight mentions, in Bill Clinton & Al Gore, *Putting People First* (1992) at 15, 51, 69, 83, 101, 127, 142, and 171. Discussions of the other vetoed bills he would sign took place for campaign finance (26, 52) and voter registration (65). Discussions of proposed bills took place for the Freedom of Choice Act (170), the Violence Against Women Act (49, 172), the Brady Bill (50, 57, 73, and 105), the Community Reinvestment Act (55, 114, 149), and the workplace fairness bill (126).

15. *Putting People First* speaks on wetlands (96), for citizen environmental suits (95), for enforcement of the Clean Air Act (93), on Saddam Hussein at 137–138 (quoted in text; see also 123), on burden sharing (135), and on the civil rights act (64).

16. At least Clinton made clear that he would seek it from Congress, not follow C. Boyden Gray's subterranean attempts to claim a line-item veto by presidential fiat or usurpation.

17. For a description of congressional budget procedure, *see* Charles Tiefer, *Congressional Practice and Procedure* 849–919 (1989).

18. Surprisingly little has been written about the role of the budget process in tax legislation, *but see* Tiefer, *supra*, at 900–908.

19. 1989 *Congressional Quarterly Almanac* 79 ("invisible" and "thinly detailed") and 85 ("nonbudget budget," optimistic economic assumptions).

20. *United States v. Amadeo DeCarolis et al.*, Nos 1:91-cr-78-MHS et seq., slip op. at 13 (filed Aug. 24, 1993).

21. Warren Christopher, *Ceasefire Between the Branches: A Compact in Foreign Affairs*, 60 Foreign Affairs 989 (1982).

22. *Id.*, at 997 (quotes about "executive supremacy") and 1001 (sharing information and the hostage briefings).

23. The quote and Lake's background are from Dick Kirschten, *Muscled Up?: Foreign Policy*, 25 National Journal 454, 458 (February 20, 1993). The wiretapping of Lake and others is discussed in Seymour M. Hersh, *The Price of Power: Kissinger in the Nixon White House* 197 (1983).

24. The initial spring 1993 Somalia authorizations came in enactment by the Senate of S. J. Res. 45, 103d Cong., 1st Sess., and by the House of the same resolution as amended. Janet Hook et al., *Clinton Controls Fall Agenda, Although Not its Results*, 51 Cong. Q. Week. Rep. 2295, 2332 (Sept. 4, 1993). September enactment of the resolution occurred as an amendment to H.R. 2401, 103d Cong., 1st Sess., the defense authorization bill. Carroll J. Doherty, *Contrary Paths to Peacekeeping Converge in Wake of Violence*, 51 Cong. Q. Week. Rep. 2655 (Oct. 2, 1993). *See id.* at 2657 (quoting President Clinton's news conference of Sept. 27) (box labeled "Bosnia Ground Rules").

25. Arthur M. Schlesinger, Jr., *The Imperial Presidency* 138 (1974).

26. Barry M. Blechman, *The Politics of National Security: Congress and U.S. Defense Policy* 186 (1990).

27. Executive Order 12866 is in Pub. Papers 1925 (Sept. 30, 1993). For a description of the order's preparation, and the changing role of OIRA, see Viveca Novak, *The New Regulators,* 25 National Journal 1801 (July 17, 1993).

28. Judge Harold Greene's opinion regarding the need for congressional authorization of war with Iraq came on December 13, 1990, in *Dellums v. Bush,* 752 F. Supp. 1141 (D.D.C. 1990). Judge Marvin H. Shoob gave his conclusions about the issues in the BNL matter on October 5, 1992, in *United States v. Christopher P. Drogoul,* No. 91-CR-78-ALL (N.D.Ga.).

29. *See, e.g., Crockett v. Reagan,* 720 F.2d 1355 (D.C. Cir. 1983); *Lowry v. Reagan,* 676 F. Supp. 333 (D.D.C. 1987); *Dellums v. Smith,* 797 F.2d 817 (9th Cir. 1984).

30. For general treatments of the large role that congressional-executive interaction, rather than judicial decisions, plays in checks and balances, see Louis Fisher & Neal Devins, *Political Dynamics of Constitutional Law* (1992), and Louis Fisher, *The Politics of Shared Power: Congress and the Executive* (1981).

31. Charles Tiefer, *The Flag-Burning Controversy of 1989–90: Congress' Valid Role in Constitutional Dialogue,* 29 Harv. J. Legis. 357, 396–397 (1992).

32. The case for an active judicial role is made well in Michael J. Glennon, *Constitutional Diplomacy* 313–325 (1990).

33. For the full history, see Frank J. Smist, Jr., *Congress Oversees the United States Intelligence Community, 1947–1989* (1990).

34. The text of a speech by Robert Gates from which this quote and the subsequent ones are taken is reprinted in American Bar Association Standing Committee on Law and National Security, *National Security Law Report,* February 1993, at 1-3 (emphasis on "welcome" in the original text).

About the Book and Author

In *The Semi-Sovereign Presidency*, Capitol Hill insider Charles Tiefer shows how George Bush used the executive office to circumvent Congress, thwart official Washington, and confound the public will. Even Bush partisans may be surprised to discover the president's unprecedented use of executive signing statements to modify or, in effect, abrogate acts of Congress—even popular, bipartisan efforts like the 1991 Civil Rights Act; his commissioning of the "Quayle Council" to derail regulatory legislation such as the Clean Air Act of 1990; and his catapulting of the National Security Council into foreign policy prominence outstripping that of the Departments of Defense and State. As Tiefer details for the first time here, "Iraqgate," the hidden courtship of Saddam Hussein prior to the Gulf War, is perhaps the most dramatic example of Bush's executive fiat—a relationship conducted by way of Bush National Security Directives and similarly obscured from the public eye.

Bush chose an essentially negative approach to governing partly because he was unwilling to engage Congress on matters of principle head to head and was equally unwilling to make his principles public—addressing himself to the nation as his predecessor had so effectively done. But, as Tiefer persuasively argues, it was Bush's belief in the sovereignty of executive power—an almost monarchical conception of the presidency—that was his primary modus operandi and ultimately his downfall.

Bush and his approach to power are interesting not just to students and scholars of the presidency but to all citizens concerned about the country and its leadership.

Charles Tiefer is acting general counsel to the U.S. House of Representatives and author of the authoritative reference work *Congressional Practice and Procedure*.

Index